CCNP™ Exam Notes™: Advanced Cisco® Router Configuration

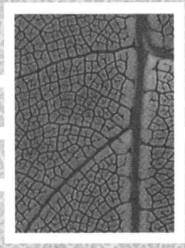

Todd Lammle

San Francisco • Paris • Düsseldorf • Soest • London

Associate Publisher: Neil Edde
Contracts and Licensing Manager: Kristine O'Callaghan
Editor: Jeff Gammon
Technical Editor: Shawn Zudal
Book Designer: Bill Gibson
Graphic Illustrator: Tony Jonick
Electronic Publishing Specialist: Bill Gibson
Project Team Leader: Teresa Trego
Proofreaders: Emily Hsuan, Laura Schattschneider, and Rich Ganis
Indexer: Rebecca Plunkett
Cover Designer: Archer Design
Cover Photograph: Image Bank

Library of Congress Card Number: 99-65193
ISBN: 0-7821-2540-9

Manufactured in the United States of America

10 9 8 7 6 5 4 3 2 1

Acknowledgments

I'd like to acknowledge Brian Horakh of www.networkstudyguides.com. He helped me develop many of the questions in this book that will help the reader get a firm grasp of the real exam.

I happily acknowledge Neil Edde and thank him for supplying motivation, patience, and insight whenever I needed them.

Much thanks also goes out to Jeff Gammon, who edited this book. I appreciate his care in editing and all of the late nights and extra hours that he devoted to making this a better book for its readers.

I appreciate Shawn Zudal's attention and care in helping me to keep this book technically in tune.

Last, but certainly not least, I appreciate the production crew at Sybex. Thanks to Project Team Leader Teresa Trego and Electronic Publishing Specialist Bill Gibson for corralling my manuscript and turning it into this good-looking book!

Table of Contents

Introduction   *ix*

Chapter 1   Overview of Scalable Networks   1

  ▪ Describe the key requirements of a scalable
    internetwork. 2

  ▪ Select a Cisco IOS feature as a solution for a
    given internetwork requirement. 7

Chapter 2   Introduction to Managing Traffic and Access   15

  ▪ Describe causes of network congestion. 17

  ▪ List solutions for controlling network
    congestion. 20

  ▪ Introduction to Managing Traffic and
    Access 27

  ▪ Configure IP standard access lists. 30

  ▪ Limit virtual terminal access. 37

  ▪ Configure IP extended access lists. 40

  ▪ Verify access list operation. 44

  ▪ Configure an alternative to using
    access lists. 50

  ▪ Configure an IP helper address to manage
    broadcasts. 52

Chapter 3   Managing Novell IPX/SPX Traffic   59

  ▪ Describe IPX/SPX traffic management
    issues. 61

  ▪ Filter IPX traffic using IPX access lists. 66

  ▪ Manage IPX/SPX traffic over WAN. 73

  ▪ Verify IPX/SPX filter operation. 76

Chapter 4   Configuring Queuing to Manage Traffic   85

- Describe the need for queuing in a large network. 87

- Describe weighted fair queuing operation. 89

- Configure priority. 93

- Configure custom queuing. 98

- Verify queuing operation. 102

Chapter 5   Routing Protocol Overview   107

- List the key information routers need to route data. 108

- Compare distance vector and link-state protocol operation. 112

Chapter 6   Extending IP Addresses Using VLSMs   121

- Given an IP address, use VLSMs to extend the use of the IP address. 123

- Given a network plan that includes IP addressing, explain if a route summarization is or is not possible. 128

- Define private addressing and determine when it can be used. 133

- Define network address translation and determine when it can be used. 136

Chapter 7   Configuring OSPF in a Single Area   141

- Explain why OSPF is better than RIP in a large internetwork. 143

- Explain how OSPF discovers, chooses, and maintains routes. 149

- Configure OSPF for proper operation. 155

- Verify OSPF operation. 159

Chapter 8   **Interconnecting Multiple OSPF Areas**   **165**

- Describe the issues with interconnecting multiple areas and how OSPF addresses. **166**

- Explain the differences between the possible types of areas, routers, and LSAs. **170**

- Configure a multiarea OSPF network. **176**

- Verify OSPF operation. **181**

Chapter 9   **Configuring EIGRP**   **185**

- Describe Enhanced IGRP features and operation. **187**

- Configure Enhanced IGRP. **194**

- Verify Enhanced IGRP operation. **197**

Chapter 10   **Optimizing Routing Update Operation**   **201**

- Select and configure the different ways to control route update traffic. **203**

- Configure route redistribution in a network that does not have redundant paths between dissimilar routing processes. **206**

- Configure route redistribution in a network that has redundant paths between dissimilar routing processes. **210**

- Resolve path selection problems that result in a redistributed network. **215**

- Verify route redistribution. **220**

Chapter 11   **Connecting Enterprises to an Internet Service Provider**   **223**

- Describe when to use BGP to connect to an ISP. **224**

- Describe methods to connect to an ISP using static and default routes, and BGP. **227**

Chapter 12   WAN Connectivity Overview   235

- Compare the differences between WAN connection types: dedicated, asynchronous dial-in, dial-on-demand, and packet switched services. 237

- Determine when to use PPP, HDLC, LAPB, and IETF encapsulation types. 241

- List at least four common issues to be considered when evaluating WAN services. 247

Chapter 13   Configuring Dial-on-Demand Routing   251

- Describe the components that make up ISDN connectivity. 253

- Configure ISDN BRI. 257

- Configure Legacy dial-on-demand routing (DDR). 260

- Configure dialer profiles. 268

- Verify DDR operation. 274

Chapter 14   Customizing DDR Operation   277

- Configure dial backup. 279

- Verify dial backup operation. 283

- Configure MultiLink PPP operation. 291

- Verify MultiLink PPP operation. 295

- Configure snapshot routing. 302

- Configure IPX spoofing. 306

Chapter 15   Bridging Overview   311

- Define routable and nonroutable protocols and give an example of each. 313

- Define various bridging types and describe when to use each type. 317

**Chapter   16   Configuring Transparent Bridging and
                   Integrated Routing and Bridging   321**

▪ Configure transparent bridging.   322

▪ Configure integrated Routing and
  Bridging (IRB).   330

Chapter   17   Configuring Source-Route Bridging   337

▪ Describe the basic functions of source-route
  bridging (SRB).   339

▪ Configure SRB.   342

▪ Configure source-route transparent
  bridging (SRT).   347

▪ Configure source-route translational bridging
  (SR/TLB).   350

▪ Verify SRB operation.   358

Chapter   18   Managing AppleTalk Traffic   365

▪ Identify potential sources of congestion in an
  AppleTalk network.   367

▪ Configure zone filters.   370

▪ Configure RTMP filters.   374

▪ Configure NBP filters.   379

Chapter   19   Configuring T1/E1 and ISDN PRI Options   383

▪ Identify channelized T1 and E1
  configuration.   385

▪ Identify ISDN PRI configuration
  commands.   390

Index   *395*

Introduction

The *CCNP Exam Notes* is intended to start you out on an exciting new path toward obtaining your CCNP certification. It reaches beyond popular certifications like the MCSE and CNE to provide you with an indispensable factor in understanding today's network: insight into the Cisco world of internetworking.

If you've purchased this book, you are probably chasing one of the Cisco professional certifications: CCNA/CCNP, CCDA/CCDP, or CCIE. All of these are great goals, and they are also great career builders. Glance through any newspaper and you'll find employment opportunities for people with these certifications. These ads are there because finding qualified network administrators is a challenge in today's market. The certification means you know something about the product, but, more importantly, it also means you have the ability, determination, and focus to learn—the greatest skills any employee can have!

You've probably also have heard all the rumors about how hard the Cisco tests are. Believe it or not, the rumors are true! Cisco has designed a series of exams that truly challenge your knowledge of their products. Each test not only covers the materials presented in a particular class but it also covers the prerequisite knowledge for that course.

Is This Book for You?

The *CCNP Exam Notes* covers everything you need to know to pass Cisco's Advanced Cisco Router Configuration (ACRC) exam (640-403). The ACRC exam is a required exam in the CCNP certification process. Each chapter begins with a list of the ACRC test objectives that are detailed in it (so make sure to read over them before working through the chapter). This book teaches you how to perform advanced configurations on Cisco routers using multiple protocols.

And it covers all of the advanced topics you'll need to understand, including the Cisco three-layer hierarchical model, distance-vector and link-state routing protocols, bridging, queuing, and more!

The Sybex Exam Notes books are designed to be succinct, portable exam review guides. They can be used either in conjunction with a more complete study program—supplemented by books, CBT courseware, or practice in a classroom/lab environment—or as an exam review for those who don't feel the need for more extensive test preparation. It isn't our goal to "give the answers away" but rather to identify the topics on which you can expect to be tested and to provide sufficient coverage of those topics.

Perhaps you've been working with Cisco internetworking technologies for years now. The thought of paying lots of money for a specialized Cisco exam preparation course probably doesn't sound too appealing. What can they teach you that you don't already know, right? Be careful, though. Many experienced network administrators, even CCIEs, have walked confidently into testing centers only to walk sheepishly out of them after failing a Cisco exam. As they discovered, there's the Cisco of the real world but also the Cisco of the Cisco certification exams. It's the goal of the Exam Notes books to show you where the two both converge and diverge. After you've finished reading through this book, you should have a clear idea of how your understanding of the technologies involved matches up with the expectations of the Cisco test makers.

Or perhaps you're relatively new to the world of Cisco internetworking, being drawn to it by the promise of challenging work and higher salaries. You've just waded through an 800-page Cisco ACRC study guide or taken a class at a local training center. Lots of information to keep track of, isn't it? Well, by organizing the Exam Notes books according to the Cisco exam objectives, and by breaking up the information into concise, manageable pieces, we've created what we think is the handiest exam review guide available. Throw it in your briefcase and carry it to work with you. As you read through the book, you'll be able to quickly identify those areas that you know best and those that require more in-depth review.

The goal of the Exam Notes series is to help Cisco certification candidates familiarize themselves with the subjects on which they can expect to be tested in the certification exams. For complete, in-depth coverage of the technologies and topics involved in Cisco networking, we recommend the Cisco Certification Study Guide series from Sybex.

How is This Book Organized?

As previously mentioned, this book is organized according to the official exam objectives list prepared by Cisco for the ACRC exam (640-403). Within each chapter, the individual exam objectives are addressed in turn. Each objective section is further divided according to the type of information presented, as explained in the following paragraph.

Critical Information

This section presents the greatest level of detail on information that is relevant to the objective. This is the place to start if you're unfamiliar with or uncertain about the technical issues related to the objective.

Necessary Procedures

Here you'll find instructions for procedures that usually require a lab computer to be completed. From logging into a router to configuring EIGRP and OSPF routing, the information in these sections addresses the hands-on requirements for the ACRC exams.

NOTE   Not every objective has a hands-on procedure associated with it. For such objectives, the Necessary Procedures section is omitted.

Exam Essentials

This section consists of a concise list of the most crucial subject areas that you'll need to fully comprehend prior to taking the Cisco exam. This section can help you to identify those topics that might require extra study.

Key Terms and Concepts

This section is a mini-glossary of the most important terms and concepts related to the specific objective being presented. Since some objectives are interrelated, certain terms are sometimes repeated from objective to objective. You'll understand what all of those technical words mean within the context of the related subject matter.

Sample Questions

For each exam objective, we've included a selection of questions similar to those you'll encounter on the actual Cisco exam. Answers and explanations are provided so you can gain some insight into the test-taking process.

How Do You Become a CCNP?

The CCNP certification is a new certification in the new line of Cisco certifications. With the new certification programs, Cisco has created a stepping-stone approach to Cisco Certified Internetwork Associate (CCIE) certification. You can become a CCNP by passing the CCNA exam and four other exams, one of which is the ACRC exam (640-403). Once you are a CCNP, you have completed all the coursework and acquired all the knowledge you need to attempt the CCIE lab.

Why Become a CCNP?

Cisco has created a certification process—not unlike Microsoft's or Novell's—to give administrators a set of skills and prospective employers an authenticated way to measure those skills. Becoming a CCNP can be the initial step of a successful journey toward a new or refreshed, highly rewarding and sustainable career.

As you study for the ACRC exam, this point can't stress this enough: It's critical that you have some hands-on experience with Cisco routers. If you can get your hands on some 2500 routers, you're set! But if you can't, we've worked hard to provide dozens of configuration examples throughout this book to help network administrators (or people who want to become network administrators) learn what they need to know to pass the ACRC exam.

SEE ALSO One way to get the hands-on router experience you'll need in the real world is to attend one of the seminars offered by Globalnet System Solutions, Inc. (http://www.lammle.com), produced by the author of this book. And check out the router simulator available at www.routersim.com. It can help you get the hands-on experience you need at a fraction of the cost of real routers.

It can also be helpful to take an Introduction to Cisco Router Configuration (ICRC) course at an Authorized Cisco Education Center, but be aware that this class doesn't cover all of the test objectives. If you decide to take the class, reading this book in conjunction with the hands-on course will give you the knowledge you need for certification. There are hundreds of Cisco Authorized Training Centers around the world; see the Cisco Web page (http://www.cisco.com) for the location nearest you.

Where Do You Take the Exams?

You may take the exams at any one of the more than 800 Sylvan Prometric authorized testing centers around the world. For the location of a testing center near you, call 800-204-3926. For testing centers outside the United States and Canada, contact your local Sylvan Prometric registration center.

To register for a Cisco Certified Network Professional exam:

1. Determine the number of the exam you want to take. (The ACRC exam number is 640-403.)

2. Register with the Sylvan Prometric testing center nearest you, either via phone at 1-800-204-3926 or at www.sylvanprometric.com. You will need to pay in advance for the exam. At this writing, registration costs $100 per exam, and the test must be taken within one year of payment. You can sign up for an exam as early as six weeks in advance or as late as one working day prior to your exam date. Same-day registration isn't available for the Cisco tests. (If something comes up and you need to cancel or reschedule your exam appointment, contact Sylvan Prometric at least 24 hours in advance.)

3. When you schedule the exam, you'll be provided with instructions regarding all appointment and cancellation procedures, the ID requirements, and information about the testing center location.

What the Cisco ACRC Exam Measures

The CCNP program was not only created to provide a solid introduction to the Cisco internetwork operating system (IOS) and to Cisco hardware but to internetworking in general, making it helpful to you in areas not exclusively Cisco's. It's hard to say at this point in the certification process, but it's not unrealistic to imagine that future network managers—even those without Cisco equipment—could easily require Cisco certifications of their job applicants.

To meet the ACRC certification skill level, you must be able to understand or do the following:

- Install and/or configure a network to increase bandwidth, quicken network response times, and improve reliability and quality of service.

- Maximize performance through campus LANs, routed WANs, and remote access.

- Improve network security.

- Create a global intranet.

- Provide access security to campus switches and routers.

- Provide increased switching and routing bandwidth, end-to-end resiliency services.

- Provide custom queuing and routed priority services.

Tips for Taking Your Cisco ACRC Exam

The ACRC test contains around 70 questions, which are to be answered in 90 minutes. You must schedule the test at least 24 hours, or one business day, in advance (unlike the Novell or Microsoft exams), and you aren't allowed to take more than one Cisco exam per day.

Many questions on the exam will have answer choices that, at first glance, look identical—especially the syntax questions! Remember to read through the choices carefully, because a "close" answer won't cut it. If you choose an answer in which the commands are in the wrong order or there is even one measly character missing, you'll get the question wrong. Some of the exam questions are multiple-choice and some are fill-in-the-blank. Unlike Microsoft or Novell tests, the exam has answer choices that are really similar in syntax; some syntax will be dead wrong, but, more than likely, it will just be very *subtly* wrong. Some other syntax choices may be almost right except that the variables are shown in the wrong order.

Also, never forget that the right answer is the Cisco answer. In many cases, they'll present more than one correct answer, but the *correct* answer is the one Cisco recommends.

Here are some general tips for exam success:

- Arrive early at the exam center so you can relax and review your study materials—particularly IP tables and lists of exam-related information.

- Read the questions *carefully*. Don't jump to conclusions. Make sure you're clear on *exactly* what the question is asking.

- Don't leave any unanswered questions. These will be counted against you.

- When answering multiple-choice questions that you're not sure about, use a process of elimination to get rid of the obviously incorrect answers first. Doing this will greatly improve your odds should you need to make an "educated guess."

- Because the hard questions will eat up the most time, save them for last. You can move forward and backward through the exam.

- If you are unsure of the answer to a question, choose one of the answers anyway. Mark the question so that if you have time, you can go back to it and double-check your answer. Remember, an unanswered question is as bad as a wrong one, so answer questions even if you're not certain of the correct choice; if you don't and you run out of time or forget to go back to the question, you'll get it wrong for sure.

Once you have completed an exam, you'll be given immediate online notification of your pass or fail status, plus a printed Examination Score Report indicating whether you passed or failed, along with your exam results by section. (The test administrator will give you the printed score report.) Test scores are automatically forwarded to Cisco within five working days after you take the test, so you don't need to send your score to them. If you pass the exam, you'll receive confirmation from Cisco, typically within two to four weeks.

There's one more thing you can do to prepare. Visit Brian Horakh's Web site (http://www.networkstudyguides.com) and go through the exercises and practice test questions he provides. This will really help you keep abreast of any changes made to the test.

How to Contact the Author

Todd Lammle can be reached at his integration and consulting company, located in Colorado, at todd@lammle.com.

How to Contact the Publisher

Sybex welcomes reader feedback on all of their titles. Visit the Sybex Web site at http://www.sybex.com for book updates and additional certification information. You'll also find online forms for submitting comments or suggestions regarding this or any other Sybex book.

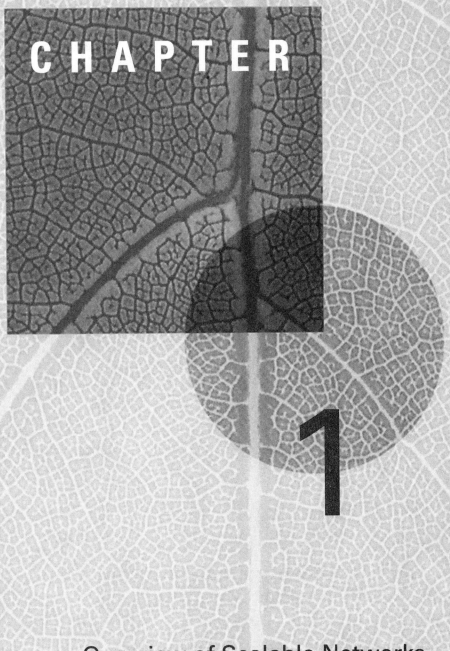

CHAPTER

1

Overview of Scalable Networks

Cisco ACRC Exam Objectives Covered in This Chapter:

▶ **Describe the key requirements of a scalable internetwork.** *(pages 2 – 7)*

▶ **Select a Cisco IOS feature as a solution for a given internetwork requirement.** *(pages 7 – 14)*

For an internetwork to realize its full potential, it must be able to efficiently connect many different networks together to serve the organizations depending on it. The key requirements of a scalable internetwork are based on an ideal design using the Cisco hierarchical model to simplify management, which permits well-planned growth that honors the network's requirements. The essential areas focused on in this chapter are important not only to know for the test but also for everyday network administration, troubleshooting, and design. All good network designers must focus on answering the question of whether or not their design meets the criteria listed in this chapter before proceeding with purchasing or implementation. Finding a vendor who can provide these benefits and then properly implement the equipment so as to achieve the desired result is mandatory, especially if you want peace of mind and to get a good night's sleep.

The Cisco internetwork operating system (IOS) has many features that can help administrators create a dependable and growth-oriented network. This chapter covers the features of the Cisco IOS. These objectives are the foundation for the rest of the objectives, so you should learn as much of this chapter as possible.

▶ Describe the key requirements of a scalable internetwork.

Today's internetworks are experiencing extraordinary growth due to increasing demands for connectivity both in businesses and homes. Therefore, it is very important for internetworks to be scalable. Scalable networks should be able to grow without changing the entire network. If a network is built correctly, growth can happen without any noticeable change to the core network.

It is now vital for administrators to understand what a scalable network is, as well as what is required to effectively manage its incessant growth. This section will focus on the following five specific keys to a scalable internetwork. The internetwork must be:

- Reliable and available

- Responsive

- Efficient

- Adaptable

- Easily accessible while being secure

Memorizing these areas will help you on the exam in two basic ways. You'll benefit if there is a test question directly relating to these areas and also if there is a question about a subject for which one of these areas is the underlying foundation.

Critical Information

Since a scalable internetwork undergoes continual growth, it must be both flexible and easily appended. An ideal design is based on the hierarchical model to both simplify management and permit well-planned growth that honors the network's requirements. The following sections present a more detailed account of the mandatory requirements of a scalable internetwork.

Reliability and Availability

The Cisco internetwork operating system provides features for implementing redundancy, load balancing, and reachability with protocols, such as the Enhanced Interior Gateway Routing Protocol (EIGRP) and Open Shortest Path First (OSPF). Strategies like tunneling and dial backups, which are also included in the Cisco IOS, can also help keep an internetwork up and running.

Responsiveness

Because network growth often occurs on a daily basis, the administrator's duty to maintain the network's responsiveness can become overwhelming. The Cisco IOS provides solutions to this issue, such as queuing that is configured by an administrator to keep latency to a minimum.

Efficiency

Efficiency, in a nutshell, boils down to keeping the bandwidth from becoming saturated. A central goal of this book is to arm you with information on fine-tuning your router in order to optimize the existing bandwidth on your internetwork. You'll learn how to achieve that objective through innovative techniques such as snapshot routing, access lists, and dial-up routing.

Adaptability

The internetwork that is designed to respond masterfully to change while managing both routed and non-routable protocols is a true prize. The Cisco IOS provides valuable bridging features to help you win that prize.

Accessibility and Security

It is a network administrator's foremost obligation (some might call it an obsession) to meet business requirements by ensuring that network resources remain available to users at all times, while also keeping any and all hackers out. The Cisco IOS provides dedicated and switched WAN support, such as Frame Relay, SMDS, X.25, and ATM, to equip networking professionals with options to meet cost, location, security, and traffic requirements. The Cisco IOS also provides exterior routing support with the Exterior Gateway Protocol (EGP) and Border Gateway Protocol (BGP) to permit routing on the Internet with maximum security.

Exam Essentials

Understand and be able to list the five keys to a scalable internetwork. An internetwork must be:

- Reliable and available
- Responsive
- Efficient
- Adaptable
- Easily accessible while being secure

Remember the difference between a routed and a routing protocol. Routed protocols are protocols that send user data through an internetwork (e.g., IP and IPX). Routing protocols are protocols that update routing tables with neighbor routers (e.g., RIP, IGRP, and OSPF).

Key Terms and Concepts

ATM (asynchronous transfer mode) An international standard for cell relay in which multiple service types, such as voice, video, and data, are conveyed in fixed-length (53-byte) cells.

BGP (Border Gateway Protocol) Generally used as an external routing protocol to control routing updates between autonomous systems (e.g., Internet Service Providers).

Cisco IOS (internetwork operating system) Cisco's proprietary internetwork operating system is the operating system that runs Cisco routers and switches.

EGP (Exterior Gateway Protocol) Was generally used as the primary external routing protocol between autonomous systems before it was essentially replaced by BGP.

EIGRP (Enhanced Interior Gateway Routing Protocol) Enhanced version of IGRP that was developed by Cisco with superior convergence properties and operating efficiencies.

Frame Relay An industry-standard, packet-switched, Data–Link-layer protocol that handles multiple virtual circuits using HDLC encapsulation between connected devices; generally considered to be a replacement for X.25.

Internetwork A collection of networks, interconnected by routers and other devices, that generally functions as a single network.

Latency The time a frame takes to get from the source host to the destination host.

Non-routable protocol A protocol at layer two of the OSI model that cannot be routed by routing protocols but must be bridged to its destination instead. These protocols don't have a logical address but do have a physical address.

OSPF (Open Shortest Path First) A hierarchical IGP routing algorithm with features like least-cost routing, multi-path routing, and load balancing.

Routable protocol A protocol at layer three of the OSI model that can be routed by routing protocols. These protocols have a logical address and a physical address.

SMDS (Switched Multimegabit Data Service) A high-speed, packet-switched, datagram-based, WAN networking technology offered by some telephone companies.

X.25 An older, slower, Data Link layer protocol that has essentially been replaced by Frame Relay.

Sample Questions

1. Which of the following terms identifies the characteristics of a scalable internetwork?

   A. Reliability

   B. Responsiveness

   C. Efficiency

   D. Adaptability

E. Accessibility

F. All of the above

Answer: F—The Cisco IOS provides all of the characteristics of a scalable network.

2. What types of dedicated and switched WAN support does the Cisco IOS provide?

A. Frame Relay

B. SMDS

C. ATM

D. X.25

E. All of the above

Answer: E—Cisco WAN support can use all of these methods.

Select a Cisco IOS feature as a solution for a given internetwork requirement.

Today's internetworks vary widely in their use, size, requirements, and load. This objective covers the rich features available with Cisco's IOS that allow an administrator to implement a variety of solutions in almost any internetworking situation. Multiple routing protocols, queuing techniques, load balancing techniques, security and control measures, and dial-up services, each having their own strengths and options, are all available with Cisco's latest IOS releases.

It is imperative that you know most, if not all, of Cisco's IOS features in order to be able to recommend, design, and troubleshoot on the job. Knowing these features will allow you to pick the most appropriate hardware and software for the task at hand and will allow you to implement them in such a way as to lessen future redesign and troubleshooting work.

This section lists each of the main features of the IOS and which of the key requirements of a scalable internetwork they contribute to. Be sure to come to a good understanding of the implementation and configuration of the features themselves.

Critical Information

Due to the many IOS features, a full description of each would take many more pages. Each feature of Cisco's IOS contributes in some way to the five key requirements of a scalable network. The following outline categorizes these many features.

Reliability and Availability

Some Cisco IOS features that provide stability and availability are described in the following paragraphs.

Reachability OSPF, EIGRP, and Novel Link State Protocol (NLSP) all use expanded metrics that can go beyond the hop-count limitations of distance-vector routing algorithms. These routing protocols analyze a combination of factors to establish the real cost of a path to a network, making Cisco routers able to support very large internetworks.

Convergence Scalable routing protocols can converge quickly because of each router's complete understanding of the internetwork and ability to detect problems.

Alternate paths routing Because OSPF and EIGRP build a complete map of the internetwork, a router can easily reroute traffic to an alternate path if a problem occurs.

Load balancing Through the EIGRP and OSPF routing algorithms, the Cisco IOS is able to perform load balancing. This allows for redundant links and for more bandwidth to be available to locations needing more than just one link. For example, if two T1 WAN links were installed between buildings, the actual bandwidth between them would reach approximately 3Mbps.

Packet tunneling   Running a tunneling protocol affords the ability to communicate across WAN links that were previously unreachable. For example, if you have a WAN link that supports only TCP/IP and you want to manage a Novell NetWare server that supports only IPX, you could tunnel IPX packets inside of IP packets to achieve your goal.

Dial-backup links   You can configure dial-backup links for redundancy on your WAN links and to add extra bandwidth whenever it becomes saturated, enhancing the link's reliability and availability.

Responsiveness

Since network administrators are responsible for making sure users don't experience delays in responsiveness as an internetwork grows, they must be keenly aware of the latency factor that each piece of equipment (routers, switches, and bridges) contributes to the internetwork. The Cisco IOS provides mitigation for the latency needs of each protocol running on your internetwork with features such as those described in the following paragraphs.

Weighted fair queuing   This feature prevents a single user or network device from monopolizing the internetwork's bandwidth and causing delays for the others. It fairly allots bandwidth to all users.

Priority queuing   This feature is used to tag a particular traffic type as a priority, ensuring that important information reaches its destination in a timely fashion. However, when using it, non-priority traffic may not make it to its destination on time.

Custom queuing   This feature allows the bandwidth to be divided up into slots (large or small), according to the business requirements of various types of traffic.

Efficiency

The task of creating smoothly running, efficient LANs and internetworks is obviously very important, but optimizing the bandwidth on a WAN can be very difficult. That's the focus of this book. The best way to reduce the bandwidth usage is to reduce the amount of update traffic on the LAN that will be sent over your WAN. The Cisco IOS features that are available to help reduce bandwidth usage are outlined in the following paragraphs.

Access lists   These are used to permit or deny certain types of traffic from entering or exiting a specific router interface. They can stop basic traffic, broadcasts, and protocol updates from saturating a particular link. TCP/IP, IPX, and AppleTalk can all be filtered extensively.

Snapshot routing   Commonly used for ISDN connections when running distance-vector protocols, snapshot routing allows routers to exchange full distance-vector routing information at an interval defined by the administrator.

Compression over WANs   The Cisco IOS supports TCP/IP header and data compression to reduce the amount of traffic crossing a WAN link. Link compression can be configured, which compresses header and data information into packets. This is accomplished by the Cisco IOS prior to sending the frame across the WAN.

Dial-on-demand routing   DDR allows wide-area links to be used selectively. The administrator can use DDR to define "interesting" traffic on the router and initiate point-to-point WAN links based upon that traffic. Interesting traffic is defined by access lists, so a great deal of flexibility is afforded to the administrator. For instance, an expensive ISDN connection to the Internet could be initiated to retrieve e-mail, but not for a WWW request. DDR is an effective tool in situations where WAN access is charged according to a quantified time interval; it's best to use it in situations where WAN access is infrequent.

Reduction in routing table entries   By using route summarization and incremental updates, you can reduce the number of router processing cycles by reducing the entries in a routing table. Route summarization occurs at major network boundaries, which summarize all the routes advertised into one entry. Incremental updates save bandwidth by sending only topology changes instead of the entire routing table when transmitting updates.

Adaptability

Another important goal for an administrator is to design an internetwork that responds well to change. To achieve this goal, internetworks need to be able to perform as described in the following paragraphs.

Pass both routable and nonroutable network protocols. Examples of this would be TCP/IP, which is routable, and Microsoft's NetBEUI (NetBIOS Extended User Interface), which is not routable but only bridgeable.

Create islands of networks using different protocols. This allows you to add protocols used by the network islands to Core-layer routers, or to use tunneling in the backbone to connect the islands, which keeps you from having to add unwanted protocols to the core backbone.

Balance between multiple protocols in a network Each protocol has different requirements, and the internetwork must be able to accommodate the specific issues of each one.

The Cisco IOS also has many different features, described in the following paragraphs, that contribute to network adaptability.

EIGRP Cisco's proprietary EIGRP allows you to use multiple protocols within one routing algorithm. EIGRP supports IP, IPX, and AppleTalk.

Redistribution This allows you to exchange routing information between networks that use different routing protocols. For example, you can update a routing table from a network running IGRP on a router participating in a RIP network.

Bridging By using source-route bridging and integrated routing and bridging, you can integrate your older networks and protocols that do not support routing into the new internetwork.

Accessibility and Security

Access routers must be both accessed and used to access a variety of WAN services, while maintaining security to keep hackers out. The Cisco IOS features that support these requirements are outlined in the following paragraphs.

Dedicated and switched WAN support   You can create a direct connection with Cisco routers using basic or digital services (a T1, for example). Cisco routers also support many different switched services, such as Frame Relay, SMDS, X.25, and ATM, to give you options to meet cost, location, and traffic requirements.

Exterior protocol support   Both Exterior Gateway Protocol and Border Gateway Protocol are supported by the Cisco IOS. BGP (discussed in detail later in this book) is used mostly by Internet Service Providers and has largely replaced EGP.

Access lists   These are used to filter specific kinds of traffic from either entering or leaving a Cisco router.

Authentication protocols   Cisco supports both Password Authentication Protocol (PAP) and Challenge Handshake Authentication Protocol (CHAP) for providing authentication on WAN connections using PPP.

You must have a solid understanding of these key requirements and where each of the IOS features fits. The key requirements and IOS features that have been explained in this section are the very foundation of what makes Cisco the leader in routing/switching technology.

SEE ALSO   For further study on each area, please reference the ACRC Study Guide by Sybex (ISBN# 0-7821-2403-8).

Exam Essentials

You will need to understand how the Cisco IOS can provide solutions for internetworks. This objective has covered the features available with Cisco's IOS that allow an administrator to implement a variety of solutions in almost any internetworking situation.

Remember the differences between the types of queuing. Weighted fair queuing gives every type of traffic a chance to get across the wire. Priority queuing gives specific types of traffic priority, and everything else must wait on these priority queues to empty before being processed. Custom queuing allocates a specified amount of bandwidth to each type of traffic based on time slicing.

Understand that Cisco will test heavily on their own proprietary implementations. You must have a good understanding or EIGRP and HDLC, both of which are Cisco proprietary protocols.

Key Terms and Concepts

Convergence   The speed and ability of a group of internetworking devices running a specific routing protocol to agree on the topology of an internetwork after a change in that topology.

Exterior Routing Protocols   Routing protocols that route between autonomous systems rather than inside them.

Redistribution   Allowing information discovered through one routing protocol to be distributed in the update messages of another routing protocol.

Snapshot routing   A routing technique that allows dial-up service functions within a Cisco router to call another Cisco router and pass updates for a specified amount of time, after which they disconnect and go into a quiet mode for a specified amount of time.

WAN (wide area network)   Generally, a network connected over serial connections via some type of long-distance medium (e.g., analog phone lines).

Sample Questions

1. Which Cisco IOS features are available to help reduce bandwidth usage? (Choose all that apply.)

   A. Access lists

   B. Snapshot routing

   C. Compression of WANs

   D. TTL

   E. DDR

   F. Incremental updates

   Answer: A, B, C, E, F—Everything listed can reduce bandwidth usage if configured correctly.

2. Which Cisco IOS features serve to provide stability and availability? (Choose all that apply.)

   A. Reachability

   B. Convergence

   C. Alternative path routing

   D. Snapshot routing

   E. Tunneling

   F. Dial backup

   G. Load balancing

   Answer: C, D, E, F—By configuring alternate paths and dial-backup lines, a Cisco router can provide network stability. Snapshot routing and tunneling can provide availability in a Cisco internetwork.

CHAPTER

2

Introduction to Managing
Traffic and Access

Cisco ACRC Exam Objectives Covered in This Chapter:

▶ **Describe causes of network congestion.** *(pages 17 – 20)*

▶ **List solutions for controlling network congestion.**
(pages 20 – 26)

▶ **Introduction to Managing Traffic and Access** *(pages 27 – 30)*

▶ **Configure IP standard access lists.** *(pages 30 – 36)*

▶ **Limit virtual terminal access.** *(pages 37 – 39)*

▶ **Configure IP extended access lists.** *(pages 40 – 43)*

▶ **Verify access list operation.** *(pages 44 – 49)*

▶ **Configure an alternative to using access lists.** *(pages 50 – 52)*

▶ **Configure an IP helper address to manage broadcasts.**
(pages 52 – 58)

The objectives in this chapter are important for you to
know when implementing Cisco routers in the real world. To be successful on the ACRC exam, you must thoroughly understand the
objectives discussed in this chapter.

Knowing the syntax, rules, and uses of standard access lists, extended
access lists, and IP helper addresses will save valuable time during configuration—helping you to avoid reading reference books, which might
make you appear as an amateur to your customer. And, most importantly, it will also assure accurate router configurations the first time
around. Making sure your access lists are properly configured the first
time through will undoubtedly save you many hours of troubleshooting.

Many of the exam's questions will require that you type in the answer
instead of selecting the usual multiple-choice type answers. Be prepared, because this part of the test will count against you if you
mistype even a single character.

Describe causes of network congestion.

As more and more users connect to a network, a network's performance begins to wane as the added users fight for more bandwidth. Like too many cars getting onto a freeway at rush hour, this increased utilization causes increased network congestion as more users try to access existing network resources. With the combination of today's more powerful workstations, audio and video to the desktop, and network-intensive applications, 10Mbps Ethernet networks no longer offer enough bandwidth to fulfill the business requirements of typical large companies today.

It is not difficult to understand why one needs to know the causes of network congestion before being able to troubleshoot, design, and administer networks. As this section points out, there are many reasons why network congestion can become a serious problem. Most companies heavily rely on their network; some even *are* their network (e.g., an ISP). Therefore, network congestion can be a corporation killer if left untreated. The costs to troubleshoot, repair, and upgrade a network can become astronomical if problems are left unattended for long periods of time. This objective is tested with few direct questions, but it forms the foundation of several questions on other subjects, such as LAN segmentation.

Critical Information

An internetwork is the communication structure that works to tie LANs and WANs together. Its primary goal is to quickly and efficiently move information anywhere within a corporation, upon demand, and with complete integrity. Today's users have become increasingly dependent on their networks. Just make a group of users' server or hub go offline and watch the chaos that results around the office. Where this has led—and what this means for corporations that want to remain competitive in today's global market—is that the networks companies depend on today have to efficiently manage, on a daily basis, some or all of the following:

- Graphics and imaging
- Files in the gigabyte range
- Client/server computing
- High network traffic loads

To be able to amply meet these needs, an Information Services (IS) department must provide the following to users:

- More bandwidth
- Bandwidth on demand
- Low delays
- Data, voice, and video capabilities on the same media

Also, today's networks must be adaptable; they must be ready to suit the applications of tomorrow. In the not-too-distant future, networks will need to be equipped to handle the following:

- High-definition imaging
- Full-motion video
- Digitized audio

In short, for an internetwork to satisfactorily realize its purpose, it must be able to efficiently connect many different networks together to serve the organizations that depend on it. This connectivity must happen regardless of the type of physical media involved. Companies expanding their networks must also overcome the limitations of physical and geographic boundaries. The Internet serves as a model to facilitate this growth.

Exam Essentials

You should understand and be able to explain the primary reason for network congestion.   Too many users trying to use the same bandwidth at the same time is the main cause for network congestion.

Remember the basics of internetworking.   Keeping in mind some of the basics of networking—like CSMA/CD for Ethernet and token passing for architectures like FDDI and Token Ring—will greatly help you answer questions about network congestion.

Understand why adding more bandwidth isn't always the best answer for resolving network congestion.   At some point, adding more bandwidth is going to be impractical or cost prohibitive. Learning to make the most of available bandwidth is a valuable tool in an engineer's bag of tricks.

Key Terms and Concepts

CSMA/CD (Carrier Sense Multiple Access/Collision Detection)
Ethernet's contention-based protocol for getting traffic across the wire, which stipulates that only one node may transmit at any one time.

FDDI (Fiber Distributed Data Interface)   A 100Mb implementation of a token-passing protocol that is used mainly for campus backbones.

Internetwork   Communication structure that works to tie LANs and WANs together. Routers create internetworks.

Sample Questions

1. What is a benefit of bridge segmentation?

    A. Regeneration and propagation

    B. Segmenting or breaking up your network into smaller, more manageable pieces

    C. LAN queuing

    D. Bridges begin forwarding the frame before reception is complete

    Answer: B—Bridges break up a network into collision domains, but the network is still one large broadcast domain.

2. By which of the following methods does cut-through switching provide better performance than other switching methods?

    A. LAN queuing

    B. Microsegmentation

    C. Receiving the entire frame onto onboard buffers, running a CRC, and then forwarding the frames out of the destination port

    D. Forwarding the frame before reception is complete

    Answer: D—It only has to read the header of the frame before it starts forwarding the frames to the destination.

List solutions for controlling network congestion.

Congestion usually causes users to scream for more bandwidth. However, simply increasing bandwidth cannot always solve the problem. One way to solve congestion problems and to increase the networking performance of your LAN is to divide a single Ethernet segment into multiple network segments. This maximizes the available bandwidth.

Understanding network segmentation is one of the most valuable tools available for Ethernet network design, troubleshooting, upgrading, and performance optimizing. Most network consultants and experienced administrators will look for improper segmentation the moment they hear anything about network congestion. This should be considered to be part of "Basic Networking 101" since it is a starting point for network design and troubleshooting.

This objective will give you a thorough understanding of duplex modes, segmentation, Ethernet/Fast Ethernet, FDDI/Token Ring, and bridging/switching. You should also be aware that the questions will be presented in both direct and indirect formats.

Critical Information

The following list contains some of the ways to control network congestion. Each of these methods is covered in detail in the following paragraphs.

- Physical segmentation
- Network switching technology
- Using full-duplex Ethernet devices
- Using Fast Ethernet
- Using FDDI

Physical Segmentation

Physical segmentation allows you to break up collision domains and broadcast domains. The three main ways to control network congestion involve segmentation with bridges, routers, and LAN switches.

Segmentation with a Bridge

A bridge can segment or break up your network into smaller, more manageable pieces. This helps to reduce network congestion. However, if a bridge is placed incorrectly in your network, it can cause more harm than good.

Bridges perform at the MAC sublayer of the Data Link layer. They create separate physical and logical network segments to reduce the traffic loads. There are solid advantages to bridging. By segmenting a logical network into multiple physical pieces, it secures network reliability, availability, scalability, and manageability.

Bridges work by examining the MAC or hardware addresses in each frame and then forwarding the frame to the other physical segments (only if necessary). These devices dynamically build a forwarding table of information comprised of each MAC address and the segment on which that address is located.

Bridges will forward packets and multicast packets to all other segments to which they're attached. Because, by default, the addresses from these broadcasts are never seen by the bridge, and hence are not filtered, broadcast storms can result. The same problem can happen with switches because, theoretically, switch ports are bridge ports. A Cisco switch is really a multi-port bridge that runs the Cisco IOS and performs the same functions as a bridge.

It is important to remember that bridges create smaller collision domains, but the network is still one large broadcast domain.

Segmentation with a Router

As you know, routers work at the Network layer and are used to route packets to destination networks. Routers, like bridges, use tables to make routing decisions. However, routers only keep information on how to get to remote networks—not to hosts—in their tables, using that information to route packets through an internetwork. Routers use IP addresses instead of hardware addresses when making their routing decisions.

Routers maintain a routing table for each protocol on the network, and a Cisco router will keep a routing table for AppleTalk, a different one for IPX, and still another one for IP.

The following information will help you to understand some of the benefits of routers:

Manageability   Multiple routing protocols give the network manager who's creating an internetwork a lot of flexibility.

Increased functionality   Cisco routers provide features that address the issues of flow, error and congestion control, fragmentation, reassembly, and control over a packet's lifetime.

Multiple active paths   Using protocols, DSAPs, SSAPs, and path metrics, routers can make informed routing decisions and interpret the next layer protocol. This allows routers to have more than one active path between networks.

Segmentation with LAN Switches

LAN switching is a great strategy for LAN segmentation. LAN switches improve performance by employing frame switching, which permits high-speed data exchanges.

Just like bridges, switches use the destination MAC address to ensure that the packet is forwarded to the right outgoing port. Cut-through LAN switching begins forwarding the packet before reception is complete, keeping latency to a minimum. Store-and-forward LAN switching receives the entire frame onto the onboard buffers, runs a CRC, and then forwards the frame out of the destination port.

The following are three different switching methods:

Port-configuration switching   Allows a port to be assigned to a physical network segment under software control. It's the simplest form of switching.

Frame switching   Used to increase available bandwidth on the network. Frame switching allows multiple transmissions to occur in parallel. This is the type of switching performed by all Catalyst switches.

Cell switching (ATM)   Similar to frame switching; ATM uses small, fixed-length cells that are switched on the network. It's the switching method used by all Cisco Lightstream switches.

A LAN switch supplies you with considerably higher port density at a lower cost than standard bridges. Since LAN switches permit fewer users per segment, the average available bandwidth per user increases. This fewer-users-per-segment trend is known as microsegmentation, which lets you create dedicated segments.

When you have one user per segment, each one enjoys instant access to the full lot of available bandwidth instead of competing for it with other users. Because of this, the collisions that are so common with shared, medium-sized networks that use hubs just don't happen.

Network Switching Technology

As network usage increases, more Token Ring and FDDI LAN switches are being used, but Ethernet LAN switches are still the most common type of switch. LAN switches uniquely support some very cool new features, including the following:

- Numerous, simultaneous conversations

- High-speed data exchanges

- Low latency and high frame-forwarding rates

- Dedicated communication between devices

- Full-duplex communication

- Media rate adaptation (both 10Mbps hosts and 100Mbps hosts can work on the same network)

- The ability to work with existing 802.3-compliant network interface cards and cabling

Thanks to dedicated, collision-free communication between network devices, file-transfer throughput is increased. Many conversations can occur simultaneously by forwarding or switching several packets at the same time, which expands network capacity by the amount of supported conversations.

Full-duplex communication fully doubles throughput, and media rate adaptation allows the LAN switch to translate between 10Mbps and 100Mbps to allocate bandwidth on an as-needed basis. Another benefit is that changing over to LAN switches doesn't require changing the existing hubs, network interface cards, or cabling.

Full-Duplex Ethernet Devices

By using full-duplex devices, you can theoretically double your bandwidth on your network. Attaching devices to full-duplex switch ports allows the devices to transmit and receive simultaneously. Theoretically, since each transmitted and received signal has its own wires to use, collisions or fragmentation should not happen.

Fast Ethernet

Fast Ethernet runs at 100Mbps, which is 10 times as fast as 10BaseT Ethernet, which runs at 10Mbps. The best thing about Fast Ethernet is that it uses the same signaling techniques as 10BaseT, which allows you to run both types of devices together on your network. This means you can upgrade your network a piece at a time instead of having to upgrade the whole network all at once.

FDDI

Fiber Distributed Data Interface is a token-based media access network. It typically runs at 100Mbps and has a mature, dependable specification. It was the fastest network around until Fast and Gigabit Ethernet came out. However, it works well under heavy loads and does not have collisions, because of its token-based media access.

***

Exam Essentials

You should be able to list the three key types of LAN segmentation and understand how segmentation is used to thwart network congestion. The three key types of equipment used to segment LANs are bridges, routers, and switches. Re-read the preceding section to make sure you fully understand the difference between each device.

Remember that there is no contention in a full-duplex environment. This is why servers are attached directly to switches. When connected in a full-duplex mode, they can transmit and receive simultaneously.

Remember that there is no contention in a token-based system. This is why FDDI is commonly used as a backbone solution. This is also why a token-based system is more efficient under a heavy load than a contention-based system like Ethernet.

Key Terms and Concepts

Cut-through switching   A packet-switching approach that streams data through a switch so that the leading edge (destination address) of a packet exits the switch at the output port before the packet finishes entering the input port.

Full-duplex communications   Mode that allows a device to both transmit and receive at the same time.

Latency   The measurement of when a frame enters a switch to the time it leaves the switch.

Store-and-forward switching   A packet-switching technique in which the entire frame is copied to the switch's on-board buffer and a CRC is run before being forwarded out the appropriate port.

Sample Questions

1. What is LAN segmentation with switches also called?

   A. Filtering

   B. Microsegmenting

   C. Bridging

   D. Routing

   Answer: B—Microsegmenting is the old industry term for switching.

2. By which of the following methods do routers filter a network? (Choose all that apply.)

   A. Logical address

   B. IP address

   C. Digital signaling

   D. Hardware address

   E. IPX address

   Answer: A, B, E—Routers use third-layer logical addresses to create smaller collision and broadcast domains.

Introduction to Managing Traffic and Access

Cisco has created their own three-layer hierarchical model, which you can follow when building or designing a scalable internetwork. This hierarchical model makes addressing and device management easier because mapping network addresses to the hierarchy reduces the odds that you'll have to reconfigure them as the network grows. Plus, if you know where all devices that do similar things are placed within the hierarchy, it is much easier to consistently configure all routers within a particular layer. To be able to manage traffic and access, you must understand the Cisco hierarchical model.

Understanding Cisco's three-layer hierarchical model will also enable you to make more resilient, growth-oriented network designs, allow you to recognize a good or bad design when you see one, and assure that you only spend as much money as is needed to purchase the most appropriate products for the required tasks.

Critical Information

This section will present for you the three-layer Cisco hierarchical model. Figure 2.1 shows the Cisco three-layer model, and the layers of the hierarchical model are as follows:

- Core layer
- Distribution layer
- Access layer

FIGURE 2.1: The Cisco three-layer hierarchical model

The Core Layer

The primary function of the Core layer is to provide an optimized and reliable transport structure. This is essential for the entire enterprise internetwork and may include LAN and WAN backbones. Services that enhance communication between routes in a different logical group or are located at different sites function at the Core layer. Its routers provide maximum reliability and availability, and if a LAN or WAN circuit falters here, Core routers can usually maintain connectivity.

The Distribution Layer

The Distribution layer's *raison d'être* is to provide access to various parts of the internetwork as well as to services. This represents the campus backbone. Distribution-layer routers govern access to Core-layer resources, and it's vital for Distribution-layer routers to utilize bandwidth efficiently. They must also fulfill the quality-of-service (QOS) requirements of various protocols by exerting a policy-based form of traffic control that sequesters local and backbone environments.

The Access Layer

The Access layer provides access to corporate resources for a workgroup or users on a local segment. Routers at the Access layer manage traffic by restricting all service requests and broadcasts to the access media, and they must provide connectivity while sustaining the network's integrity. The routers situated at the point of access must determine the legitimacy of users dialing in while requiring only minimal authentication steps from them.

Exam Essentials

Memorize the three layers of Cisco's hierarchical model. You should be able to list the three layers Cisco uses for its hierarchical internetworking model, as previously described in this section, and understand how these three layers are implemented to contribute to the areas of a scalable internetwork.

Remember what each layer does. The Core layer provides an optimized and reliable transport structure. The Distribution layer provides access to various parts of the internetwork as well as to services, and the Access layer provides access to corporate resources for a workgroup or users on a local segment.

Key Terms and Concepts

Access layer Provides access to corporate resources for a workgroup or users on a local segment.

Core layer Provides an optimized and reliable transport structure.

Distribution layer Provides access to various parts of the internetwork as well as to services.

Sample Questions

1. Choose the three layers Cisco uses for building its hierarchical internetwork model.

   A. Fundamental

   B. Distribution

   C. IGRP

   D. Core

   E. Backbone

   F. Access

   Answer: B, D, F—Distribution, Core, and Access are the three layers in the Cisco hierarchical model.

2. What is the primary function of the Core layer?

   A. To distribute client/server router information

   B. To provide an optimized and reliable transport structure

    C. To provide access to various parts of the internetwork as well as to services

    D. To provide access to corporate resources for a workgroup or users on a local segment

Answer: B—Core-layer routers provide maximum reliability and availability.

Configure IP standard access lists.

There are two types of access lists: standard and extended. (Extended access lists are covered in detail later in this chapter.) The standard access list is relatively limited in the functions it can provide. It can filter based only upon the source address of the incoming or outgoing packet. The valid numerical assignment for a standard access list is 1–99. Standard access lists are very common and easily configured. Memorizing them isn't time consuming and saves time when configuring a Cisco router for basic filtering.

Both standard and extended access lists can be tricky. Practice as much with routers and study this objective as much as necessry to grab a firm understanding of what the objective is asking.

Critical Information

A standard access list is a sequential list of *permit* or *deny* statements based on the source IP address of a packet. When a packet reaches a router, the packet has to follow a different procedure based on whether it's trying to enter or leave an interface. If there's an access list on the interface, the packet must go through every line in it until the packet matches the specified criteria. If the packet goes through the entire list without a match, it is dropped. For the packet to be forwarded, there has to be a permit statement at the end of the list allowing that or the packet will simply be dropped.

In Cisco IOS, there's an implied deny statement at the end of the access list, so, if the purpose of your access list is to deny a few criteria but forward everything else, you must include a permit statement as the final line of the access list. However, you don't have to end the access list with a deny statement if the list's purpose is to permit only certain criteria and drop the rest; this is automatically understood.

If you're thinking that access lists have the potential to create a lot of overhead on a router, you're right. They can also cause delays because packets have to be checked against every line in the access list until either they're matched or the list ends. So, when you write an access list, it's really important to plan ahead and write it as efficiently as possible. Place the lines that will receive the most matches at the top of the list, and, as lines are added, try to place them according to their projected usage. Be aware of the possibility that the most-matched line may not end up where you write it, depending on whether it is a permit or deny statement. Sometimes the IOS will re-order the statements based on the condition. Finally, the shorter the list, the less overhead and delay it will introduce.

The wildcard mask is the last part of the command. The wildcard mask should be written in a four-octet IP address format. The decimal value of each octet converts into a stream of binary zeros and ones. The zeros represent significant bits, which means that the value must be matched exactly. The ones represent insignificant bits, which means that the value does not have to be matched exactly. Examples of wildcard masks and their corresponding network addresses are listed in Table 2.1.

TABLE 2.1: Network Addresses and Wildcard Masks

Network Address	Wildcard Mask (Decimal)	Wildcard Mask (Binary)
172.16 .10.0	0.0.0.255	00000000.00000000.00000000.11111111
172.16 .0.0	0.0.15.255	00000000.00000000.00001111.11111111
172.16 .20.4	0.0.0.3	00000000.00000000.00000000.00000011

These examples show that any address being compared to the IP address and wildcard mask must match the binary value for every place that has a zero assigned.

The first example shows that network 172.16.10.0 has a wildcard mask of 0.0.0.255. This means, as long as the first three octets match exactly, that the last octet does not matter. It can be any value between zero and 255.

The second example is similar in that the Class B network must be matched, but the third octet needs to match only every 16th host/network.

For the third example, the last two bits of the last octet do not matter.

Included here are some sample access lists for you to read through, with an explanation following each list.

```
access-list 1 deny    172.16.40.6
access-list 1 permit 172.16.20.6
```

This access list is pretty simple and straightforward. The first line identifies the access list as access-list 1. The condition of the first line is to deny any packet that matches the source address specified (in this case, 172.16.40.6). The second line, also identified as part of access list one, specifies that the access list will permit any packet that matches the source address of 172.16.20.6. What happens to a packet that doesn't match either of those lines? Remember that in Cisco IOS the last line (although it may be invisible) of an access list is a *deny any* statement by default. So, if you want packets that don't match the specified source addresses to be forwarded, you must add a *permit any* statement at the end of the list or the packets will be dropped. The following access list two includes a permit any statement:

```
access-list 2 deny    10.0.0.0 0.255.255.255
access-list 2 deny    192.168.0.0 0.0.255.255
access-list 2 permit any
```

In this list, the private networks of 10.0.0.0 and 192.168.0.0 are denied, and everything else is permitted. Access list two has also used the source wildcard mask, indicating that any possible IP address within the Class A address space of 10.0.0.0 will be denied. The same thing was done for 192.168.0.0, indicating that every possible IP address within that Class C supernet range will also be denied. This is because trying to enter a single line for each and every one of the possible Class A and Class C addresses would be an impossibly huge task. Also, notice that access list two ends with permit any. If it didn't, nothing would be forwarded.

Finally, when writing a standard access list for any purpose, plan exactly which source addresses will be blocked and which ones will be permitted. After obtaining a preliminary draft of the networks that will be included in your access list, determine which networks can be aggregated into a single line using wildcard masks so that the list will be shorter, packets will experience less delay, and the router processor won't experience as much load. If you want packets that don't match any line on the list to be forwarded, don't forget to add the *permit any* statement so they won't be dropped.

Creating an Access List

Now that you know how the standard access list works, this section shows you how they're written. The command is given with the following syntax:

```
access-list access-list-number [deny | permit] source
[source-wildcard]
```

The access-list-number command is an integer between one and 99. After the list number, either a deny or a permit statement must be added to tell the router what to do if a packet matches this line of the access list. The *source* is either the source IP host address or the source IP network address. It's the part of the line used to match the packets being compared against the access list, and it can be entered as a four-octet IP address or as the word *any*, which will match any IP address. If more than one host or network needs to be designated, the *source-wildcard* can be added.

To apply an access list directly to an interface, use the following command:

```
ip access-group access-list-number [ in | out ]
```

The *access-list-number* is the number of the list being applied to the interface. If the packet to be forwarded should be checked before its exit onto the line, the out option should be used. If packets coming from outside the router are to be checked against the access list before gaining entry, choose the in option. Following is an example of how an access list is applied to an interface and an output excerpt from the running-configuration file showing how the commands were received.

```
Router_C#config term
Enter configuration commands, one per line.  End with
CNTL/Z.
Router_C(config)#access-list 10 deny 172.16.10.0
0.0.0.255
Router_C(config)#access-list 10 deny 172.16.20.0
0.0.0.255
Router_C(config)#access-list 10 permit 172.16.30.0
0.0.0.255
Router_C(config)#int s0
Router_C(config-if)#ip address 172.16.40.6
255.255.255.252
Router_C(config-if)#ip access-group 10 in
Router_C(config-if)#^Z
Router_C#

interface Serial0
 ip address 172.16.40.6 255.255.255.252
 ip access-group 10 in
!
access-list 10 permit 172.16.30.0 0.0.0.255
access-list 10 deny   172.16.20.0 0.0.0.255
access-list 10 deny   172.16.10.0 0.0.0.255
```

Exam Essentials

There are several key points to keep in mind with standard access lists. By memorizing these key factors, you will save yourself time and mistakes.

Memorize the syntax for the *access-list* command. access-list is a global command. By using access-list 1, you are specifying that you are creating a standard access list because the number you are using is between one and 99.

Keep in mind the implied "deny any" at the end of every access list and that access lists filter from top to bottom. Each packet that enters a router is matched to the access list, line by line. If it doesn't match any lines, it is automatically dropped.

Understand the concept of wildcard masks—especially those with variable length. Practice working wildcard masks on paper. This should be easy for you to accomplish before taking the exam.

Understand how to apply access lists to physical interfaces using the *access-group* command. The access-group 10 in command is an example of applying an access list to an interface.

Remember that you should place standard access lists as close to the destination router as possible in order to exercise the most control. By placing access lists close to the destination network or router, you could save packets from traversing an internetwork and then getting dropped at the end. It is better to drop the packets as soon as possible.

Key Terms and Concepts

access-group command Applies a standard or extended access list to a logical or physical interface.

access-list command Creates and makes entries into a standard or extended access list.

Wildcard mask A subnet-mask group that defines a group of hosts or networks.

Sample Questions

1. What is the criterion used to match a packet on a standard access list?

   A. Full IP address

   B. Domain name

   C. Source IP address and wildcard mask

   D. IP address or host name

   E. User access

   F. MAC address or IP address

   Answer: C—Standard access lists can only filter on source IP addresses.

2. What is the proper syntax for writing a standard access list?

   A. `ip access-list access-list-number [deny | permit] source [source-wildcard]`

   B. `access-list access-list-number [deny | permit] source [source-wildcard]`

   C. `access-list access-list-number [deny | permit] source [source-mask]`

   D. `access-list access-list-number [deny | permit] [protocol] source [source-wildcard] destination [destination-wildcard]`

   Answer: B—`access-list 10 permit 172.16.50.0 0.0.0.255` is an example of how to filter using a standard access list.

Limit virtual terminal access.

Just as there are physical ports or interfaces, such as E0 or S1 on the router, there are also virtual ports. These virtual ports are called virtual terminal lines, numbered vty 0 through vty 4. Understanding how to access and restrict access to virtual terminal ports (vty ports) is critical. If left unguarded, vty ports can invite trouble.

It is important to know the theory and syntax of using and restricting vty ports if you want to implement any type of effective network security strategy. Try practicing this on Cisco routers if possible. It is important, when studying for the exam, that you understand this objective fully.

Critical Information

Cisco thinks this is important because the vty ports on a router can be a hole waiting to be taken advantage of. You can set an extended access list to stop Telnet from being received on a router, which can be cumbersome. What happens if you miss an interface or a source address? It is easier to add a standard access list right to the vty ports. By using a standard access list, you can simply specify which source hosts you want to be able to Telnet into the router.

Restricting virtual terminal access is not necessarily a traffic control mechanism but is more a technique for increasing network security. For security purposes, vty access can be blocked to or from the router.

Necessary Procedures

By default, access lists are effective only for packets that travel through the router—not ones that originate from the router. This leaves a security hole. The five virtual terminals on the router are vulnerable to unrestricted access, but you can apply standard access lists to them as well.

The vty ports are numbered zero through four. The good news is that you can implement security and configure all of these ports at the same time. Here's how:

```
RouterA#config t
RouterA#access-list 50 permit 172.16.30.0 0.0.0.255
RouterA(config)#line vty 0 4
RouterA(config-line)#access-class 50 in
RouterA(config-line)#^Z
RouterA#
```

Notice that the access-class command was used instead of access-group. The access-class command syntax is as follows:

```
access-class access-list-number [in | out]
```

The *access-list-number* in this command is a value from one to 99, meaning that it must be a standard access list. Remember that standard access lists match source IP addresses only.

TIP It is sometimes recommended that you configure the last vty port (vty 4) differently than the others (vty 0–3). This way, you will have a back door into the router. Each vty connection will use the first available line at the lowest number not in use. It is generally recommended that all vty ports be set to the same values.

Exam Essentials

Remember that vty ports use the *access-class* command, rather than the *access-group* command, to apply the access list to the port. Practice limiting vty access on a router.

Remember that, by default, there are five vty ports on a Cisco router. The five ports are vty 0–4.

Key Terms and Concepts

access-class command   Applies a standard or extended access list to a virtual terminal interface.

line command   Places the router in line configuration mode so that vty ports may be configured.

Vty (Virtual TeleType) ports: The five default virtual interfaces used on a router for Telnet.

Sample Questions

1. Which command is issued to apply a standard access list to a virtual interface?

   A. access-class access-list-number [in | out]

   B. access-list access-list-number [in | out]

   C. access-group access-list-number [in | out]

   D. ip access-class access-list-number [in | out]

   Answer: A—The access-class command is used to apply an access list to a line.

2. Which command is used to apply an access list to a physical interface?

   A. access-class access-list-number [in | out]

   B. access-list access-list-number [in | out]

   C. access-group access-list-number [in | out]

   D. ip access-group access-list-number [in | out]

   Answer: D—The ip access-group command is used to apply an access list to an interface.

Configure IP extended access lists.

Extended access lists offer filtering on port numbers, session-layer protocols, and destination addresses, in addition to filtering by source address. While all of these extended filtering features make this kind of access list much more powerful, they can also produce a greater amount of overhead on a router because of their potential complexity. Although it is difficult to completely memorize the syntax due to all of the variations, it is highly recommended that you become very familiar with how the syntax is structured. This will greatly impact how efficient you become in working with Cisco routers.

Critical Information

The primary difference between extended access lists and standard access lists is the syntax of the command. A packet must follow the same basic process when arriving at an interface, no matter whether it has an extended access list or a standard access list applied to it. The only difference is the much-greater scope of criteria available to specify with extended access lists. Because extended access lists are complex and can create a lot of overhead and delay on routers, it's even more important to strategically place them so they'll be most efficient and so their burden on the network will be minimized.

Extended lists can be applied using the `access-group` command on any given interface, and each interface can have two access groups applied to them—one inbound and one outbound.

There are some important considerations when deciding where to apply an extended access list. For example, if the list's purpose is to provide security, it should be applied to the interface where the machines are connected. However, if the list is for stopping certain types of traffic from transiting the network, it should be applied as close as possible to the origin of the unwanted traffic, which avoids the problem of wasted bandwidth. You don't want traffic to move across the core just to be denied on the destination router's side.

An extended access list can also become long; if it does, examine it to see whether it can be streamlined by applying it closer to the edge devices. Another good strategy—if the same list is applied outbound to the majority of the interfaces on the router—is to apply it inbound instead, on the interface that points upstream. All of these tricks can really help to manage access lists by providing ways to implement them efficiently.

Necessary Procedures

Syntax is where the real differences between standard and extended access lists lie. The syntax for extended lists varies considerably from the syntax for the simpler standard lists.

The following syntax is used to configure extended access lists:

```
access-list access-list-number [deny | permit]
[protocol | protocol-keyword] [source-address source
wildcard mask | any] [destination-address destination
wildcard mask | any] [protocol-specific options]
```

The following descriptions are for the syntax of the main extended-access-list command:

- *access-list-number* is an integer value between 100 and 199.

- deny | permit is the condition that's applied to a specific line in the access list.

- *protocol* is the session-layer protocol. (EIGRP, GRE, ICMP, IGMP, IGRP, IP, IPinIP, NOS, OSPF, TCP, and UDP are all options.)

- *protocol-keyword* can be ICMP, IGMP, TCP, UDP, and host. These keywords allow other protocol-specific commands. The host command specifies that a single host address will follow.

- *source-address source wildcard mask* is the IP address and wildcard mask. (The *any* option specifies any source IP address.)

- *destination-address destination wildcard mask* is the IP address and wildcard mask. (The *any* option specifies any destination IP address.)

- The log command enables logging for the access list.

As you choose among these different options, additional ones not listed above will become available. These special options are the protocol keywords.

Something to note is that the syntax for TCP lines is significantly different from the syntax of normal extended access lists. The command is as follows:

```
access-list access-list-number [permit | deny] tcp
[source source-wildcard | any] [operator source-port |
source-port] [destination destination-wildcard | any]
[operator destination-port | destination-port]
[established]
```

Exam Essentials

Remember the number range (100–199) for an extended access list and that it filters on source addresses, destination addresses, session-layer protocols, and application port numbers. For example, access-list 110 permit tcp 172.16.10.0 0.0.0.255 host 172.16.50.1 eq telnet log is how you can specify both source and destination IP addresses, IP header protocol field (TCP) and upper-layer service (Telnet).

Remember that extended access lists do *not* filter IP based on port number. Only TCP or UDP can be filtered by port number. For example, access-list 110 permit ip any any eq ftp log will never work. The protocol must be TCP or UDP for the access list to filter based on upper-layer service or protocols.

Remember as many industry standard port numbers as possible (e.g., *telnet/23, ftp/21, smtp/25, pop3/110,* etc.). Even though you really don't have to memorize this, it will help to study the port numbers.

Key Terms and Concepts

access-group command   Used to set an access list on an interface.

access-list command   Used to set an access list in a router.

Extended access list   Lets you filter by source and destination IP address, Network-layer protocol, and Transport-layer protocol.

Syntax   How commands are structured or put together—the order, types, values, and names of the parts.

Sample Questions

1. What is the effect of the following configuration line?

   ```
   Access-list 101 permit tcp any host 138.99.88.77 eq smtp
   ```
   A. All e-mail traffic to 138.99.88.77 is passed.

   B. All e-mail traffic from 138.99.88.77 is passed.

   C. All e-mail to 138.99.88.77 is filtered.

   D. All e-mail from 138.99.88.77 is filtered.

   Answer: A—The access list allows any source packets with a destination IP address of 138.99.88.77 with SMTP in the Transport-layer header to be passed.

2. What range of integers is used to signify an extended access list?

   A. 101–199

   B. 1–99

   C. 100–200

   D. 100–199

   Answer: D—You must specify the access-list command (100–199) when creating extended access lists.

Verify access list operation.

It is important to check your access lists for accuracy. By using a few commands, you will be able to check how your access lists are set and how they are applied to an interface. Knowing how to check your access lists by protocol (e.g., IP) and how to ascertain which interfaces have access lists set is very important when working in a production environment.

If you make an error when working with access lists on your Cisco router, it is possible to shut the router down. What might be worse is that you could cause a small but annoying error in your internetwork that is very hard to troubleshoot.

Critical Information

This is a small but important objective. The following commands are for verifying access lists:

- `show access-lists` shows you all configured access lists on your router.

- `show ip access-lists` shows only IP access lists on your router.

- `show access-list 187` shows only access list 187.

- `show ip access-list 187` also shows only access list 187.

The following commands are for verifying which interfaces have IP access lists applied:

- `show running-config` shows the current configuration of your router.

- `show ip interface` shows the configured parameters of the router's interfaces.

Necessary Procedures

This section demonstrates and more closely defines the commands previously discussed.

Executing the show access-lists command displays the following information about the access lists configured on the router:

```
Router_B#show access-lists
Standard IP access list 1
    deny    172.16.40.6
    permit 172.16.20.6
Standard IP access list 2
    deny    10.0.0.0, wildcard bits 0.255.255.255
    deny    192.168.0.0, wildcard bits 0.0.255.255
    permit any
Standard IP access list 3
    deny    10.1.3.10
    deny    10.1.2.10
    permit 10.1.4.10
Extended IP access list 110
   permit tcp host 172.16.50.2 host 172.16.10.2 eq 8080
(47 matches)
   permit tcp 172.16.30.0 0.0.0.255 host 172.16.10.2 eq
8080 (11 matches)
   permit tcp any any eq www (33 matches)
Router_B#show ip access-lists
Standard IP access list 1
    deny    172.16.40.6
    permit 172.16.20.6
Standard IP access list 2
    deny    10.0.0.0, wildcard bits 0.255.255.255
    deny    192.168.0.0, wildcard bits 0.0.255.255
    permit any
Standard IP access list 3
    deny    10.1.3.10
    deny    10.1.2.10
    permit 10.1.4.10
```

```
Extended IP access list 110
  permit tcp host 172.16.50.2 host 172.16.10.2 eq 8080
(47 matches)
  permit tcp 172.16.30.0 0.0.0.255 host 172.16.10.2 eq
8080 (11 matches)
  permit tcp any any eq www (33 matches)
Router_B#show access-list 3
Standard IP access list 3
    deny    10.1.3.10
    deny    10.1.2.10
    permit 10.1.4.10
```

This information gives you a summary of each access list on the router. The access list type is defined as a standard access list, along with the number assigned to it. Each line of the list is displayed individually; if you look at access list two, you can see that the command breaks the line down into its different components. The show access-lists command also specifies which network is matched using which wildcard mask.

The show ip access-lists command shows the same information. However, it is a useful command if you have multiple protocols configured with access lists.

The show access-list command is also helpful if you have many access lists configured. It allows you to see only the list specified.

To see which interfaces have access lists applied, you can use the show running-config and/or the show ip interface commands. The show running-config command will show you your current router configuration. Notice the following interface Ethernet 0 configuration:

```
RouterA#show running-config
Building configuration...

Current configuration:
!
version 11.3
no service password-encryption
!
```

```
hostname RouterA
!
enable secret 5 $1$YMNO$Pz1r4tEg1E91wcKrNUIOHO
enable password password
!
!
interface Ethernet0
 ip address 172.16.10.1 255.255.255.0
 ip access-group 110 out
 no mop enabled
!
interface Serial0
 ip address 172.16.20.1 255.255.255.0
 no ip mroute-cache
!
interface Serial1
 no ip address
 shutdown
!
router rip
 redistribute connected
 network 172.16.0.0
!
ip classless
access-list 110 permit tcp host 172.16.50.2 host
    172.16.10.2 eq 8080
access-list 110 permit tcp 172.16.30.0 0.0.0.255 host
    172.16.10.2 eq 8080
access-list 110 permit tcp any any eq www
access-list 110 deny   ip any any log
!
line con 0
line aux 0
line vty 0 4
 password password2
 login
!
end
RouterA#
```

The show ip interface command will show you all configured options for your interface. The access list information is bolded. The show running-config command is easier to read.

```
RouterA#sh ip interface e0
Ethernet0 is up, line protocol is up
  Internet address is 172.16.10.1/24
  Broadcast address is 255.255.255.255
  Address determined by non-volatile memory
  MTU is 1500 bytes
  Helper address is not set
  Directed broadcast forwarding is enabled
  Multicast reserved groups joined: 224.0.0.9
  Outgoing access list is 110
  Inbound  access list is not set
  Proxy ARP is enabled
  Security level is default
  Split horizon is enabled
  ICMP redirects are always sent
  ICMP unreachables are always sent
  ICMP mask replies are never sent
  IP fast switching is enabled
  IP fast switching on the same interface is disabled
  IP multicast fast switching is enabled
  Router Discovery is disabled
  IP output packet accounting is disabled
  IP access violation accounting is disabled
  TCP/IP header compression is disabled
  Probe proxy name replies are disabled
  Gateway Discovery is disabled
  Policy routing is disabled
  Network address translation is disabled
```

Exam Essentials

Know the commands that show access lists. The show access-list, sh ip access-list, and sh access-list 187 commands will show you access list information.

Know the commands that show which interfaces have access lists set. The show run and sh ip int commands show you which interfaces have access lists applied.

Key Terms and Concepts

show running-config command   Used on a Cisco router to see the configuration a router is running.

show startup-config command   Used on a Cisco router to see the configuration that will be used when the router is rebooted.

show ip interface command   Used on a Cisco router to see the interface default configuration. This command can also show you what interfaces have an access list set.

Sample Questions

1. Which command(s) may be issued to provide specific information on access list functionality?

   A. show ip access-list 34

   B. show access-list 34

   C. debug ip icmp

   D. show ip icmp packets

   E. Answer: A, B—Both selections will show access list 34.

2. Which command(s) can be used to see which interfaces have access lists set?

   A. show ip access-list 34

   B. show run

   C. sh int access-list

   D. sh ip int

   Answer: B, C—show running-config and show ip interface will show you which interfaces have access lists set.

Configure an alternative to using access lists.

U sing an access list can be overkill when all you really want to do is localize traffic to its own network; you may just be creating unnecessary overhead. There's a better way to isolate traffic. With the Cisco IOS, pointing to a software interface of Null 0 can create static routes. Null 0 doesn't exist on the router as a physical, virtual, or logical interface; it exists only in the IOS software. This is important information when extra CPU cycles and WAN bandwidth become scarce. This technique is often used when you have overloaded routers in a production environment.

If you can practice this on Cisco routers, then consider that a bonus. When studying for the ACRC exam, you must understand this objective.

Critical Information

The Null 0 interface is like a dump where packets are simply dropped without any CPU processing. Null interfaces are often used for this very reason; they don't require any processor time. Packets are sent to the Null 0 via an entry in the routing table. The route is entered in the routing table by configuring a static route like the following:

```
ip route [destination] [mask] null 0
```

If you use this configuration, any destination address listed in the static router will be routed to Null 0 and subsequently dropped. This is an effective way to eliminate unwanted traffic from transiting your WAN, because the static route can be implemented anywhere you want. Null 0 static routes can also be used to summarize routes for redistribution into other routing protocols. For example, if you had a lot of 30-bit networks and you wanted to summarize them to your interior routing protocol, you would place one static route to Null 0 and summarize, and then you would redistribute static.

Necessary Procedures

In Figure 2.2, you can see that network 10.1.2.0 hangs off Router C. If you want to prevent packets from being sent across the WAN to network 10.1.2.0, you can use the null 0 command. If a packet hits Router A with a destination of network 10.1.2.0, the static route will forward it to the Null 0 dump.

FIGURE 2.2:   Static route to Null 0

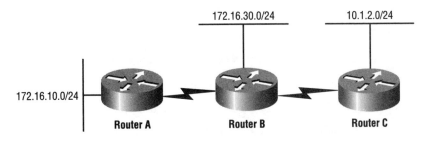

Here is a sample configuration to block packets destined for network 10.1.2.0:

```
RouterA#conf t
RouterA(config)#ip route 10.1.2.0 255.255.255.0 null 0
RouterA(config)#^Z
```

Exam Essentials

Understand the exact syntax of, and the reasons for using, the *null 0* command.   Remember that the null 0 command can be used instead of access lists to save CPU cycles.

Remember what a null interface is.   Null 0 doesn't exist on the router as a physical, virtual, or logical interface; it exists only in the IOS software.

Key Terms and Concepts

ip route command   Used to build a static route.

Null 0 interface   A software interface that can be used as a bit bucket for unwanted packets.

Static route   A route that the administrator builds by hand instead of letting a routing algorithm build the routing entry.

Sample Questions

1. When are Null 0 interfaces used in place of an access list?

   A. When RIP is the only protocol running on the router

   B. When security needs to be configured on a loopback interface

   C. When saving CPU utilization

   D. When globally denying access to a network

   Answer: C—Null interfaces can be used to save CPU cycles.

2. Which is the correct usage of the null 0 command?

   A. ip route 10.1.2.0 255.255.255.0 null 0

   B. ip route null 0 10.1.2.0 255.255.255.0

   C. ip null 0 route 10.1.2.0 255.255.255.0

   D. ip route 10.1.2.0 null 0 255.255.255.0

   Answer: A—You use the null 0 command instead of a next-hop address.

Configure an IP helper address to manage broadcasts.

By default, routers don't forward broadcast messages to prevent broadcast storms. While this generally is good, it can create a problem. What if a client needs access to a server on a different network? If that client doesn't have the IP address of the server, it will send out a broadcast requesting it, but since the router won't forward a broadcast, the server won't receive the client's request. This problem is a very common one, considering the widely used IP protocol. DHCP servers, BootP servers, and the like are integral parts of today's networks. Learning why this function is needed and how it's implemented is very useful in working with large internetworks.

Learning the default port numbers that are enabled when using IP helper addressing and protocol forwarding is a very handy thing.

Critical Information

Cisco has a solution to routers being default broadcast-blocking devices: the IP helper address command. Helper addresses convert the broadcast message into a unicast, or a directed-broadcast message, destined for the server. The helper command syntax is as follows:

    ip helper-address *address*

Eight protocols and ports (in parentheses) are forwarded by default using the `ip helper-address` command. These are:

- TFTP (69)

- DNS (53)

- Time (37)

- TACACS (49)

- BOOTP client (68)

- BOOTP server (67)

- NetBIOS name service (137)

- NetBIOS datagram service (138)

You can use the `forward-protocol` command in conjunction with the IP helper address. The `forward-protocol` command allows the IP helper address to refine the type of broadcasts it will convert and forward. The following syntax is for the forward-protocol command:

```
ip forward-protocol [udp[port] | nd | sdns]
```

This command is used to permit and deny certain UDP port numbers and is also applied to the interface with the IP helper addresses. It works somewhat like an access list.

Necessary Procedures

To configure your router's LAN interface to forward broadcasts to a server located on a different subnet, you use the ip helper-address command, as demonstrated below:

```
Router_A#conf t
Router_A(config)#int e0
Router_A(config-int)#ip helper-address 172.16.30.10
Router_A(config-int)#^Z
Router_A#
```

Notice that the Ethernet port is configured with the IP address of the server. This interface will receive the broadcast and will then make it a unicast packet with the destination IP address of 172.16.30.10.

If multiple servers exist on a different subnet than the client, the broadcast address of the server's subnet may be used. The router will turn the broadcast into a multicast packet. Figure 2.3 illustrates how this is done.

The following configuration text shows how a helper address may be configured for multiple servers on the same subnet:

```
Router_A#conf t
Router_A(config)#int e0
Router_A(config-int)#ip helper-address 172.16.30.255
Router_A(config-int)#^Z
Router_A#
```

FIGURE 2.3: Configuring helper addresses

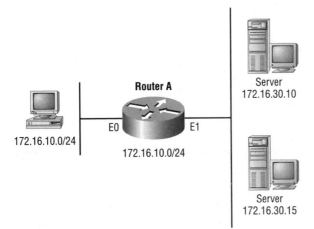

When multiple servers exist on different subnets, the interface will need multiple ip helper-address lines. Figure 2.4 shows servers on different networks.

FIGURE 2.4: Multiple servers and multiple subnets

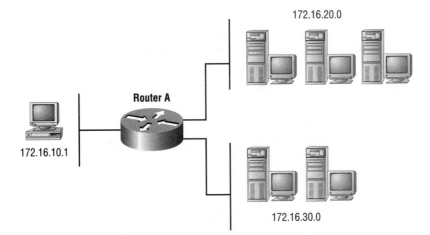

The configuration would look similar to the following:

```
Router_A#conf t
Router_A(config)#int e0
Router_A(config-int)#ip helper-address 172.16.30.255
Router_A(config-int)#ip helper-address 172.16.20.255
Router_A(config-int)#^Z
Router_A#
```

The ip forward-protocol command can be used to allow only certain broadcasts through the router. As mentioned in the Critical Information section, eight ports are forwarded by default when using the ip helper-address command. You can use the ip forward-protocol command to prevent unwanted ports from being broadcasted through the router. Here is an example of using the ip forward-protocol command in conjunction with the ip helper-address command:

```
Router_A#conf t
Router_A(config)#int e0
Router_A(config-int)#ip helper-address 172.16.30.10
Router_A(config-int)#exit
Router_A(config)#no ip forward-protocol udp 69
Router_A(config)#no ip forward-protocol udp 37
Router_A(config)#no ip forward-protocol udp 49
Router_A(config)#no ip forward-protocol udp 68
Router_A(config)#no ip forward-protocol udp 137
Router_A(config)#no ip forward-protocol udp 138
Router_A(config)#^Z
Router_A#
```

Notice that the ip forward-protocol command is a global command, not an interface command. The configuration above configures Ethernet E0 to send both BootP server and DNS broadcast requests to server 172.16.30.10. Everything else is blocked by using the ip forward-protocol command.

Exam Essentials

You must remember how to configure a router to forward broadcasts to multiple servers on a network subnet. To configure a router to forward broadcasts to multiple servers on a subnet, you must specify the broadcast address of the subnet using the ip helper-address command.

Remember the default protocols enabled with the ip *helper-address* command. The default ports forwarded when you use the ip helper-address command are: TFTP (69), DNS (53), Time (37), TACACS (49) , BOOTP client (68), BOOTP server (67), NetBIOS name service (137), NetBIOS datagram service (138).

Remember the reason for using the ip *forward-protocol* command. This command will give you a more granular control over the enabled protocols and ports that can be forwarded.

Key Terms and Concepts

BootP (Bootstrap Protocol) Used basically like DHCP in that it makes a request for an IP address, but it does this in order to may boot from the network instead of locally.

Broadcast Used to send a message to all devices on a subnet or network.

DHCP (Dynamic Host Configuration Protocol) A server protocol/ service used to give out IP addresses from a pre-assigned pool of addresses to host devices on the network that make requests to it.

Multicast Message to multiple specified devices on a subnet or network.

Unicast Message with the destination of a single IP address.

Sample Questions

1. If clients need to reach multiple servers on network 172.16.30.0/ 24, which command will allow the clients to reach all of the servers?

   A. ip helper address 172.16.30.0

   B. ip helper address 172.16.30.255

   C. ip helper-address 172.16.30.0

   D. ip helper-address 172.16.30.255

   Answer: D—You must understand what the subnet broadcast address is in order to use this command.

2. Which command is used to refine the broadcast domain in conjunction with IP helper addresses?

   A. ip forward-protocol [udp[port] | nd | sdns]

   B. forward-helper [udp[port] | nd | sdbs]

   C. ip helper-protocol [udp[port] | nd | sdbs]

   D. None of the above

   Answer: A—The ip forward protocol command can be used to allow or deny only certain UDP broadcasts through the router.

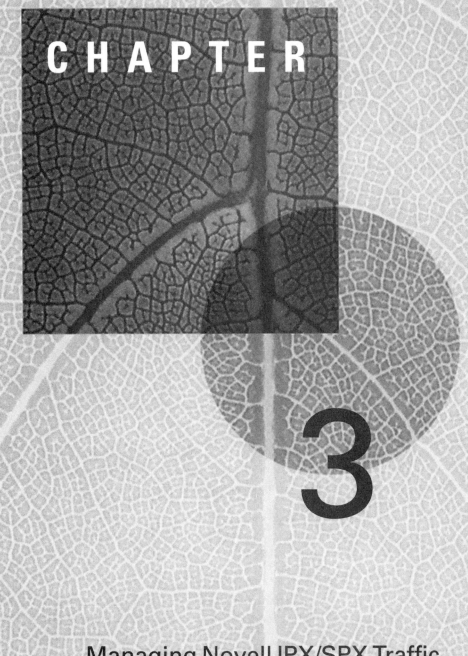

CHAPTER

3

Managing Novell IPX/SPX Traffic

Cisco ACRC Exam Objectives Covered in This Chapter:

▶ Describe IPX/SPX traffic management issues. *(pages 61 – 66)*

▶ Filter IPX traffic using IPX access lists. *(pages 66 – 73)*

▶ Manage IPX/SPX traffic over WAN. *(pages 73 – 76)*

▶ Verify IPX/SPX filter operation. *(pages 76 – 84)*

Most network administrators have encountered Internetwork Packet Exchange (IPX) at some point in their careers, and there are usually two reasons for this. First, Novell NetWare uses IPX as its default protocol; and second, it was the most popular network operating system during the late 1980s and early 1990s. Therefore, millions of IPX networks have been installed.

Novell, however, is changing things with the release of NetWare 5. Now TCP/IP is the default communications protocol instead of IPX, although Novell still supports IPX. This is because, considering the multitude of installed IPX clients and servers, it would be impractical to yank the support for it. No, there's little doubt that IPX will be around for a while! And considering that, it's no surprise that the Cisco IOS provides full support for large IPX internetworks.

This chapter covers IPX configuration on a Cisco router. However, the objectives more specifically concern traffic issues that are created when IPX routing is configured on a Cisco router.

SEE ALSO To learn about IPX addressing and configuration issues, read the Sybex *CCNA Study Guide,* Chapter 9.

This is an important chapter to read because it can provide you with the commands that are necessary to create a healthy, functional IPX internetwork. When studying this chapter, keep in mind that you need to understand the different ways to filter IPX on an internetwork.

Describe IPX/SPX traffic management issues.

Internetwork Packet Exchange is a protocol suite that was developed by Novell in the early 1980s to run with their NetWare operating system. As you are probably aware, this operating system (OS) became very popular. One of the reasons for its popularity is that IPX is a very resilient protocol stack. It provides auto addressing of hosts and can perform IPX RIP routing right out of the box and with very little configuration. Because the protocol stack was developed to help users get up and running with little effort, IPX can be hard on bandwidth with larger internetworks, because IPX uses many broadcasts to get the job done.

Coverage of this objective will include the different parts of the protocol stack that can use excessive amounts of bandwidth if they are not properly configured. This is an important objective to read and understand before reading the other objectives in this chapter. This section shows you the Novell protocol stack and compares it to the OSI reference model.

Critical Information

Novell IPX is quite similar to XNS (Xerox Network Systems), which was developed by Xerox in the 1960s. IPX even shares a likeness with TCP/IP and is really a family of protocols that coexists and interacts to empower sound network communications.

Novell IPX Protocol Stack

IPX doesn't map directly to the OSI model, but its protocols still function in layers. When designing IPX, engineers were more concerned with performance than with strict compliance to existing standards or models. Figure 3.1 on the next page illustrates the IPX protocols, layers, and functions relative to those of the OSI reference model:

FIGURE 3.1: IPX protocol stack and the OSI model

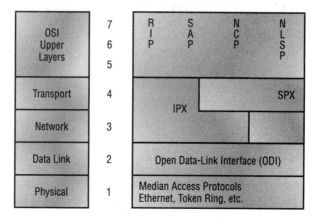

IPX

IPX performs functions at layers three and four of the OSI model. It controls the assignment of IPX addresses (software addressing) on individual nodes, governs packet delivery across internetworks, and makes routing decisions based on information provided by the routing protocols RIP or Novell Link State Protocol (NLSP). IPX is a connectionless protocol (similar to TCP/IP's UDP), so it doesn't require any acknowledgement that packets were received from the destination node. To communicate with the upper-layer protocols, IPX uses *sockets*. These are similar to TCP/IP ports in that they're used to address multiple, independent applications running on the same machine.

SPX

Sequenced Packet Exchange (SPX) adds connection-oriented communications to the otherwise connectionless IPX. Through it, upper-layer protocols can ensure data delivery between source and destination nodes. SPX works by creating *virtual circuits* or *connections* between machines, with each connection having a specific *connection ID* included in the SPX header.

RIP

Routing Information Protocol (RIP) is a distance-vector routing protocol that is used to discover IPX routes through internetworks. It employs ticks (1/18 of a second) and hop counts (number of routers between nodes) as metrics for determining preferred routes.

SAP

Service Advertising Protocol (SAP) is used to advertise and request services. Servers use it to advertise the services they offer, and clients use it to locate network services.

NLSP

NetWare Link Services Protocol (NLSP) is an advanced link-state routing protocol developed by Novell. It is intended to replace both RIP and SAP.

NCP

NetWare Core Protocol (NCP) provides clients with access to server resources. Functions such as file access, printing, synchronization, and security are all handled by NCP.

IPX's Internetworking Capability

What does the presence of routing protocols, connection-oriented and connectionless-oriented transport protocols, and application protocols indicate to you? All of these factors add up to the fact that IPX is capable of supporting large internetworks running many applications. Understanding how Novell uses these protocols clears the way for you to include third-party devices (such as Cisco routers) into an IPX network.

IPX, SAP, and RIP Updates

NetWare servers use SAP to advertise the services they offer by sending out SAP updates every 60 seconds. These broadcasts announce all services that the servers have learned about from other servers, not just the ones they specifically furnish. All servers receiving the SAP broadcasts incorporate the information into their own SAP tables; they then rebroadcast the data in their own SAP updates. Because SAP information is shared among all Novell servers, all servers eventually become aware of all available services and are thereby equipped to respond to client *get nearest server* (GNS) requests. As new services are introduced, they're added to SAP tables on local servers and are rebroadcasted until every server knows they exist and where to get them.

As far as SAP is concerned, Cisco routers act just like other NetWare servers. By default, SAP broadcasts won't cross Cisco routers. A Cisco router catalogs all SAPs heard on any of the IPX-enabled interfaces in its SAP table. As a default, the router then broadcasts the whole table from each of those interfaces at 60-second intervals, unless the settings are changed—just as NetWare servers do. This is an important point, especially with WAN links. The router isolates SAP broadcasts to individual segments and passes along only the summarized information to each segment.

Each SAP contains a service type, the most common of which are:

- 3 for print queue

- 4 for file server

- 7 for print server

RIP information is exchanged between servers much the same way that SAP information is. Servers build routing tables that contain entries for the networks they're directly connected to, and they then broadcast this information to all IPX-enabled interfaces. Other servers on those segments receive the updates and then broadcast the RIP tables on their IPX interfaces. Just as SAP information travels from server to server until all servers are enlightened, RIP information is proliferated until all servers and routers know of the internetwork's routes. As with SAP, RIP information is broadcast at 60-second intervals.

Exam Essentials

Remember the Novell protocol stack. You need to have a firm understanding how IPX, SPX, RIP, and SAP work in an internetwork environment.

Understand what a SAP does and how a Cisco router uses this information. Service Advertising Protocol is used by Novell routers to let hosts know about network services, like file and print services. Cisco routers gather this information and create tables. It then can respond to a client GNS broadcast. Since broadcasts are not forwarded by default, the router basically proxies for the server.

Remember how RIP works with IPX. IP RIP and IPX RIP are two different protocols and use different metrics. IP RIP is broadcasted by default every 30 seconds and only contains a hop count. IPX RIP is broadcasted every 60 seconds by default and contains hops and ticks. The tick is 1/18 of a second, and it is IPX's way of providing link speed.

Remember how often SAP broadcasts are sent out. Service Advertising Protocol uses broadcasts to advertise services available from a NetWare server. These are broadcasted on the local LAN every 60 seconds. Cisco routers receive these SAPs and build SAP tables.

Key Terms and Concepts

GNS (get nearest server) Used by a Novell client to locate a server on the network. Cisco routers may also respond on behalf of the server.

Hop Metric used in distance-vector routing algorithms to find the best path to a remote network.

IPX (Internetwork Packet Echange) The connectionless protocol at the heart of the IPX protocol stack. It is similar to IP in that it provides device addressing and routing of datagrams through an internetwork.

RIP (Routing Information Protocol) Used by default on Net-Ware and Cisco routers when Novell is configured. It is used to update routers about network information.

SAP (Service Advertising Protocol) Used by servers to learn about other services on the network. By default, a SAP broadcast won't cross a Cisco router, which catalogs all of the SAPs it has received on any of its IPX-enabled interfaces into its own SAP table. The router then broadcasts the whole table from each of those interfaces at 60-second intervals.

Tick Used in IPX RIP routing tables to measure the time it takes to get to a remote network in 1/18th of a second.

Sample Questions

1. Which protocol is used by a client to locate a NetWare server on an IPX/SPX network?

   A. GNS

   B. SAP

   C. IPX

   D. SPX

   Answer: A—Get nearest server is used to locate a Novell server on an IPX/SPX network.

2. How often, by default, are SAP broadcasts sent out?

   A. Every 10 seconds

   B. Every 30 seconds

   C. Every 60 seconds

   D. Every 10 minutes

   Answer: C—RIP and SAP information is broadcasted every 60 seconds by default.

Filter IPX traffic using IPX access lists.

Filtering IPX can be confusing. Because of the way that extended IPX lists can filter by network addresses and sockets, they can become difficult to comprehend. Just as IP access lists use port addresses to identify separate services running on a host, IPX uses a *socket* address to identify services provided by a server. This objective shows you the different ways that you can filter IPX using access lists.

IPX access lists fall into the following three categories:

- Standard access lists

- Extended access lists

- SAP filters

It is very important that you read the section concerning this objective because it will explain how to configure all three access lists using the Cisco help screens. You really need to understand the material covered in this objective.

Critical Information

The information concerning this objective will show you the three different types of IPX access lists and how to set them to filter IPX traffic. The following access lists will be demonstrated:

Extended IPX access lists   Allow filtering based upon any of the following criteria: source network/node, destination network/node, and IPX protocol at the Network layer (SAP, SPX, etc.). This either points to a protocol at the Network layer or to the next protocol at the Transport layer. IPX socket extended access lists live in the 900–999 range.

IPX SAP filters   Control IPX SAP traffic and use access lists in the 1000–1099 range. The commands to set this access list on an interface are `ipx sap-input-filter` and `ipx output-sap-filter`. You do not use the in/out parameters.

Standard IPX access lists   Provide the ability to permit or deny packets based on source and/or destination IPX addresses. You cannot filter based on socket or protocol, but only on source and destination IPX network/node.

Necessary Procedures

This section shows you how to build the three types of IPX access lists by using the help screens.

Standard IPX Access Lists

This section shows you the steps for creating a standard IPX access list using the Cisco IOS help facility.

```
access-list number permit/deny source destination
```

```
Router(config)#access-list ?
  <1-99>       IP standard access list
  <100-199>    IP extended access list
  <1000-1099>  IPX SAP access list
  <1100-1199>  Extended 48-bit MAC address access list
  <1200-1299>  IPX summary address access list
  <200-299>    Protocol type-code access list
  <300-399>    DECnet access list
  <400-499>    XNS standard access list
  <500-599>    XNS extended access list
  <600-699>    Appletalk access list
  <700-799>    48-bit MAC address access list
  <800-899>    IPX standard access list
  <900-999>    IPX extended access list

Router(config)#access-list 810 ?
  deny    Specify packets to reject
  permit  Specify packets to permit

Router(config)#access-list 810 permit ?
  -1           Any IPX net
  <0-FFFFFFFF> Source net
  N.H.H.H      Source net.host address
  <cr>

Router(config)#access-list 810 permit 30 ?
  -1           Any IPX net
  <0-FFFFFFFF> Destination net
  N.H.H.H      Destination net.host address
  <cr>

Router(config)#access-list 810 permit 30 4d  ?
  <cr>
```

After you create the list, you still need to apply this to an interface with the ipx access-group command, as shown here.

```
Router(config)#int e0
Router(config-if)#ipx access-group 810 ?
  in   inbound packets
  out  outbound packets
  <cr>
Router(config-if)#ipx access-group 810 in
```

Extended IPX Access Lists

Extended IPX access lists can be complicated. You can filter based on source and destination IPX address, IPX protocol at the Network layer (protocol), and IPX/SAP address at the Transport layer (sockets). The following is presented to show you the steps for creating an extended IPX access list using the Cisco IOS help facility.

```
access-list number permit/deny protocol source socket
destination socket log

RouterA(config)#access-list ?
  <1-99>     IP standard access list
  <100-199>  IP extended access list
  <1000-1099> IPX SAP access list
  <1100-1199> Extended 48-bit MAC address access list
  <1200-1299> IPX summary address access list
  <200-299>  Protocol type-code access list
  <300-399>  DECnet access list
  <600-699>  Appletalk access list
  <700-799>  48-bit MAC address access list
  <800-899>  IPX standard access list
  <900-999>  IPX extended access list

Router(config)#access-list 910 ?
  deny    Specify packets to reject
  permit  Specify packets to permit

Router(config)#access-list 910 permit ?
  -1      Any IPX protocol type
```

```
              <0-255>  Protocol type number (DECIMAL)
              <cr>

Router(config)#access-list 910 permit -1 ?
    -1              Any IPX net
    <0-FFFFFFFF>  Source net
    N.H.H.H         Source net.host address
    <cr>
Router(config)#access-list 910 permit -1
40.3cb2.0000.4c3a ?
    <0-FFFFFFFF>  Source Socket (0 for all sockets)
HEXIDECIMAL
    H.H.H           Source host mask
    N.H.H.H         Source net.host mask
    <cr>
Router(config)#access-list 910 permit -1
40.3cb2.0000.4c3a 0 ?
    -1              Any IPX net
    <0-FFFFFFFF>  Destination net
    N.H.H.H         Destination net.host address
    <cr>
Router(config)#access-list 910 permit -1
40.3cb2.0000.4c3a 0 -1 ?
    <0-FFFFFFFF>  Destination Socket (0 for all sockets)
HEXIDECIMAL
    <cr>
Router(config)#access-list 910 permit -1
40.3cb2.0000.4c3a 0 -1 4 ?
    <cr>
```

At this point, you still need to apply this access list to an interface with the ipx access-group command.

IPX SAP Filters

IPX SAP filters were created to make it easier to filter based on an IPX service or a complete server. You can still do the same thing with an extended IPX access list, but it is more complicated. IPX SAP filters help simplify the configuration. Here is an example:

```
access-list 1010 permit/deny source service type
```

```
RouterA(config)#access-list ?
<1-99>     IP standard access list
<100-199>  IP extended access list
<1000-1099> IPX SAP access list
<1100-1199> Extended 48-bit MAC address access list
<1200-1299> IPX summary address access list
<200-299>  Protocol type-code access list
<300-399>  DECnet access list
<600-699>  Appletalk access list
<700-799>  48-bit MAC address access list
<800-899>  IPX standard access list
<900-999>  IPX extended access list
RouterA(config)#access-list 1010 ?
deny  Specify packets to reject
permit Specify packets to forward
RouterA(config)#access-list 1010 permit ?
-1       Any IPX net
<0-FFFFFFFF> Source net
N.H.H.H     Source net.host address
RouterA(config)#access-list 1010 permit
11.0000.0000.0001 ?
<0-FFFFFFFF> Service type-code (0 matches all
services)
N.H.H.H     Source net.host mask
<cr>
RouterA(config)#access-list 1010 permit
11.0000.0000.0001 0 ?
WORD A SAP server name
<cr>
RouterA(config)#access-list 1010 permit
11.0000.0000.0001 0
```

Once you create the filter, you need to apply it to an interface. However, it is different than a standard or extended access list because you use the `ipx input-sap-filter` or `ipx output-sap-filter` command. Here is an example to stop a SAP from entering an interface:

```
RouterA(config)int s0
RouterA(config-if)ipx input-sap-filter 1010
```

Exam Essentials

Remember the different types of IPX access lists available.   You can filter IPX with a standard access list, an extended access list, and a SAP filter.

Remember the number range of each type of IPX access list. Standard IPX access lists are numbered from 800–899. Extended IPX access lists are numbered from 900–999. And IPX SAP filters are numbered from 1000–1099.

Remember what parameters are used to filter with standard IPX access lists.   Standard IPX access lists can filter both by source and destination host/network address. The difference is that IP standard can only filter by source host/network.

Remember what parameters are used to filter with extended IPX access lists.   Extended access lists can be more complicated and take more practice to master. You can filter based on source and destination IPX address, IPX protocol at the Network layer (protocol), and IPX/SAP address at the Transport layer (sockets).

Remember what parameters are used to filter with IPX SAP filters.   SAP filters can filter based on a socket and service type provided by either a network or a specific node.

Key Terms and Concepts

Access list   Command used in Cisco routers to create filters. You can create IP, IPX, and AppleTalk filters.

Socket   Used in Unix, AppleTalk, and IPX, from a lower-layer protocol to point to an upper-layer process. It is similar in concept to a TCP/IP port.

Sample Questions

1. What is the proper range for an extended IPX access list?

  A. 800–899

  B. 900–999

  C. 1000–1099

  D. 1100–1199

  Answer: B

2. Which of the following would you use to prevent SAPs from being broadcasted from a specific server?

  A. Standard IPX access list

  B. Extended IPX access list

  C. IPX SAP filter

  D. IP access list

  Answer: C

Manage IPX/SPX traffic over WAN.

Cisco routers exchange RIP and SAP tables with each other just like NetWare servers do, and their exchanges occur at the default update interval of every 60 seconds. If you are dealing with a slow WAN link, that default is likely to be more frequent than necessary. Also, if your router's SAP tables are sufficiently large, these events will surely eat up more serial link time than you're likely to find acceptable.

This chapter shows you how to control and manage IPX/SPX traffic over a WAN link. This is important to understand because, even with a T1 WAN link (1.544Mbps), IPX/SAP broadcasts can eat up a lot of bandwidth. When studying this objective, keep in mind that you must understand IPX filtering, which includes WANs.

Critical Information

By default, Cisco routers collect RIP and SAP information and store this information in their routing and SAP tables. They then broadcast this information out of every active interface every 60 seconds. This can eat up precious bandwidth, especially on a WAN. Following are the two ways to solve bandwidth issues when using NetWare:

Reduce the SAP update interval By changing the SAP interval to to a higher number of seconds instead of the default of 60 seconds, you can save an enormous amount of bandwidth. Use the `ipx sap-interval` command to change the interval.

Reduce the RIP update interval You can change the interval for RIP updates to save bandwidth with the `ipx update-time` command. Remember that you must change this on all routers if you use this command. Also, you cannot set this on an interface like you can with the `sap-interval` command because this is a global command.

Necessary Procedures

This section will present the commands you can use to save bandwidth on a WAN link when running IPX on your Cisco internetwork.

The *ipx sap-interval* Command

The following example configures Router A to broadcast the entire SAP table every 10 minutes instead of every 60 seconds over serial 0. When modifying the default SAP update interval, you must make sure to configure the same update interval on the serial interfaces of both routers. If they don't agree, services may expire from one table before updates are received. Therefore, they won't be continuously advertised.

```
Router#config t
Enter configuration commands, one per line.  End with
CNTL/Z.
RouterA(config)#interface serial0
```

```
RouterA(config-if)#ipx sap-interval ?
<0-2147483647>  Minutes (0=update only at boot &
shutdown)
RouterA(config-if)#ipx sap-interval 10
RouterA(config-if)#^Z
```

RIP Update Intervals

To change the default RIP update timer from 60 seconds, use the ipx
update-timer command.

```
Router(config-if)#ipx update-time ?
<10-4294967295>  Routing update timer

Router(config-if)#ipx update-time 600
```

The ipx update-time command is in seconds; 600 seconds is 10 minutes, for example.

Exam Essentials

Understand why you need to change the SAP timer. By changing the SAP update frequency, you can save a large amount of bandwidth, especially on networks with large SAP tables.

Remember how to set the update time. You can change the SAP
update frequency by using the ipx sap-interval command.

Remember the SAP timer is set in minutes, not seconds. When
you use the ipx sap-interval command on an interface, the command is followed by the update in minutes, not seconds.

Key Terms and Concepts

IPX (Internetwork Packet Exchange) The connectionless protocol at the heart of the IPX protocol stack. It is similar to IP in that
it provides device addressing and routing of datagrams through an
internetwork.

RIP (Routing Information Protocol)   Used by default on Net-Ware and Cisco routers when Novell is configured. It is used to update routers about network information.

Sample Questions

1. What is the default SAP interval on a Cisco router?

   A. 30 seconds

   B. 60 seconds

   C. 30 minutes

   D. 60 minutes

   Answer: B—By default, RIP and SAP information is set to 60 seconds.

2. Which of the following would set the IPX SAP timer to 10 minutes?

   A. `ipx sap-interval 60 10`

   B. `ipx sap-interval 10`

   C. `ipx sap-interval 600`

   D. `ipx sap-holddown 60 10`

   E. `ipx sap-holddown 10`

   F. `ipx sap-holddown 600`

   Answer: B—You can change the frequency of a SAP interval being sent out an interface by using the `ipx sap-interval` command.

Verify IPX/SPX filter operation.

Almost every chapter of this book contains information about how to configure Cisco routers with different types of commands.

Most of those chapters, if not all of them, also discuss the ways to verify the configuration once the routers are up and running. This chapter is no exception because this objective section covers how to verify the configuration of IPX access lists.

This is an important objective because you must be able to verify how your access lists are affecting the internetwork. When studying for the exam, it is important to understand how to verify your router's configuration.

Critical Information

This objective section shows you the commands you can use to verify the configuration of IPX access lists on your Cisco router internetwork. There are quite a few possible commands, as you will begin to see in the following example concerning the help screen:

```
Router#sh ipx ?
    accounting    The active IPX accounting database
    cache         IPX fast-switching cache
    compression   IPX compression information
    eigrp         IPX EIGRP show commands
    interface     IPX interface status and configuration
    nasi          Netware Asynchronous Services Interface
                  status
    nhrp          NHRP information
    nlsp          Show NLSP information
    route         IPX routing table
    servers       SAP servers
    spx-protocol  Sequenced Packet Exchange protocol
                  status
    spx-spoof     SPX Spoofing table
    traffic       IPX protocol statistics
```

There are four important commands that are used to verify IPX/SPX filter operation. They are show ipx servers, show ipx interfaces, show ipx traffic, and show access-lists. Each of these commands is described on the following page.

- show ipx servers displays the contents of the router's SAP table. This is built by collecting SAPs sent by servers on LANs connected to a Cisco router.

- show ipx interface is used to see which interfaces have IPX enabled, as well as which, if any, of the access lists that have been discussed in this chapter have been applied. The show ipx interface command also shows the IPX address of an interface; the show interface command only shows the hardware address.

- show ipx traffic will display information about the total number of IPX packets both sent and received. Information on routing and SAP is included here.

- show access-list is used to display all of the access lists currently configured on your router.

- show proto, an additional command, is used to show you routed protocol information, including addresses.

Necessary Procedures

This section shows you each of the previously listed commands. It is important that you come to understand the outputs of the commands, which are presented in the following sections.

The *show ipx servers* Command

The show ipx servers command displays the contents of the router's SAP table. The output should look similar to the following example:

```
RouterA#show ipx servers
Codes: S - Static, P - Periodic, E - EIGRP, N - NLSP, H
- Holddown, + = detail
9 Total IPX Servers

Table ordering is based on routing and server info
```

```
   Type Name              Net    Address   Port   Route Hops
Itf
P   4  BORDER1          350ED6D2.0000.0000.0001:0451    2/
01  1  Et0
P   4  BORDER2            1.0000.0000.0001:0451   2/01  1
Et0
P  107 BORDER1          350ED6D2.0000.0000.0001:8104    2/
01  1  Et0
P  107 BORDER2            1.0000.0000.0001:8104   2/01
1 Et0
P  26B BORDER_____
350ED6D2.0000.0000.0001:0005   2/01  1 Et0
P  278 BORDER_____   1.0000.0000.0001:4006
2/01   1 Et0
P  278 BORDER_____
350ED6D2.0000.0000.0001:4006   2/01  1 Et0
P  3E1 BORDER1          350ED6D2.0000.0000.0001:9056    2/
01  1  Et0
P  3E1 BORDER2            1.0000.0000.0001:9056   2/01
1 Et0
RouterA#
```

The *show ipx interface* Command

You can use the show ipx interface command to see which interfaces have IPX enabled, as well as which, if any, of the access lists that have been presented have been applied. The output reads as seen in the following example:

```
RouterA#show ipx interface
Ethernet0 is up, line protocol is up
  IPX address is CC715B00.0000.0c47.6f4f, ARPA [up]
line-up,   RIPPQ: 0, SAPPQ: 0
  Delay of this IPX network, in ticks is 1 throughput 0
link   delay 0
  IPXWAN processing not enabled on this interface
  IPX SAP update interval is 1 minute(s)
  IPX type 20 propagation packet forwarding is disabled
  Incoming access list is not set
  Outgoing access list is not set
```

```
IPX helper access list is not set
SAP GNS processing enabled, delay 0 ms, output filter
list  is not set
SAP Input filter list is not set
SAP Output filter list is not set
SAP Router filter list is not set
Input filter list is not set
Output filter list is not set
Router filter list is not set
Netbios Input host access list is not set
Netbios Input bytes access list is not set
Netbios Output host access list is not set
Netbios Output bytes access list is not set
Updates each 60 seconds, aging multiples RIP: 3 SAP: 3
SAP interpacket delay is 55 ms, maximum size is 480 bytes
RIP interpacket delay is 55 ms, maximum size is 432 bytes
IPX accounting is disabled
IPX fast switching is configured (enabled)
RIP packets received 1850, RIP packets sent 1
SAP packets received 1850, SAP packets sent 1
```

The *show ipx traffic* Command

The show ipx traffic command will display information about the
total number of IPX packets both sent and received. Information on
routing and SAP is included here. The output reads as shown in the
following example:

```
RouterA#show ipx traffic
System Traffic for 0.0000.0000.0001 System-Name:
RouterA
Rcvd:  13388 total, 1579 format errors, 0 checksum
errors, 0  bad hop count,
    926 packets pitched, 12462 local destination, 0
multicast
Bcast: 13386 received, 2 sent
Sent:  2 generated, 0 forwarded
    0 encapsulation failed, 0 no route
SAP:  0 SAP requests, 0 SAP replies, 9 servers
```

```
    1850 SAP advertisements received, 0 sent
    0 SAP flash updates sent, 0 SAP format errors
RIP:  2 RIP requests, 0 RIP replies, 3 routes
    1848 RIP advertisements received, 0 sent
    0 RIP flash updates sent, 0 RIP format errors
Echo:  Rcvd 0 requests, 0 replies
    Sent 0 requests, 0 replies
    0 unknown: 0 no socket, 0 filtered, 0 no helper
    0 SAPs throttled, freed NDB len 0
Watchdog:
    0 packets received, 0 replies spoofed
Queue lengths:
    IPX input: 0, SAP 0, RIP 0, GNS 0
    SAP throttling length: 0/(no limit), 0 nets pending
lost      route reply
    Delayed process creation: 0
EIGRP: Total received 0, sent 0
    Updates received 0, sent 0
    Queries received 0, sent 0
    Replies received 0, sent 0
    SAPs received 0, sent 0
NLSP:  Level-1 Hellos received 0, sent 0
    PTP Hello received 0, sent 0
    Level-1 LSPs received 0, sent 0
    LSP Retransmissions: 0
    LSP checksum errors received: 0
    LSP HT=0 checksum errors received: 0
    Level-1 CSNPs received 0, sent 0
    Level-1 PSNPs received 0, sent 0
    Level-1 DR Elections: 0
    Level-1 SPF Calculations: 0
    Level-1 Partial Route Calculations: 0
RouterA#
```

The *show access-list* Command

You can use the show access-list command to display all of the access lists currently configured on your router. The output reads as follows:

```
RouterA#show access-list
Novell access list 910
    deny -1 50 0 10 0
Novell SAP access list 1010
    permit 11.0000.0000.0001 0
```

The *show proto* Command

The "show protocol" command (show proto) will show you information about all of your routed protocols. For example, in the output that follows, you can get IP, IPX, and AppleTalk information, which includes interface addresses.

```
Router#show proto
Global values:
    Internet Protocol routing is enabled
    Appletalk routing is enabled
    Novell routing is enabled
Ethernet0 is up, line protocol is down
    Internet address is 172.16.10.1/24
    AppleTalk address is 110.137, zone Sales
    Novell address is 200.0000.0c3e.da86
Serial0 is down, line protocol is down
    Internet address is 172.16.20.1/24
    AppleTalk address is 333.73, zone Marketing
    Novell address is 100.0000.0c3e.da86
Serial1 is administratively down, line protocol is down
    Internet address is 172.16.30.1/24
    Novell address is 300.0000.0c3e.da86
```

Exam Essentials

Remember the commands used to verify IPX connectivity.
There are quite a few commands, but the ones you need to remember
are show ipx servers, show ipx interface, show ipx traffic,
show access-list, and show proto.

Remember how to find the IPX address of an interface. The
show ipx interface and show proto commands will show you your
addresses set for each interface.

**Remember how to view the servers on your internetwork from
your Cisco router.** The show ipx servers command displays the
contents of the router's SAP table, which is built by collecting the
SAPs sent by servers on LANs connected to a Cisco router.

Key Terms and Concepts

SAP (Service Advertisement Protocol)   Used by Services to learn
about other services on the network. By default, a SAP broadcast
won't cross a Cisco router, which catalogs all the SAPs it has
received on any of its IPX-enabled interfaces into its own SAP
table. The router then broadcasts the whole table from each of
those interfaces at 60-second intervals.

Socket   Used in Unix, AppleTalk, and IPX, from a lower-layer
protocol to point to an upper-layer process. It is similar in concept
to a TCP/IP port.

Sample Questions

1. Which of the following displays the contents of the router's
SAP table?

   A. show ipx servers

   B. show ipx services

C. show ipx sap-table

D. show ipx sap servers

Answer: A—Cisco routers collect SAP broadcasts from servers connected to LANs and build a SAP table. The show ipx servers command will display this table.

2. Which of the following displays the information about the total number of SAP packets sent and received?

A. show ipx traffic

B. show traffic ipx

C. debug ipx traffic

D. debug traffic ipx

Answer: A—The show ipx traffic command shows you the statistics of SAP being sent and received.

CHAPTER

4

Configuring Queuing to
Manage Traffic

Cisco ACRC Exam Objectives Covered in This Chapter:

▶ **Describe the need for queuing in a large network.**
(pages 87 – 89)

▶ **Describe weighted fair queuing operation.** *(pages 89 – 93)*

▶ **Configure priority.** *(pages 93 – 98)*

▶ **Configure custom queuing.** *(pages 98 – 102)*

▶ **Verify queuing operation.** *(pages 102 – 106)*

I t is important for you to have an understanding of queuing when configuring an internetwork or building a large internetwork. One of the first things you need to understand is that queuing is used for packets headed out of an exit port. You cannot queue ports for packets that come into a router. However, you can queue an exit port for packets that enter a specific port.

This chapter discusses the need for queuing. Has Cisco created routers that are so good that they no longer need to be administratively queued? Maybe. Cisco definitely has good routers that make good decisions on their own. However, administrators can help them to make even better decisions to meet their business requirements. Correctly queuing Cisco routers can also prove helpful in preventing some users from hogging the bandwidth, as well as helping users that have time-sensitive needs, like video.

When studying for your ACRC exam, be sure to practice the different queuing methods on a Cisco router, if possible. It is important to understand the fundamental differences between the queuing methods and how the commands are used to configure each type of queuing method on a Cisco router.

Describe the need for queuing in a large network.

This objective covers why Cisco routers need queuing. It will discuss the reasons why certain types of queuing are used. This is important information to understand when creating or maintaining Cisco routers in a large internetwork. Reread this objective as much as necessary to understand the different queuing methods.

Critical Information

Queuing is necessary in situations involving traffic that is sensitive to delay, such as with video. In some cases, you may need to tune your queuing configuration so that bursty traffic does not affect your other network applications. Queueing does not replace buffers because it merely decides in which order information is to be transmitted, nor does it decide which information will be transmitted or improve link speeds.

Each algorithm has a distinct way of processing the queues it uses. Because of these differences, queuing can be adapted to the needs of individual networks. Since administrators need a way of handling bandwidth problems and network congestion, queuing is a cost-effective way of dealing with these problems.

The significant characteristics of each queuing algorithm are outlined in the following list:

FIFO (first in, first out)   The first packet received is the first to be sent out.

Weighted fair queuing   Shares equally with all traffic but gives low-volume traffic higher priority. Instead of assigning priorities to each packet, this algorithm tracks the session that a packet belongs to. There is no queue list to configure or apply to the interface.

Priority queuing   A very stringent algorithm that can cause one type of traffic to monopolize available bandwidth, because as long as there are high-priority packets in the queue, they'll be processed first. Other traffic is processed only when there's available bandwidth left over from high-priority traffic. It gives you four queues.

Custom queuing   An equitable, controllable algorithm that allows administrators to configure the amount of bandwidth reserved for specified traffic types. All traffic will be processed in turn. Custom queuing allows for the configuration of 16 queues.

Exam Essentials

Remember when to use queuing.   Queuing is used when you have bursty or time-sensitive data.

Understand what queuing does.   Queuing does not speed up a link but decides instead which order information will be transmitted in.

Remember the types of queuing.   First in first out (FIFO), weighted fair, priority, and custom queuing are the four types of queuing supported by Cisco.

Key Terms and Concepts

Bandwidth   The rated throughput capacity of a given network medium or protocol.

Queueing   The spelling of the command used to set or check on the queues. For example, *show queueing*, not *show queuing*, is the correct spelling of the command.

Queuing   Small amounts of buffers reserved for putting packets into an administratively assigned order before being sent from a router.

Sample Questions

1. Which of the following applications call for queuing in order to improve network efficiency? (Choose all that apply.)

A. Bursty traffic

B. Lack of buffers

C. Slow network links

D. Video conferencing

Answer: A, C, D—Queuing is used when you have bursty traffic, slow network links, and have applications that are time sensitive (e.g., video).

2. Which of the following terms are the four types of queuing available on all Cisco routers?

A. FIFO

B. Weighted fair

C. Session

D. Cut-through

E. Priority

F. Store-and-forward

G. Custom

Answer: A, B, E, G—The four types of queuing are first in, first out; weighted fair; priority; and custom queuing.

Describe weighted fair queuing operation.

Weighted fair queuing is the default for most WAN links connected to Cisco routers. (Any link connected to a Cisco router that is 2.048Mbps or less is the default.) The idea of weighted fair queuing is to not let one user or network device monopolize the bandwidth. It does this by making low-volume traffic pass through before high-volume traffic can be transmitted.

It is important for you to understand the different queuing operations and how they are configured. This will help you when configuring Cisco routers and when taking the ACRC exam.

Critical Information

Weighted fair queuing provides equal amounts of bandwidth to each conversation that traverses the interface using a process that refers to the timestamp found on the last bit of a packet as it enters the queue.

Weighted fair queuing automatically assigns a high priority to all low-volume traffic. Figure 4.1 demonstrates how the timing mechanism for priority assignment occurs. The algorithm determines which frames belong to either high-volume or low-volume conversations and forwards out the low-volume packets from the queue first. This timing convention assigns an exiting priority to the remaining packets. In Figure 4.1, packets are labeled A through H. As depicted in the diagram, packet A will be forwarded out first because it's part of a low-volume conversation, even though the last bit of session B arrived before the last bit of the packets associated with packet A. The remaining packets are divided between the two high-traffic conversations, with their timestamps determining the order in which they will exit the queue.

F I G U R E 4.1: Priority assignment using weighted fair queuing

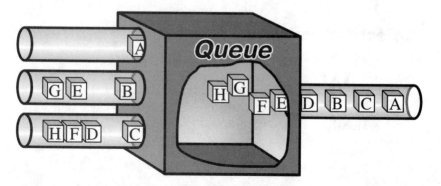

Each of the pipes in Figure 4.1 represents a conversation. The most common elements used to establish a conversation are as follows:

- Source and destination IP addresses

- MAC addresses

- Port numbers

- Type of service

- The DLCI number assigned to an interface

Necessary Procedures

This section shows you how to set up weighted fair queuing. There is not too much to the configuration as shown below. A sample command string looks like the following example:

```
fair-queue {congestive-discard-threshold [dynamic-
queues [reservable-queues]]}

Router_C#config t
Enter configuration commands, one per line. End with
CNTL/Z.
Router_C(config)#int s0
Router_C(config-if)#fair-queue 96
Router_C(config-if)#^Z
Router_C#
```

The fair-queue 96 command changed the default queue of 64 to 96 conversations that can exist within the queue.

The following list explains all of the possible command strings for weighted fair queuing:

- congestive-discard-threshold is a value from one to 512 that specifies the number of conversations that can exist within the queue. Once this number is exceeded, the conversations that follow won't be allocated their equal amount of bandwidth. Without a place in the queue, new conversations will be dropped. The default value is 64.

- dynamic-queues establishes dynamically to handle conversations that don't have special requirements. The valid values for this option are 16, 32, 64, 128, 256, 512, 1024, 2048, and 4096, with the default value being 256.

- deservable-queues defines the number of queues established to handle conversations. The available range is from zero to 1000, with the default being zero. These queues are for interfaces that use RSVP (Resource Reservation Protocol).

Exam Essentials

Remember when weighted fair queuing is used. Weighted fair queuing is used to make sure not one user or device can monopolize the bandwidth. Weighted fair queuing automatically assigns a high priority to all low-volume traffic.

Understand what the congestive-discard-threshold option is used for. This option specifies the number of conversations that can exist within the queue.

Remember how to change the congestive-discard-threshold option. The fair-queue command is used to change the congestive-discard-threshold.

Key Terms and Concepts

DLCI (data link connection identifier)   Used to identify a permanent virtual circuit in a Frame Relay network.

Queuing   Small amounts of buffers reserved for putting packets into an administratively assigned order before being sent from a router.

Sample Questions

1. Which of the following describes the interfaces to which weighted fair queuing is automatically assigned?

   A. Faster than or equal to 2.048Mb

   B. Slower than or equal to 2.048Mb

   C. Not configured with any other algorithm

   D. Running a T3

   Answer: B—Weighted fair queuing is assigned to all interfaces that have a speed of 2.048Mb or less.

2. Which of the following examples would change weighted fair queuing on an interface?

   A. (Router) Config# `fair-queue interface e 0 128`

   B. (Router) Config-if# `enable fair-queue 96`

   C. (Router) Config# `fair-queue 128 interface e 0`

   D. (Router) Config-if# `fair-queue 128`

   Answer: D—From the interface configuration, you use the `fair-queue` command to set the congestive-discard-threshold option.

Configure priority.

Priority queuing happens on a packet basis instead of on a session basis, and it is ideal in network environments that carry time-sensitive applications or protocols. When congestion occurs on low-speed interfaces, priority queuing guarantees that traffic that is assigned a high priority will be sent first. In turn, if the queue for high-priority traffic is always full and monopolizing bandwidth, packets in the other queues will be delayed or dropped.

It is important for you to understand why to use priority queuing instead of other types of queuing. Priority queuing is not configured as much on Cisco routers since weighted fair queuing has become that router's default. However, you must still understand how to configure priority queuing for the exam.

Critical Information

The priority queuing header information consists of either the TCP port or the protocol being used to transport the data. When a packet enters the router, it is compared against a list that will determine its priority, and then it is forwarded to the corresponding queue.

The four different priorities that can be assigned to a packet during priority queuing are high, medium, normal, and low, with a separate dispatching algorithm to manage the traffic in all four priorities. Figure 4.2 shows how these queues are serviced; you can see that the algorithm starts with the high-priority queue, processing all of the data there. When that queue is empty, the dispatching algorithm moves down to the medium-priority queue, and so on down the priority chain, performing a cascade check of each queue before moving on. So if the algorithm finds packets in a higher-priority queue, it will process them first before moving on, and this is where problems can develop. Traffic in the lower queues can be totally neglected in favor of the higher ones if they're continually busy with new packets arriving.

Implementing priority queuing on an interface requires the following three steps:

- A priority list must be created that the processor will use to determine packet priority.

- If desired, the size of the queues can be adjusted.

- The priority list can be applied to the desired interfaces.

Priority queuing uses priority lists to differentiate the different traffic types. Priority lists number from one to 16. Once the list is applied to the interface, it is implicitly applied outbound. All packets will be checked against the priority list before entering their corresponding queue. The ones that don't match will be placed in the default queue.

F I G U R E 4.2:   Dispatching algorithm in priority queuing

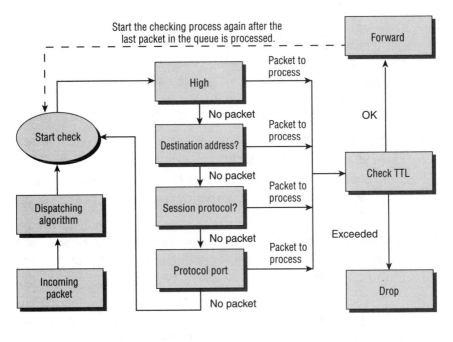

Necessary Procedures

This section shows you how to configure priority queuing. Some examples of working configurations will be used to illustrate this topic. Following is the priority queuing command string:

```
priority-list list-number {[protocol protocol-name] |
[interface interface-type] (high | medium | normal |
low) | default | queue-limit]} queue-keyword
```

A sample output is shown in the following example:

```
!
interface Serial0
 ip address 172.16.40.6 255.255.255.252
 priority-group 1
!
```

```
priority-list 1 protocol ip high gt 1500
priority-list 1 protocol ip low lt 256
priority-list 1 protocol ip normal
priority-list 1 interface Serial1 normal
priority-list 1 interface Ethernet0 high
priority-list 1 queue-limit 40 80 120 180!
```

The following points explain each line in the configuration:

- The list-number command identifies the list, and the valid values for it are one through 16.

- protocol directs the list to assign priorities based on the protocol, and protocol-name defines which protocol to match.

- With interface, the physical interface is listed along with the type of queue that pertains to it. Next, after specifying the protocol or interface, the type of queue needs to be defined—high, medium, normal, or low.

- The same priority-list command is used to configure a default queue for traffic that doesn't match the priority list and that you do not want to be placed in the normal queue.

- queue-limit is used to create the size limits of the queue. Configuring the size of the queues must be handled carefully because, if a packet is forwarded to the appropriate queue but the queue is full, the packet will be discarded—even if there is bandwidth available. This means that enabling priority queuing on an interface can be useless (even destructive) if queues aren't accurately configured to respond to actual network needs. It's really important to make the queues large enough to accommodate congestion so the influx of packets can be accepted and stored until they can be forwarded.

- queue-keyword allows packets to be compared by their byte-count, existing access list, protocol port number, or name and fragmentation.

Exam Essentials

Remember when to use priority queuing.   Priority queuing happens on a packet basis instead of on a session basis and is ideal in network environments that carry time-sensitive applications or protocols.

Remember the type and amount of queues used with priority queuing.   Priority queuing can assign four different priorities to a packet: high, medium, normal, and low.

Key Terms and Concepts

Bandwidth   The rated throughput capacity of a given network medium or protocol.

Queueing   The spelling of the command used to set or check on the queues.

Sample Questions

1. The header information that priority queuing uses consists of either the _____ or the _____ being used.

   A. *TCP port number* or the *TTL*

   B. *TCP port number* or the *protocol*

   C. *Frame type* or the *protocol*

   D. *Media type* or the *TTL*

   Answer: B—Priority queuing can use either the protocol field in a Network-layer header or the port field in a Transport-layer header to make queuing decisions.

2. Which of the following do you use to determine a packet's priority in priority queuing?

   A. The packet's protocol type

B. An access list

C. The packet's TTL

D. A priority list

E. The packet's destination

Answer: D—An administrator creates a priority list and then applies it to an interface that sets a packet's priority.

Configure custom queuing.

Custom queuing functions are based upon the concept of sharing bandwidth among traffic types. Custom queuing offers the ability to customize the amount of actual bandwidth used by a specified traffic type. This is important because this type of queuing is typically used when configuring queuing on a Cisco router. There are many options to configure when assigning custom queuing to an interface, and this objective covers all of the configuration options you will need to know for the ACRC exam.

Critical Information

In custom queuing, varying amounts of the total bandwidth are reserved for various specific traffic types, and if the bandwidth isn't being fully utilized by its assigned traffic type, other types can access it. The configured limits go into effect during high levels of utilization or when congestion on the line causes different traffic types to compete for bandwidth.

Figure 4.3 shows each queue being processed, one after the other. Once this begins, the algorithm checks the first queue, processes the data within it, and then moves to the next queue; if it comes across an empty one, it will simply move on without hesitating. The amount of data that will be forwarded is specified by the *byte-count* for each queue, which directs the algorithm to move to the next queue once it's been attained. Custom queuing permits a maximum of 16 configurable queues.

FIGURE 4.3:   Custom queuing algorithm

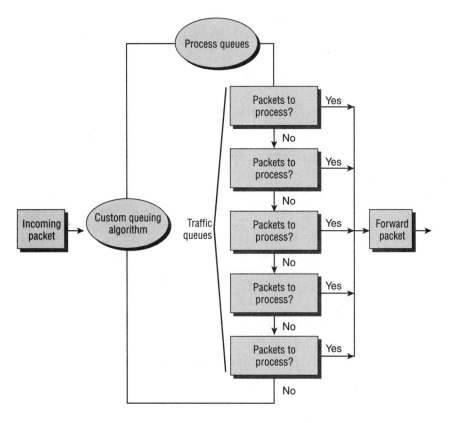

Figure 4.4 shows how the bandwidth allocation via custom queuing looks relative to the physical connection. Bandwidth allocations are configured by using the frame size of the protocols and configuring the byte-count for each different queue.

FIGURE 4.4:   Bandwidth allocation using custom queuing

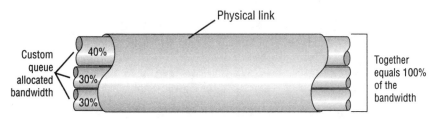

Necessary Procedures

This section shows you how to configure custom queuing on Cisco routers. The first step while enabling custom queuing is to configure a list that will be used to separate types of incoming traffic into their desired queues. Then you configure a default queue for the traffic that is unassigned to any of the other queues.

Once your specific and default queues are defined, the capacity or size of each queue can be adjusted, or you can just stick with the default settings. When that is complete, you have to specify the transfer rate or byte-count for each queue. This is important; the byte-count determines the percentage of bandwidth reserved for a specified queue. After these parameters are set, apply them to an interface.

The commands used to configure the queuing list, default queue, queue size, and transmit rate follow, but the command syntax for this configuration is shown first:

```
queue-list list-number {default | interface [interface-
type interface-number] | lowest-custom | protocol
[protocol-name] | queue [queue-number byte-count |
limit ] | stun } queue-number queue-keyword keyword-
value
```

The following example is a sample configuration:

```
!
interface Serial0
ip address 172.16.40.1 255.255.255.0
custom-queue-list 1
!
queue-list 1 protocol ip 2 tcp telnet
queue-list 1 protocol ip 3 tcp www
queue-list 1 protocol ip 4 udp snmp
queue-list 1 protocol ip 5
queue-list 1 default 6
queue-list 1 interface Ethernet0 1
queue-list 1 queue 1 limit 40
queue-list 1 queue 2 byte-count 1000
```

```
queue-list 1 queue 3 byte-count 4000
queue-list 1 queue 4 byte-count 500
queue-list 1 queue 5 byte-count 4000
```

The following points explain the configuration:

- When the interface option is specified, you must supply the *interface-type* and *interface-number* as well. The *interface-type* is the type of physical interface, and the *interface-number* is the physical port of the interface.

- The protocol option also requires additional information. Obviously, the *protocol-name* must be specified. After supplying the *queue-number*, the *keyword-value* may be supplied to refine the protocols and port numbers used for filtering.

- The limit option allows you to change the size of the queue.

- The byte-count command option specifies the rate at which the queues will be emptied.

Exam Essentials

Understand why custom queuing is used. Custom queuing functions are based upon the concept of sharing bandwidth among traffic types.

Remember the amount of configurable queues with custom queuing. Custom queuing permits a maximum of 16 configurable queues.

Key Terms and Concepts

Default Designates a custom queue for packets that don't match the queue-list command.

Interface Assigns priorities for packets incoming on the specified physical interface.

Lowest-custom option Specifies the lowest queue number considered a custom queue.

> **Protocol option** Indicates that the packets are to be sorted by protocol.
>
> **Stun** Establishes queuing priority for STUN packets.

Sample Questions

1. Which command do you use to create a custom queue list?

   A. custom-list

   B. queue-list

   C. priority-list

   D. custom-queue-list

   Answer: B—The global configuration queue-list command is used to create a custom queue.

2. Which of the following are valid protocols that may be used in the same custom queueing configuration?

   A. AppleTalk

   B. TCP/IP

   C. DECnet

   D. IPX

   Answer: A, B, C, D—All of the protocols are supported.

▶ Verify queuing operation.

Once queuing is set up, you need to be able to verify the operation. This is important because you need to verify that you actually helped the network and didn't harm it. You can do this by looking at some particular commands on your Cisco routers.

Verifying the queuing options is just as important as assigning the queues to the correct port. This is important for both keeping your network running in top form and for taking the ACRC exam.

Critical Information

To see the queuing information, you use the show queueing command. Please notice the spelling. When using a queuing command, you must spell it *queueing*, not *queuing*. Following is the template for gathering queueing information:

```
show queueing [fair | priority | custom]
```

The following list describes what each command will show you:

- show queueing fair gives you the output information about fair queuing (if fair queuing is used). It also shows you the discard threshold or number of packets the queue can hold.

- show queueing priority shows you the priority list number, queues, and command arguments for each queue.

- show queueing custom is output information that gives you a breakdown of the custom queue list, detailing queue assignments and any limits or byte-counts assigned to the queue.

There is one more command to be aware of when trying to view your queue information. This command is show queue, and it is shown on the following line:

```
show queue [interface-type interface-number]
```

This command shows you the size of the input and output queues and the number of drops. You can just type show queue to see all queues or to add an interface number to view.

Necessary Procedures

The commands discussed previously can be used to see the current conditions of queues. The following sections present a sample output of each command.

Verifying Fair Queuing

Use the show queueing fair command, a sample of which follows, to view the fair queues:

```
Router_C#show queueing fair
Current fair queue configuration:

Interface  Discard    Dynamic      Reserved
           threshold  queue count  queue count
Serial0    96         256          0
Serial1    64         256          0

Current priority queue configuration:
Current custom queue configuration:
Current RED queue configuration:
Router_C#
```

Verifying Priority Queuing

Use the show queueing priority command, a sample of which follows, to view the current priority queue configuration:

```
Router_C#show queueing priority
Current priority queue configuration:

List   Queue Args
1    high   protocol ip     gt 1500
1    low    protocol ip     lt 256
1    normal protocol ip
1    normal interface Serial1
1    high   interface Ethernet0
1    high   limit 40
1    medium limit 80
1    normal limit 120
1    low    limit 160
Router_C#
```

Verifying Custom Queuing

Use the show queueing custom command, a sample of which follows, to view the current custom queue configuration:

```
Router_B#show queueing custom
Current custom queue configuration:

List  Queue Args
1     6     default
1     1     interface Ethernet0
1     2     protocol ip      tcp port telnet
1     3     protocol ip      tcp port www
1     4     protocol ip      udp port snmp
1     5     protocol ip
1     1     limit 40
1     2     byte-count 1000
1     3     byte-count 4000
1     4     byte-count 500
1     5     byte-count 4000
Router_B#
```

Showing Queuing

Use the show queue *interface* command, a sample of which follows, to view the queue on an individual interface:

```
Router_C#show queue serial0
 Input queue: 0/75/0 (size/max/drops); Total output
drops: 0
 Queueing strategy: weighted fair
 Output queue: 0/1000/96/0 (size/max total/threshold/
drops)
     Conversations 0/1/256 (active/max active/max total)
     Reserved Conversations 0/0 (allocated/max allocated)
```

Exam Essentials

Remember the commands needed to view queues. show queueing fair, show queueing priority, or show queueing custom will show you the specific information about a queue.

Remember the spelling of the commands, and be able to type the answer. Remember that the command to view a queue is typed a specific way (e.g., show queueing fair).

Key Terms and Concepts

Queueing   The spelling of the command used to set or check on the queues.

Queuing   Small amounts of buffers reserved for putting packets into an administratively assigned order before being sent from a router.

Sample Questions

1. Which queuing algorithm guarantees that certain protocols will be dispatched first?

   A. FIFO

   B. Weighted fair queuing

   C. Priority queuing

   D. Custom queuing

   Answer: C—Priority queues can set up queuing by protocol.

2. Which queuing algorithm uses byte-count limits to determine how much priority to give each protocol?

   A. FIFO

   B. Weighted fair queuing

   C. Priority queuing

   D. Custom queuing

   Answer: D—Custom queuing can use the size of a packet to make queuing decisions.

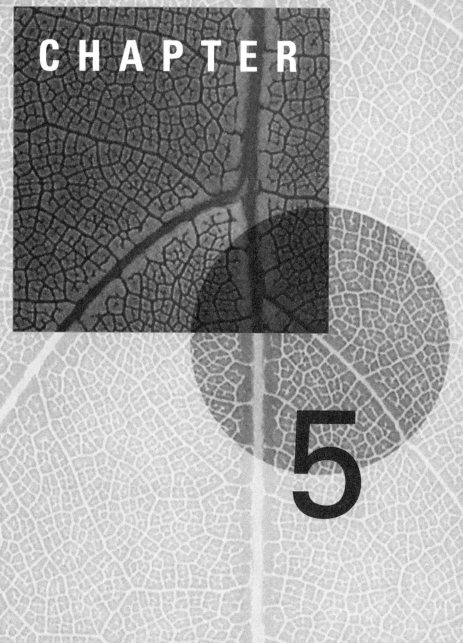

CHAPTER

5

Routing Protocol Overview

Cisco ACRC Exam Objectives Covered in This Chapter:

▶ **List the key information routers need to route data.**
(pages 108 – 111)

▶ **Compare distance vector and link-state protocol operation.**
(pages 112 – 120)

Routers use a table of information to determine the best path to a remote network. This table is called a routing table. Routers keep a routing table for every protocol configured on the router. For example, a router will have a routing table for IP and different routing tables for IPX as well as AppleTalk. As an administrator, it is your job to help the routers create an efficient routing table. You can do this by running routing algorithms that work well in your internetwork environment.

This chapter explains how routers use routing tables to route packets to remote internetworks. It also explains the differences between the distance-vector and link-state routing algorithms. This can help you when deciding how to create routing tables in your production environment. It is also extremely important to know the difference between link-state and distance-vector routing on the ACRC exam.

List the key information routers need to route data.

As mentioned in the introduction, routers build routing tables, which are used to hold map routes to remote networks. Routers then use these maps to find the best paths to the remote network. Think of a router as a mail person and the routing table as a city map. The mail person can't work without the map, and the map is useless if the mail person doesn't use it. In other words, a router cannot do much without a routing table.

The following section presents the information used in routing tables and how routers gather this information. This is probably the most important information for a router to gather. As a network administrator, it is imperative that you help your routers gather correct and efficient information.

Routing tables are built using either administratively assigned routing paths or dynamic-routing algorithms. The two types of dynamic-routing algorithms will be discussed in the next objective section.

Critical Information

As you probably already know, the primary function of a router is to route packets that are received on an interface out of an exit interface on the router to reach a remote network. Routers create network maps of the internetwork and then use this information when a packet needs to be routed. Dynamic-routing protocols can be used to build routing tables in routers.Dynamic-routing protocols can use a variety of metrics to determine the best path to a single destination. How each protocol determines the best path is unique. However, most scalable dynamic routing protocols use one or a combination of the following values:

Bandwidth Speed of the line, measured in kilobits (thousands of bits).

Delay Delay of the line, as measured on a router's interface.

Load Measured load of the line, where 1 is great and 255 is saturated.

Reliability Measured amount of line drops.

Hop counts Number of routers a packet must traverse to get to the remote network.

If you use a routing algorithm that uses only the hop count, the router can make poor decisions in a large internetwork. For example, if you had many links going to many destinations—some fast, some slow— the router will choose the shortest route, even if it is only a 56K link and faster links are available.

However, in a large internetwork, you should choose a routing algorithm that uses *speed of the line* and *delay of the line* to determine the best path to an internetwork. Link-state routing algorithms (discussed in the next objective section) and some hybrid routing algorithms use bandwidth (speed of the line) and delay of the line by default when trying to find the best path to a network. Load, reliability, maximum transmission unit (MTU), and hop count can be configured by an administrator to also be used if needed.

Exam Essentials

Understand the metrics used by different routing algorithms. Link-state routing algorithms can use bandwidth and delay of the line by default. Reliability, MTU, load, and hop count can be configured by an administrator to be used if necessary.

Remember that basic routing algorithms only use hop count as a metric. Routing Information Protocol (RIP) is an older distance-vector routing algorithm that uses only the hop count to determine the best path to a network. Distance-vector routing is presented in the next objective.

Key Terms and Concepts

Distance-vector routing algorithm Uses distance as a way to determine the best path to a remote network.

Hop count Routing metric used to measure the distance between routers.

Link-state routing algorithm A routing algorithm that allows each router to broadcast or multicast information regarding the cost of reaching all its neighbors to every node in the internetwork.

MTU (maximum transmission unit) The maximum size of a packet, in bytes, that an interface can handle.

RIP (Routing Information Protocol)   Distance-vector routing algorithm that uses only the hop count as a way of determining the best path to a remote network.

Sample Questions

1. Which of the following are valid metrics for determining the best path with link-state routing?

   A. Bandwidth

   B. Delay

   C. Load

   D. Hops

   E. Protocol

   F. Media type

   G. Reliability

   Answer: A, B, C, D, G

2. Which of the following metrics are used by default in a link-state or hybrid routing environment?

   A. Bandwidth

   B. Delay

   C. Load

   D. Hops

   E. Reliability

   Answer: A, B—Only bandwidth (speed of the line) and delay of the line are used to determine the best route to an internetwork. The other metrics must be set by an administrator to be used.

Compare distance vector and link-state protocol operation.

As networks grow, the extent to which a routing protocol will scale becomes a very critical issue. Network growth imposes a great number of changes to the network environment. The number of hops between end systems, the number of routes in the route table, the different ways a route was learned, and route convergence are all seriously affected by network growth. So, to maintain a stable routing environment, it's absolutely crucial to use a scalable protocol.

When the results of network growth are manifested, whether your network's routers will be able to meet those challenges is up to the routing protocol the routers are running. For instance, if you use a protocol that's limited by the number of hops that it can transverse, how many routes it can store in its table, or even the inability to communicate with other protocols, you have a protocol that will likely stunt the growth of your network.

It is very important to understand the differences between link-state and distance-vector routing algorithms. To be able to build a scalable internetwork, you must be able to create an internetwork that can grow and yet be stable and secure. Part of these requirements includes using the correct routing algorithm for your internetwork.

This objective presents the differences between link-state and distance–vector routing. Understanding the differences between these two routing algorithms is crucial to your success when designing, installing, and maintaining an internetwork, as well as when taking the ACRC exam. It is very important to understand the scalability of distance-vector routing algorithms, specifically when measured against link-state algorithms.

Critical Information

Interior routing is implemented at the Internet layer of the TCP/IP suite of protocols. An interior router can use an IP routing protocol and a specific routing algorithm to accomplish routing. Examples of interior IP routing protocols include the following:

RIP   A distance-vector routing protocol

IGRP   Cisco's proprietary distance-vector routing protocol

OSPF   A link-state routing protocol

Enhanced IGRP   Cisco's balanced-hybrid, distance-vector routing protocol

The interior routing protocols are classified into two basic categories: distance-vector and link-state algorithms. Each of these routing algorithms are explained in the following list:

- Distance-vector algorithms understand the direction and distance to any network connection on the internetwork. Distance vector listens to secondhand information to get its updates.

- Link-state algorithms (or *shortest path first*) understand the entire network better than distance-vector algorithms and never listens to secondhand information. Hence, it can make more accurate and informed routing decisions.

Distance-Vector Routing Protocols

Distance vector is a routing protocol algorithm that uses distance (metrics or hop counts) to determine the best way to a remote network. Some distance-vector routing algorithms have been expanded to look at speed of the line (bandwidth) to help in deciding the best path to a remote network. However, the protocols are still referred to as distance vector because of the way they handle convergence and loop problems.

Convergence

What happens when a link drops or a connection gets broken? All routers must inform the other routers to update their routing tables. So what is convergence time? It is the time it takes for all of the routers to update their tables when reconfigurations, outages, or link-drops occur—basically, whenever there are changes. No data is passed during this time, and a slowdown is imminent. Once convergence is completed, all routers within the internetwork are operating with the same knowledge, and the internetwork is said to have converged. If convergence didn't happen, routers would possess outdated tables and make routing decisions based on potentially invalid information.

A distance-vector network's convergence time is determined by the ability of the protocol to propagate changes within the network topology. Distance-vector protocols don't use formal neighbor relationships between routers. A router using distance-vector algorithms becomes aware of a topology change in the two following ways:

- If a router fails to receive a routing update from a directly connected router

- When a router receives an update from a neighbor notifying it of a topology change somewhere in the network

Routing updates are sent out on either default or specified time intervals, so, when a topology change occurs, it can take up to 90 seconds before a neighboring router realizes what's happened. When the router finally recognizes the change, it recalculates its route table and sends the whole thing out to all of its neighbors.

As the size of the routing table increases, so does CPU utilization, because it takes more processing power to calculate the effects of topology changes and then to converge using the new information. Also, as more routes populate a route table, it becomes increasingly complex to determine the best path and next hop for a given destination. The following list provides a summary of scalability limitations inherent in distance-vector algorithms:

- Network convergence delay

- Increased CPU utilization
- Increased bandwidth utilization

Handling Routing Loops

Since distance-vector routing algorithms have a notorious problem with routing loops, some solutions have been addressed within the protocols themselves. Following are the main solutions to this issue:

Maximum hop count A maximum number of hops has been defined for a packet. This means that if a loop does occur the packet will be dropped after traversing a certain number of routers. RIP's upper hop-count limit is 15. After 16 hops, the packet is dropped. This limits the size of an internetwork and causes scalability issues.

Split horizon Reduces incorrect routing information and routing overhead in a distance-vector network by enforcing the rule that information cannot be sent back in the direction from which it was received. However, this can be a problem in hybrid networks and must be disabled in those networks.

Poison reverse If a link goes down, the router that is directly attached to the network will send a broadcast announcing that the network is unavailable. It does this by sending the maximum hop count of the network and, therefore, preventing the link from being broadcasted as still available from any other source.

Holddown state If a link goes down, the router that is attached to the network will not send information about that network in its next update cycle. The neighbor routers will then put the route to that network in a holddown state. The routing tables will show "possible down" and will drop any packets with a destination of that remote network.

Triggered updates Holddowns use triggered updates, which reset the holddown timer when they need to let neighboring routers know of a change in the network. The following are the three instances when triggered updates will reset the holddown timer:

- HD timer expires

- The router receives a processing task proportional to the number of links in the internetwork

- Another update is received indicating that the network status has changed

Link-State Routing Protocols

The link-state routing algorithm maintains a more complex table of topology information. Routers using the link-state concept are privileged to a complete understanding and view of all of the links of distant routers, including how they interconnect. The link-state routing process uses *link-state packets* (LSPs) (or *hello packets*) to inform other routers of distant links. In addition, it uses topological databases, the shortest path first (SPF) algorithm, and, of course, a routing table.

Network discovery in link-state algorithms occurs quite differently than it does with distance-vector algorithms. First, routers exchange hello packets (LSPs) with one another, giving them a bird's-eye view of the entire network. In this initial phase, each router communicates only its directly connected links. Second, all routers compile all of the LSPs received from the internetwork and build a topological database. After that, the SPF algorithm computes how each network can be reached, finding both the shortest and most efficient paths to each participating link-state network. Each router then creates a tree structure with itself representing the root.

The results are formed into a routing table, complete with a listing of the best paths. (Again, the best paths are not simply the shortest but also the most efficient.) Once these tasks are completed, the routers can use the table for switching packet traffic.

Link-state routing protocols address the scalability issues faced by distance-vector protocols because the algorithm uses a different procedure for route calculation and advertisement, which enables them to scale along with the growth of the network.

Convergence

Link-state routers also handle convergence but in a completely different manner than distance-vector routers. When the topology changes, the routers (or router) that first become aware of the event either send information to all other routers participating with the link-state algorithm or they send the news to a specific router that's designated to consult for table updates.

A router participating in a link-state network must do the following in order to converge:

- Remember its neighbor's name, when it's up or down, and the cost of the path to that router.

- Create an LSP that lists its neighbor's name and relative costs.

- Send the newly created LSP to all other routers participating in the link-state network.

- Receive LSPs from other routers and update its own database.

- Build a complete map of the internetwork's topology from all the LSPs received, and then compute the best route to each network destination.

Whenever a router receives an LSP packet, it recalculates the best paths and updates the routing tables accordingly.

These are key differences that permit link-state protocols to function well in large networks. They don't really have any limitations when it comes to scaling other than the fact that they're a bit more complex to configure than distance-vector routing protocols.

Link-state routers send an update concerning only the *new* information, not the entire route table, so the update is a lot smaller, which saves both bandwidth and CPU utilization. Plus, if there aren't any network changes, updates are sent out only at either specified or default intervals, which differ among specific routing protocols and can range from 30 minutes to 2 hours.

Comparing Distance-Vector Routing to Link-State Routing

So, as you can see, there are quite a few major differences between the distance-vector and link-state routing algorithms. Refer to the following list for details about a few of these differences:

- Distance-vector routing gets all of its topological data from second-hand information or network gossip, whereas link-state routing obtains a complete and accurate view of the internetwork by compiling LSPs.

- Distance-vector routing determines the best path by counting hops—by metrics. Link-state routing uses bandwidth analysis plus other pertinent information to calculate the most efficient path.

- Distance-vector routing updates topology changes in 30-second intervals that are adjustable in most cases, which can result in a slow convergence time. Link-state routing can be triggered by topology changes, resulting in faster convergence times as LSPs are passed to other routers, sent to a multi-cast group of routers, or sent to a specific router.

All things considered, when it comes to routing protocols, there isn't any one solution for all networks. Routing choices shouldn't be based on what is fastest or cheapest since multi-vendor support or standards may well outweigh cost or other factors. Considerations like network simplicity, the need to set up and manage quickly and easily, or the ability to handle multiprotocols without complex configurations can be pivotal in making proper decisions for your network.

Exam Essentials

Understand the hop-count limits of distance-vector routing algorithms. RIP has a maximum hop count of 15 hops, with 16 being considered unreachable. IGRP (Cisco's proprietary distance-vector algorithm) uses a default maximum hop count of 100. However, it can be set to run up to 255 hops.

Remember the limitations of distance-vector routing compared to link-state routing. When a routing problem occurs, distance-vector routing has network convergence delay, increased CPU utilization, and increased bandwidth utilization problems. Link-state routing solves these problems by using a more efficient routing algorithm.

Remember what link–state algorithms can use for determining the best route to a remote network. Link-state algorithms (along with other hybrid protocols like EIGRP) use bandwidth and delay of the line by default to find the best way to a remote network.

Key Terms and Concepts

Distance-vector routing algorithm Dynamic routing algorithm that uses hop counts to determine the best path to a remote network.

Convergence The time it takes for all of the routers to update their tables when reconfigurations, outages, or link-drops occur.

Sample Questions

1. Which type of routing algorithm would be best to use in a large internetwork with thousands of routers?

   A. Static

   B. RIP

   C. Distance-vector

   D. Link-state

   Answer: D—Link-state routing algorithms scale well in a large internetwork.

2. Which of the following are problems associated with distance-vector routing algorithms?

   A. Increased bandwidth utilization

   B. Increased CPU utilization

C. Fast convergence

D. Network-convergence delay

Answer: A, B, D—Distance-vector routing has problems when internetwork trouble occurs. It has slow convergence, as well as high CPU and bandwidth usage when trying to solve the problems.

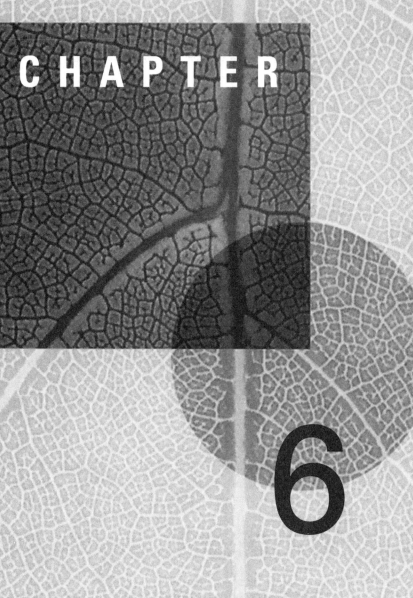

CHAPTER

6

Extending IP Addresses
Using VLSMs

Cisco ACRC Exam Objectives Covered in This Chapter:

▶ **Given an IP address, use VLSMs to extend the use of the IP address.** *(pages 123 – 128)*

▶ **Given a network plan that includes IP addressing, explain if a route summarization is or is not possible.** *(pages 128 – 133)*

▶ **Define private addressing and determine when it can be used.** *(pages 133 – 136)*

▶ **Define network address translation and determine when it can be used.** *(pages 136 – 139)*

Variable-length subnet masks (VLSMs) are used when you have more than one type or length of subnet mask configured on a router. By default, this is not possible. Cisco routers only allow you to configure the same mask on all interfaces and will give you an error message if you try to configure VLSMs. To run VLSMs on your Cisco router, you need to be running a routing algorithm that supports VLSMs, for example, EIGRP and OSPF. These routing algorithms send mask information when sending route update messages, which allow you to then use VLSMs on your routers. Configuring VLSMs allows you to assign one type of mask to a serial link, for example, and a different mask to LANs. This creates an increase in the amount of hosts that can be assigned to a LAN, without increasing the amount of valid hosts assigned to a WAN, which would never be used. This increase in availability for a LAN is made possible simply by moving the division between network and host addresses to the left. So, conversely, if you need more networks, all you have to do is move the division to the right.

VLSMs can greatly enhance potential IP address allocation and simultaneously create a hierarchical architecture within the network. So if renumbering the network is necessary to implement VLSMs, it's well worth it in the long run. If you do, you'll be able to utilize IP address space more efficiently, plus—believe it or not—network management will be much easier. For instance, just imagine how much easier it is to write access lists on a router that uses a block of addresses instead of separate networks.

This chapter shows you how VLSMs can be used in a network, as well as how to summarize a network if you need to. It also explains the private addresses that you can use on your intranet that are not routable on the Internet. And the chapter finishes by showing you how to use NAT (Network Address Translation) in your network.

This chapter is important for you to understand before building your internetwork with IP addresses and subnet masks. You can save yourself a large headache down the road if you create a VLSM that is right for your company the first time. For the ACRC exam, you need to be able to summarize a network; you will learn how to do that in this chapter.

Given an IP address, use VLSMs to extend the use of the IP address.

The specification of the host and network portions within an IP address establishes an inherent hierarchy consisting of different network lengths being advertised throughout a network or over the Internet. Using a hierarchy when implementing IP addressing provides two main benefits. First, since IP addresses can be broken down into smaller subnets to accommodate addressing requirements, address space is conserved. And second, route information can be summarized, greatly reducing the size of route tables and the need for the router to know a route to every network.

This first objective addresses why to use VLSMs when designing your network. This is important to understand before studying the other objectives in this chapter.

Critical Information

How is the length of the network prefix determined? To answer that, it will be helpful to review a little about IP addressing. In the beginning (referencing RFC 760), IP addresses weren't assigned classes.

Instead, the network portion of the address was assigned to the first octet. This allowed for only 254 IP networks. To resolve this dilemma, RFC 791 was defined and written. This RFC (Request For Comments) converted a previously classless IP address structure into specific classes—five, to be exact. The three most common ones are Classes A, B, and C. Prefix lengths were defined as 8 bits, 16 bits, and 24 bits, corresponding, respectively, to Classes A, B, and C. The first three bits in the first octet were used to determine the IP address class.

In the classfull model, in which each router interface expects a default subnet mask, each address is divided into a host and a network portion. Based on the address of the host using the VLSM, you can create the division between the two at any point desired. To understand what is meant by dividing the network and host portions, refer to Figure 6.1.

F I G U R E 6.1: VLSM subnet adjustment

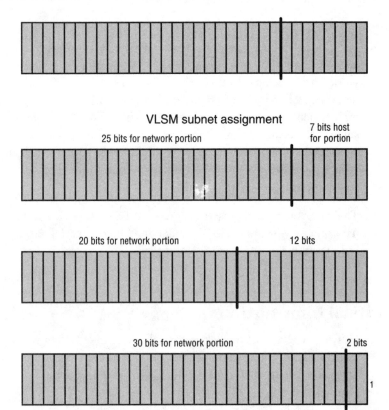

VLSM subnet assignment

25 bits for network portion

7 bits host for portion

20 bits for network portion

12 bits

30 bits for network portion

2 bits

Figure 6.1 depicts a generic 32-bit IP address. The dark line signifies the division between the network and host portions of the address. As discussed previously, in classfull IP subnets the division can take place only after 8, 16, and 24 bits. However, by using a VLSM, you can slide the division to the left or the right to adjust the subnet mask. Why is this important? Because, as the division between network and host identifying bits is moved, the number of hosts on the defined network changes respectively. For reference, consider the classfull Class C address; a Class C address contains 254 host nodes—254 because 0 and 255 are reserved for network and broadcast. As depicted in Figure 6.1, when the mask is between the 24th and 25th bit, it is a Class C address with 254 hosts. On the second sample—the first example of a VLSM-manipulated IP address—you can see that the division lies between the 25th and 26th bits. This allows 7 bits for host identification and is the equivalent of one-half of a Class C address. The numerical definition would be zero to 127, and, because 0 and 127 are reserved for network and broadcast addresses, one-half of the remaining Class C addresses gives you 126 host addresses.

Two more examples are included in Figure 6.1, with the VLSMs' equivalency to a Class C address shown at the right. In the third example, the network portion is 20-bits long, leaving 12 bits for host addresses. So, in referencing these numbers, you can see that the range is from zero to 4095. If you subtract two, you're left with 4094 possible hosts for this network. The fourth example is a network that reserves only two bits for host addresses, permitting two hosts per network.

Discontiguous IP addresses should be avoided. To implement VLSMs properly, the networks you're working with should be physically connected to the same router. Why is this important? To answer that, take a core router, for example. These routers usually have many connections from other routers and switches—even other LAN segments linked into them. To get a picture of the architecture, look at Figure 6.2.

This figure depicts a core router with several connections. Instead of using a separate Class C address for each link, VLSM can be implemented to more efficiently utilize a classfull Class B network.

FIGURE 6.2: VLSM implementation example

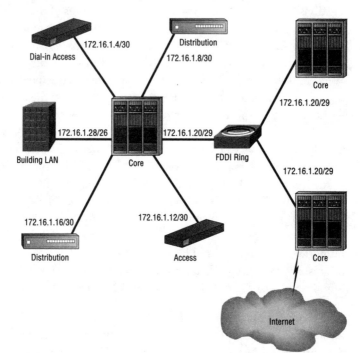

The Class B network has been broken down into six different networks, with each one providing only for the number of hosts that are necessary. When connecting two routers, only two IP host addresses are needed, and setting the subnet mask to /30 (or 255.255.255.252) defines two host IP addresses for the network. The network numbers in Figure 6.2 designate that the links connecting the core router to either a distribution or an access router will use a subnet of /30. This specifies one address for the core router interface and one IP address for the opposite end of the link.

Look at the network diagram again. Do you see subnets /26 and /29? Subnet /26 is used to connect to a switch, and using the /26 mask allocates 64 IP addresses to the switch's segment. However, remember that two of those addresses are reserved, so, in reality, 62 machines (including the switch and router) can possibly be configured on this segment. The last mask of /29 allows for even fewer hosts. There are only three routers connected to the FDDI ring, and six host addresses can be used within the 172.16.1.20 network. If more routers were added to the FDDI ring, the subnet mask could be modified to allow for more hosts.

The beauty of VLSMs is that they allow you to take a Class B address and break it down into a Class C equivalent CIDR (classless interdomain routing) block (172.16.1.0) and then create six subnets from that. Why is this useful? Because it not only conserves IP addresses but also creates a hierarchy within the core router. This gives the router different networks for each active interface and allows it to just route instead of relying on the ARP table. Can you imagine wasting an entire Class B network on one router? If the Class B were used without subnetting, the network would be flat, without a hierarchy.

Exam Essentials

Remember what VLSMs are used for.   Variable-length subnet masks are used when you have more than one type or length of subnet mask configured on a router.

Understand why you would use VLSMs on a router.   When you need more or fewer hosts on one router interface than on another interface on the same router, you can use VLSMs.

Remember that discontiguous IP addresses should be avoided. To implement VLSMs properly, the networks you're working with should be physically connected to the same router.

Key Terms and Concepts

Contiguous networks   A range of networks used in an internetwork that is the same network number.

Discontiguous networks   Different network numbers are used in the same network and are connected by a router or routers.

Subnet mask   Represented by four octets, just like an IP address, it is used to differentiate between a network, subnet, and host.

Subnet prefixes   Represented with a /#, where the number is between 1 and 32 and represents the number of binary 1s that are turned on from right to left in the four-octet subnet mask.

VLSM (variable-length subnet mask)   The usage of different subnet masks within the same network.

Sample Questions

1. What is the equivalent netmask for the prefix /20?

   A. 255.255.255.0

   B. 255.255.192.0

   C. 255.240.0.0

   D. 255.255.240.0

   E. 255.255.255.240

   Answer: D—20 bits for a subnet mask equals 255.255.240.

2. How many Class C networks can be summarized by a prefix of /22?

   A. 4

   B. 10

   C. 16

   D. 32

   Answer: A—A 22-bit mask is 255.255.252.0. This means that you have two bits for supernetting. 256 – 252 = 4 networks summarized.

Given a network plan that includes IP addressing, explain if a route summarization is or is not possible.

Route *summarization* (or *aggregation*) is a method by which contiguous networks can be grouped together and advertised as one large network. By summarizing several Class C addresses into one supernet, routing tables can be streamlined with fewer entries. A supernet is created when the division between the network and the host address portions is moved to the left. By doing this, the network prefix shrinks and absorbs all of the addresses that define individual networks.

This objective section teaches you everything you need to understand about router summarization. This is important to understand when designing an internetwork, as well as when studying for your ACRC exam.

Critical Information

Route summarization is important in large internetworks and for ISPs. The following three factors stipulate when it's good to use route summarization:

- IP networks must be contiguous, meaning that the binary enumeration must be the same for the high-order bits.

- Routing tables must have the capacity to support classless routing.

- Routing protocols must be able to manage both prefix length and subnet information along with the IP address.

Consider an example of route summarization involving three assigned /24 CIDR addresses—the equivalent of three Class C addresses. These three networks can be advertised in two ways. The first way is to advertise each individual network; if you do that, your route table will look something like the following example:

```
172.16.1.0/24
172.16.2.0/24
172.16.3.0/24
```

The second method is to summarize the three networks into one larger network and then advertise it. Doing that will make the route table look like the following example:

```
172.16.1.0/22
```

This line is one-third the size of the original route table, which represents the ability to save a lot of memory and processing power. That's why IP route summarization is such a popular thing to do. Table 6.1 details the binary breakdown of how this is done.

T A B L E 6.1: Creating a Supernet Network Address

CIDR Network	Decimal Mask	Binary to Decimal Conversion
172.16.1.0/24	255.255.255.0	10101100.000100000.000000 1.00000000
172.16.2.0/24	255.255.255.0	10101100.000100000.000000 0.00000000
172.16.3.0/24	255.255.255.0	10101100.000100000.000000 1.00000000
172.16.1.0/24	255.255.255.0	11111111.11111111.111111 11.00000000
172.16.2.0/24	255.255.255.0	11111111.11111111.111111 11.00000000
172.16.3.0/24	255.255.255.0	11111111.11111111.111111 11.00000000
172.16.1.0/22	255.255.252.0	11111111.11111111.111111 00.00000000

Each of the /24 networks has the same subnet mask. If you look closely at the last entry in the table, you'll see that it's the supernet entry for all three /24 networks. Plus you can see that the subnet mask changes for the supernet address. This is best explained by the binary mask shown in the table; the *ones* are the significant bits. The *significant bits* are the bits to which a route processor will refer in order to determine how many bits represent the network portion of the address and how many represent the host portion. The supernet mask changes from 255 to 252 in the third octet, modifying the division between network and host to the left by two bits. Now you understand how route summarization works.

Take a look at one more example of when route summarization is used. Imagine that you have the following four Class B networks assigned to you:

- `186.10.8.0/24`
- `186.10.9.0/24`
- `186.10.10.0/24`
- `186.10.11.0/24`

Remember that the first thing to do is to put these addresses into binary format, as shown in table 6.2.

T A B L E 6.2: Decimal to Binary Conversion

IP Network Address	Binary
186.10.8.0/24	10111010.00001010.000010 **00.00000000**
186.10.9.0 /24	10111010.00001010.000010 **01.00000000**
186.10.10.0 /24	10111010.00001010.000010 **10.00000000**
186.10.11.0/24	10111010.00001010.000010 **11.00000000**
Address=186.10.8.0/22	**10111010.00001010.000010** 00.00000000
Subnet=255.255.252.0	**11111111.11111111.111111** 00.00000000

After turning your network addresses into binary, you can then start from the left and move to the right until the bits no longer match up. In the preceding example, the bits stop lining up after the sixth bit of the third octet. You then use that number as your network number and mask. By turning all bits into zero after the last bit matches up, you get your summary network address, which in this case is 186.10.8.0. You would then turn on all of the bits that lined up and calculate your mask. In this example, it would be 11111111.11111111.11111100.00000000. The mask then becomes 255.255.252.0.

Exam Essentials

Understand when to use summarization. Route summarization (or aggregation) is a method by which contiguous networks can be grouped together and advertised as one large network.

Remember how to summarize. Turn your networks into binary numbers. Keep moving to the right until the binary numbers no longer match up. Add the binary numbers on the left as your network number. Turn all the bits on the left that match up into binary 1s, and that becomes your subnet mask.

Remember not to use discontiguous networks. You must use networks that are contiguous. If you do not, you can cause more overhead to your network than by not summarizing at all.

Key Terms and Concepts

Significant bits   The binary bits to which a route processor will refer in order to determine how many bits represent the network portion of the address and how many represent the host portion.

Summarization (supernetting)   The combination of network addresses into one address in order to limit the quantity of network addresses listed in a routing table.

Supernet   Any subnet that represents more than one classfull network.

Sample Questions

1. Using IGRP as the routing protocol, can the following networks be summarized: 192.168.1.0, 192.168.2.0, and 192.162.1.0?

   A. Yes

   B. No

   C. Maybe, depending on the routing protocol

Answer: B—The networks are not contiguous and, therefore, may not be summarized.

2. Is the following route summarization scenario valid—192.168.1.0, 192.168.2.0, summarized by 255.254.0.0 using EIGRP?

   A. Yes

   B. No

   C. Maybe, depending on the routing protocol

   Answer: B—The route summarization of 255.254.0.0 would create a supernet of 192.168.0.0 through 192.169.0.0.

Define private addressing and determine when it can be used.

Y ou should implement private addressing schemes with the same plan in mind as with global IP addressing schemes, assigning contiguous addresses to defined regions so you can apply summarization. Use VLSMs for subnetting to more efficiently utilize allocated networks. Finally, don't forget to run routing protocols that support classless routing.

This objective is also important to know when connecting your network to the Internet. And when studying for your ACRC exam, you must understand the address range of private addresses.

Critical Information

Another aspect of TCP/IP routing has to do with private networks. Private IP addresses can be used within a network that doesn't need to be reached by outside machines. IANA (Internet Assigned Numbers Authority) has allocated three blocks of IP addresses for private network use, as shown in Table 6.3.

T A B L E 6.3: IANA Assigned Private Networks

Network	Mask	Block
10.0.0.0	255.0.0.0	1 Class A network
172.16-31.0.0	255.240.0.0	16 Class B networks
198.168.0.0	255.255.0.0	256 Class C networks

These addresses are for use by corporate networks that don't connect to the global Internet. However, if they're used within a network that also contains a globally unique IP address, the addresses must be filtered by access lists or NAT to avoid advertising them to the Internet.

SEE ALSO NAT (Network Address Translation) is presented in detail in the next objective section in this chapter.

If a host machine is assigned a private IP address, it won't be able to communicate via TCP/IP to the outside world because private network advertisements aren't included in Internet routing tables— unless you provide the privately addressed host with a proxy server that has a globally unique address.

All of the clients' requests for information will then use the source IP address of the proxy machine instead of their own address, which allows them to communicate through it to the Internet.

TIP Remember to always consider the future of the network when you implement private addresses. Some day, some of those machines on what is presently a private network will likely need access to the Internet.

Exam Essentials

Remember what a private address is used for.   Private addresses are not forwarded on any router connected to the Internet. These addresses can be used to create a private network that cannot be routed to or from the Internet. (To route from a private network to the Internet, you need to use a NAT.)

Understand the range for Class A private networks.   The Class A range of 10.0.0.0, with any subnet mask, is reserved and cannot be routed on the Internet.

Understand the range for Class B private networks.   The Class B range of 172.16.0.0 through 172.31.0.0 is reserved and cannot be routed on the Internet.

Understand the range for Class C private networks.   The Class C range of 192.168.0.0 through 192.168.255.0 is reserved and cannot be routed on the Internet.

Key Terms and Concepts

NAT (Network Address Translation)   Used to convert a private address to a legal Internet address, or vise versa.

Proxy   A machine that maps an internal private address to a globally unique external address.

RFC 1918   Document that specifies the addresses that are not globally routable and may be assigned for private intranets.

Sample Questions

1. Which of the following is a valid private address?

   A. 209.76.25.2/16

   B. 192.16.0.0/16

    C. `172.16.0.0/16`

    D. `10.0.0.0/8`

    Answer: D—The Class A address range of `10.0.0.0` is reserved.

2. True or false: Private addresses may be globally advertised to the outside world?

    A. True

    B. False

    Answer: B—Private addresses used to keep a private network from being seen from the Internet.

Define network address translation and determine when it can be used.

Network Address Translation (NAT) is Cisco proprietary software that runs on Cisco IOS. NAT's basic function is to map private IP addresses to the globally unique IP addresses used to communicate with other Internet hosts. It is available in version 11.2 of the IOS feature set, and you enable it on a border router—one that's located between an enterprise and Internet router.

This objective section explains what NAT is and how to configure it on a Cisco router that supports this software function. This is important for you to know when connecting your network to an internetwork and when studying for the ACRC exam.

Critical Information

You can use NAT on an entirely private IP network or on one inhabited by a mix of registered and private addresses. NAT is mainly used to provide connectivity between globally and privately addressed hosts. For connectivity between the two types of hosts to be established—for it to happen at all—a source address modification of the privately addressed host must occur. NAT provides this translation.

You begin with a pool of "legal Internet" IP addresses that is specified on the router, and then you write an access list to delimit which private addresses will be allowed to be assigned registered addresses from the NAT pool. You must configure the interface connecting the enterprise router to the Internet as the NAT *outside* interface, and the other interfaces may be configured as *inside* interfaces. The `inside` / `outside` commands inform the router in which direction the translation is to occur. *Inside* tells the router that NAT should map a registered IP address back to the private IP address, and *outside* indicates the reverse—that NAT should map a private IP address to a registered IP address.

Necessary Procedures

This section uses a NAT example to show you how to configure NAT on your Cisco router. In this example, assume that the addresses 209.120.12.1 through 209.120.12.254 are legally registered IP addresses and the subnetwork 172.16.0.0 is in use internally. Below is a sample NAT configuration:

```
Router_B#config t
Enter configuration commands, one per line.  End with
CNTL/Z.
Router_B(config)#ip nat pool CCNP 209.120.12.1
209.120.12.254 netmask 255.255.255.0
Router_B(config)#access-list 55 permit 172.16.0.0
0.0.255.255
Router_B(config)#access-list 55 deny any
Router_B(config)#ip nat inside source list 55 pool CCNP
Router_B(config)#interface Ethernet 0
Router_B(config-if)#ip nat inside
Router_B(config-if)#interface Serial 0
Router_B(config-if)#ip nat outside
Router_B(config-if)#^Z
Router_B#
```

Exam Essentials

Remember when to use NAT.   Use NAT when you want to connect your network to the Internet but do not want to use valid Internet IP addresses on your hosts.

Understand how to configure NAT.   Create a NAT pool of legal registered IP addresses and then tell the device which interface is connected to the Internet and which is connected to the local network by using the NAT outside and inside commands.

Remember Cisco NAT is proprietary.   The Cisco version of Network Address Translation is proprietary and can only be used with Cisco equipment.

Key Terms and Concepts

NAT inside command   The internal IP address of a router's private interface—the one that clients see.

NAT outside command   The external IP address of a router's public interface—the one that the Internet sees. All clients using NAT appear to be coming from this address.

NAT pool   A list of addresses that is dynamically assigned to hosts as they go out.

Sample Questions

1. True or false: You must create a supernet when defining a NAT pool?

   A. True

   B. False

   Answer: B—No, with NAT, you create a pool of IP addresses to use on the Internet.

2. Which command would you use to define a global NAT pool?

   A. nat pool

   B. ip global nat pool

   C. ip nat pool

   D. ip nat pool global

Answer: C—The command ip nat pool (address pool) is used to create a NAT pool of addresses.

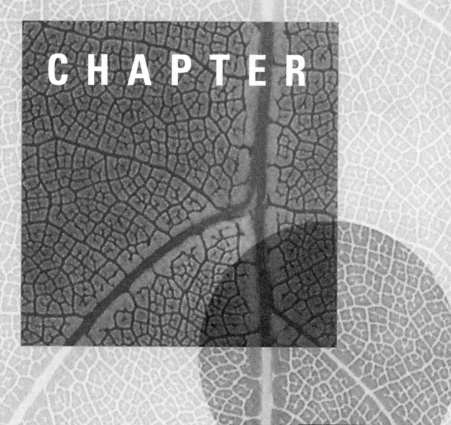

CHAPTER

7

Configuring OSPF
in a Single Area

Cisco ACRC Exam Objectives Covered in This Chapter:

▶ **Explain why OSPF is better than RIP in a large internetwork.**
(pages 143 – 149)

▶ **Explain how OSPF discovers, chooses, and maintains routes.**
(pages 149 – 155)

▶ **Configure OSPF for proper operation.** *(pages 155 – 159)*

▶ **Verify OSPF operation.** *(pages 159 – 164)*

Configuring Open Shortest Path First (OSPF) within a single area is not very difficult. However, it has more configurations than a router running Routing Information Protocol (RIP). You will need to understand what an area is and why OSPF is used in large internetworks instead of RIP before attempting the ACRC exam.

This chapter covers how to configure OSPF, verify its accuracy, and then test the configuration in both a single-area OSPF network and a multi-area OSPF network. Cisco's stand on OSPF is that if you don't need it you should use Enhanced Interior Gateway Routing Protocol (EIGRP). EIGRP is easier to configure and manage but cannot be used with routers other than Cisco's. OSPF should be used when you either need to connect to off-brand routers or you need granular control. Granular control is managed by telling OSPF routers to only advertise a subnet, part of a subnet, or a group of subnets. How to create this type of control with wild-card masks is discussed in this chapter.

The chapter's final objective teaches how to verify OSPF operation after the initial configuration of a router. This is almost as important to understand as the configuration itself. Since this is such a difficult subject, verifying and troubleshooting become a necessity.

Explain why OSPF is better than RIP in a large internetwork.

OSPF is not always a better routing protocol than RIP. However, when OSPF is used in a large internetwork, it has features that RIP lacks. For instance, RIP only uses a hop count when trying to find the best path to a remote network. OSPF can use many different methods but, by default, uses speed of the line (bandwidth) and delay of the line for finding the best path to a remote network through the internetwork.

This objective section covers the basics of OSPF, as well as the differences between RIP, a distance-vector algorithm, and OSPF, a link-state routing algorithm. When studying the ACRC material, it is imperative that you come to understand the different commands and how to verify their accuracy.

Critical Information

As networks grow, the extent to which a routing protocol will scale becomes a very critical issue. Network growth imposes a great number of changes to the network environment; the number of hops between end systems, the number of routes in the route table, the different ways a route was learned, and route convergence are all seriously affected by network growth. So, to maintain a stable routing environment, it's absolutely crucial to use a scalable protocol.

When the results of network growth are manifested, whether your network's routers will be able to meet those challenges is up to the routing protocol the routers are running. For instance, if you use a protocol like RIP that is limited by the number of hops it can transverse, by how many routes it can store in its table, or even by its inability to communicate with other protocols, you will have a protocol that will likely stunt the growth of your network. With today's ever-growing networks, this is a bad situation to be in.

Scalability Limitations of RIP

In small networks (fewer than 100 routers) where the environment is much more forgiving of routing updates and calculations, distance-vector protocols perform pretty well. However, you'll run into several problems when attempting to scale a distance-vector protocol, such as RIP, to a larger network; convergence times, router overhead (CPU utilization), and bandwidth utilization all become factors that hinder scalability.

A network's convergence time is determined by the ability of the protocol to propagate changes within the network topology. Distance-vector protocols don't use formal neighbor relationships between routers. A router using distance-vector algorithms becomes aware of a topology change in the following two ways:

- If a router fails to receive a routing update from a directly connected router

- When a router receives an update from a neighbor notifying it of a topology change somewhere in the network

Routing updates are sent out on either a default or a specified time interval, so, when a topology change occurs, it can take up to 90 seconds before a neighboring router realizes what has happened. When the router finally recognizes the change, it recalculates its routing table and sends the whole table out to all of its neighbors. This not only causes significant network convergence delays but also devours bandwidth. Just think about 100 routers sending out their entire routing tables, and imagine the impact on your bandwidth. It's not exactly a sweet scenario, and the larger the network, the worse it gets, because a greater percentage of bandwidth is needed for routing updates.

As the size of the routing table increases, so does CPU utilization, because it takes more processing power to calculate the effects of topology changes and then to converge using the new information. Also, as more routes populate a routing table, it becomes increasingly complex to determine the best path and the next hop for a given destination. The following list summarizes scalability limitations inherent in distance-vector algorithms:

- Network convergence delay

- Increased CPU utilization

- Increased bandwidth utilization

Scalability Features of OSPF

Link-state routing protocols, such as OSPF, overcome the scalability issues faced by distance-vector protocols because their routing algorithm uses a different procedure for route calculation and advertisement, which enables them to scale along with the growth of the network. OSPF uses the shortest path first (SPF) algorithm, which was first developed by Edger W. Dijkstra in 1956. Through the use of this SPF algorithm, a link-state database is developed by OSPF.

Addressing the distance-vector problem with network convergence, link-state protocols maintain a formal neighbor relationship with directly connected routers (known as neighbors) that allows for faster route convergence. OSPF establishes adjacencies with these neighbors by exchanging hello packets during a session, which cement the neighbor relationship between two directly connected routers. This relationship expedites network convergence because neighbors are immediately notified of topology changes. Hello packets are sent at short intervals (typically every 10 seconds). If an interface fails to receive hello packets from a neighbor within a predetermined hold time, the neighbor is considered to be down, and the router will then flood the update out of all physical interfaces. This is done before the new routing table is calculated, so it saves time. Neighbors receive the update, copy it, flood it out of their own interfaces, and *then* calculate the new routing table. This procedure is followed until the topology change has been propagated throughout the network.

It's noteworthy that OSPF sends an update concerning only the *new* information and not the entire routing table. This means that the update is a lot smaller, which saves both bandwidth and CPU utilization. Plus, if there aren't any network changes, updates are sent out only at either specified or default intervals, which differ among specific routing protocols and can range from 30 minutes to 2 hours.

These are key differences that permit OSPF to function well in large networks, including that it doesn't really have any limitations when it comes to scaling—other than the fact that it's a bit more complex to configure than distance-vector routing protocols.

Comparing OSPF with RIP

OSPF is an enhancement over RIP that provides a scalable routing solution. It supports several features that RIP does not (e.g., VLSM and route summarizations). The hop count was eliminated with OSPF, thus giving it limitless reachability; RIP was limited to 16 hops. And due to the fact that OSPF was used to calculate and advertise routes, network convergence is fast with OSPF. OSPF sends route updates only when changes occur in the network. A formal neighbor relationship is established with all adjacent OSPF routers.

Complete details for OSPF are found in RFC2178, and Table 7.1 briefly summarizes the features and capabilities of RIP and OSPF. Understanding this comparison is essential when studying for your ACRC exam.

TABLE 7.1: Characteristics of OSPF and RIP

Characteristic	RIP	OSPF
Type of protocol	Distance-vector	Link-state
Supports routing hierarchies	No	Yes
Convergence speed	Slow	Fast
Routing updates	Whole routing table sent	Only change is sent
Update frequency	Every 30 seconds	Every 1,800 seconds
Supports VLSM & CIDR	No (V2 only)	Yes
Can load share	No	Yes
Metric range	0–15 hops	0–65,535 hops

Exam Essentials

Understand why you would use OSPF in an internetwork. Link-state protocols maintain a formal neighbor relationship with directly connected routers. This allows each router in the internetwork to know more about the network than a distance-vector routing algorithm.

Remember why a link-state protocol works better in a large internetwork. A link-state protocol uses a different procedure for route calculation and advertisement, which enables the routers to scale along with the growth of the network.

Understand the key difference between link-state and distance-vector protocols. A link-state protocol creates neighbor relationships. A distance-vector protocol sends its complete routing table out of each active interface at a predetermined time; no neighbor relationships are formed.

Remember the key difference between OSPF and RIP. OSPF uses the Hello protocol to make peer relationships with neighbor routers. RIP only uses a hop count to find the best route to a remote network. OSPF uses speed of the line and delay of the line to find the best path to a remote network.

Key Terms and Concepts

CIDR (classless interdomain routing) Used to summarize routes, which can cut down on router table entries.

Convergence The measurement of time and the ability of routers to agree on a network topology after a change in the network.

Distance-vector routing protocol Based on distance-vector routing algorithms, every router sends its complete routing table to all of its neighbors, which can cause loops. Also called Bellman-Ford routing algorithm because of its designer.

Link-state routing protocol Based on a routing algorithm that can use both broadcasts and multicasts to all routers in an internetwork. Since link-state routers get a larger view of the network, they are not prone to routing loops. More CPU and memory in each router are required.

OSPF (Open Shortest Path First) Hierarchical interior gateway protocol that provides least-cost routing, multipath routing, and load sharing. OSPF uses the SPF routing algorithm.

RIP (Routing Information Protocol) A distance-vector routing protocol that uses a hop count as a routing metric.

Routing metric A method routers use to determine the best path to a remote network; includes shops, bandwidth, delay, load, MTU, path cost, and reliability, depending on the routing algorithm.

SPF (shortest path first) An algorithm that is used in OSPF to build routing tables.

VLSM (variable-length subnet mask) When more than one subnet mask exists for the same network number.

Sample Questions

1. When an OSPF update is detected, how is it sent to other OSPF routers?

   A. By carrier pigeon, to be manually entered by the network engineer

   B. In the form of a completely new routing table

   C. Via the Hello protocol

   D. Just the change is sent

   Answer: D—OSPF does not send its complete routing table when a change takes place like distance-vector routing algorithms do. OSPF only sends the change to its neighboring routers.

2. OSPF uses which routing algorithm to quickly calculate the network's topology?

A. CIDR

B. VLSM

C. SPF

D. Metric

Answer: C—Shortest path first routing algorithm is used to build routing tables in OSPF networks.

Explain how OSPF discovers, chooses, and maintains routes.

This objective section continues the discussion about OSPF. You will learn about how OSPF discovers neighbors and forms an adjacency. You will also learn about OSPF initializing and how OSPF maintains route information, which will show you the five basic steps that are taken when route information is exchanged (also known as database synchronization) with OSPF.

Like the other objectives in this chapter, you must understand the information presented here in order to be successful on the ACRC exam. Also, if you are maintaining an OSPF network, it is crucial that you understand the basic routing information that is used between OSPF routers. OSPF can be tuned for optimal routing but can also harm your network if misunderstood and incorrectly configured. This chapter helps you to begin the process of configuring and maintaining OSPF on Cisco routers.

Critical Information

The first step needed in order for OSPF to discover routing information outside of what it is already configured with is for it to find out who its neighbors are. Once that is complete, it can then begin to synchronize its link-state database with its neighbors' databases. This process begins as explained in the following section.

Discovering OSPF Neighbors

The Hello protocol is used to establish peering sessions between routers running OSPF, which are known as neighbors. Hello packets are multicasted out of every interface. The information that is multicasted includes the router ID, timing intervals, existing neighbors, area identification, router priority, designated and backup router information, authentication password, and stub area information. All of this information is used when establishing neighbors, which comes prior to adjacencies being formed. Once neighbors have been established, the designated router (DR) and backup designated router (BDR) need to be chosen before adjacencies, link-state information, and route information can be exchanged. The following are the only six conditions under which OSPF will form an adjacency with another router running OSPF:

- The router trying to form the adjacency is the DR.
- The router trying to form the adjacency is the BDR.
- The neighbor router is the DR.
- The neighbor router is the BDR.
- Network connectivity is through a point-to-point link.
- Network connectivity is through a virtual link.

Figure 7.1 displays a flow chart that depicts each step of the initialization process. The process starts by sending out hello packets. Every listening router will then add the originating router to the adjacency database. The responding routers will reply with all of their hello information so that the originating router can add them to its adjacency table.

After the DR and BDR are chosen, adjacencies and route information are exchanged, and the OSPF peers will continue to multicast hello packets every 10 seconds to determine if neighbors are still reachable. There is one DR and BDR per OSPF area. (An OSPF area consists of a group of routers or interfaces on a router that is assigned to a common area.)

NOTE Designated routers and backup designated routers are only present when OSPF network types are set as "Broadcast" or "NBMA."

FIGURE 7.1: OSPF peer initialization

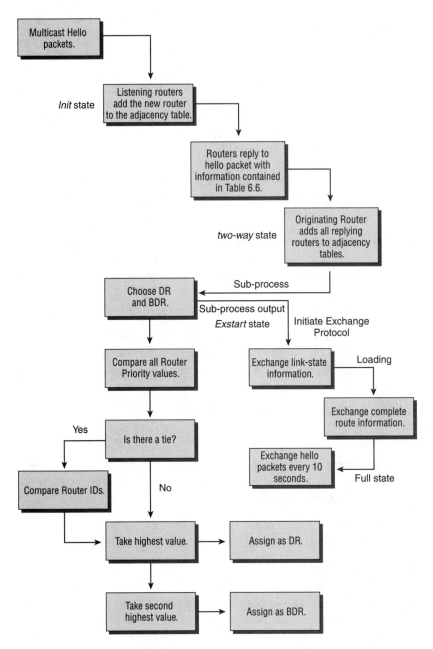

Initializing and Maintaining Route Information

Routes are discovered via the Exchange protocol (as indicated in Figure 7.1). The Exchange protocol commences discovering routes only after the DR and BDR have been chosen. The Exstart state depicted in Figure 7.1 creates peering relationships known as adjacencies with the DR, BDR, and each individual router within the area.

The following five basic steps are taken when route information is exchanged (also known as database synchronization), which happens in this order:

1. Bidirectional (two-way) communication is established—accomplished by the discovery of the Hello protocol routers and the election of a DR.

2. Exstart state—two neighboring routers form a master/slave relationship and agree upon a starting sequence that will be incremented to ensure that LSAs are acknowledged properly and that no duplication occurs. The master is the router with the highest OSPF Router ID. Database Description (DD) packets begin.

3. Exchange state—database description packets (DDPs) continue to flow as the slave router acknowledges the master's packets. At this step, OSPF is considered to be operational because the routers can send and receive LSAs.

4. Loading state—link-state requests are sent to neighbors asking for recent advertisements that have not yet been discovered. At this stage, the router builds several lists to ensure that all links are up-to-date and have been properly acknowledged. Figure 7.1 shows the fields and information contained within the link-state request packet format.

5. Full state—neighbor routers are fully adjacent because their link-state databases are fully synchronized. Data traffic can now be routed since the link-state databases are synchronized.

Now that the method for exchanging route information between OSPF routers has been discussed, it is important to also cover how OSPF selects the shortest path routes and how the router maintains the routing table.

Link-state protocols choose their routes differently than distance-vector protocols do. Bandwidth is one of the most important metrics for route selection within OSPF. The SPF algorithm is used to choose the lowest-cost link for route selection. Costs of the local router are added to the cost required to reach the destination. The route with the lowest cost is selected as the primary route. Just as with EIGRP, OSPF can hold six equal-cost routes for each destination. Changes in link-state status change the cost of the link.

Every time a link changes state, LSAs are sent to the DR and BDR. The DR relays the information to all other routers within the segment, causing the route table to be recalculated. If there are frequent link-state changes within a short period, network convergence may never be reached. OSPF prevents this problem by using holddown times. The default holddown time for route calculation is 10 seconds.

The following list summarizes how route information is calculated and shared between other routers, which typically happens in this order:

1. A link-state change occurs on Router A.

2. A multicast LSA is sent by Router A to IP Address 224.0.0.6.

3. The DR then notifies all other adjacent routers by multicasting an LSA on address 224.0.0.5.

4. Each adjacent router responds with an LSAck.

5. Other OSPF areas receive updates via LSAs sent by the DR.

6. The receiving router updates the link-state database.

7. The SPF algorithm and the link-state database are used to calculate the new routing table.

Exam Essentials

Remember how OSPF synchronizes with its neighbors. OSPF uses the Exchange protocol to discover and synchronize routes with its neighbors.

Remember how neighbors keep in touch with each other. The Hello protocol is used to ensure that each neighbor is still active.

Remember what link-state advertisements are used for. LSAs are used by OSPF to synchronize link-state databases between routers running OSPF.

Key Terms and Concepts

DR (designated router) Used to generate link-state advertisements for an internetwork running OSPF. If you have more than two OSPF routers, the designated router enables a reduction in the number of adjacencies, which can reduce the amount of routing-protocol traffic.

Hello protocol Used by OSPF systems for establishing and maintaining neighbor relationships.

LSA (link-state advertisement) Used by routers to gather routing information about neighboring routers and to maintain their routing tables.

Neighboring routers Two OSPF routers that have interfaces to a common network.

Sample Questions

1. When an LSA is sent to the DR, what is the multicast IP address?

   A. 224.0.0.4

   B. 224.0.0.5

   C. 224.0.0.6

   D. 224.0.0.7

   Answer: C—OSPF uses 224.0.0.6 as a multicast addresses when communicating to a designated router.

2. DRs and BDRs are only present on which of the following network types?

A. Point-to-point

B. Broadcast

C. ISDN

D. NBMA

Answer: B, D—Designated routers and backup designated routers are used on both broadcast and non-broadcast networks.

Configure OSPF for proper operation.

Now that the preceding objectives have helped you to learn the basics about OSPF, this objective section explains how to configure OSPF on Cisco routers. This objective teaches you how to configure your routers in a single OSPF area. It is important for you to understand how to configure both a single OSPF area and a multiple area OSPF network. (Configuring multiple areas is covered in Chapter 8.) So take a close look at the configurations presented in this objective; it covers the OSPF single-area configuration that you learned about earlier in this chapter.

When studying for the ACRC exam, remember that you must be able to both configure a Cisco router with OSPF and look at a configuration and decide where the problem is. Also, you need to understand how a single area OSPF network will work so you can both configure and troubleshoot a typical OSPF configuration.

Critical Information

When you're initializing OSPF on a router, the OSPF process is defined by a process identification number (process ID). (Unlike EIGRP's autonomous system number, OSPF's process identification number does not have to be uniform across all of the routers within the OSPF area.) The process number is just used to tell the router that OSPF is being used as a routing protocol. Instead of using the process ID to identify the OSPF area, the networks that are added to the session are assigned to an OSPF area. This means that all networks assigned to a given area make up that area. Since the OSPF areas are defined to a network number, the OSPF process looks at the network number area assigned to a router interface and then determines which subnets or networks are being advertised in the area by associating those with your configured IP addresses on your interfaces. For example:

```
Router ospf 1
Network 172.16.10.0 0.0.0.255 area 0
```

Notice that you start the configuration with `Router ospf 1`, which initializes OSPF on the router. You then tell the router which network to advertise, which can be a granular configuration. This is the best thing about OSPF; you can actually tell the routing process to only advertise a subnet or a group of subnets. Notice that you also assign the `172.16.10.0` subnet to `area 0`. This means the router will look at the configured interfaces and determine which interface is attached to network `172.16.10.0`.

Necessary Procedures

To initiate OSPF on a router, the first step is to assign the routing protocol with a process ID. After that is done, networks are added and assigned to the desired OSPF area. Following are the commands for doing this in global configuration mode:

```
router ospf process-id
network address wildcard-mask area area-id
```

The *process-id* is an integer from 1 to 65,535; the *area-id* is an integer from 0 to 4,294,967,295. Following is a configuration example:

```
Router_A#config t
Enter configuration commands, one per line.  End with
CNTL/Z.
Router_A(config)#router ospf 1
```

```
Router_A(config-router)#network 172.16.20.0 0.0.0.255
area 20
Router_A(config-router)#network 10.1.2.0 0.0.0.255 area
20
Router_A(config-router)#^Z
Router_A#

Router_A#show running-config
Building configuration...
Current configuration:
!
version 11.3
no service password-encryption
!
hostname Router_A
!
enable password aloha
!
interface Ethernet0/0
 ip address 172.16.10.1 255.255.255.0
!
interface Serial0/0
 ip address 172.16.20.5 255.255.255.252
 no ip mroute-cache
 no fair-queue
!
interface Ethernet0/1
 ip address 10.1.2.1 255.255.255.0
!
router ospf 1
 network 10.1.2.0 0.0.0.255 area 20
 network 172.16.20.0 0.0.0.255 area 20
!
ip classless
!
line con 0
line aux 0
```

```
line vty 0 4
 password aloha
 login
!
end
Router_A#
```

This example shows that the OSPF process ID was defined as 1, and two networks were added to OSPF area 20. As you can see, the configuration is quite simple, which makes sense since, as has already been stated, this configuration is the simplest form of OSPF implementation.

Exam Essentials

Remember the syntax for configuring OSPF on a router.
Following is the syntax for configuring OSPF on a router:

```
router ospf process-id
network address wildcard-mask area area-id
```

Be able to read an OSPF configuration and tell which part is valid and which part is invalid. Remember that the process ID is used after the `router ospf` command. The `process-id` option merely identifies the current OSPF session on your router; it is not significant on any other router.

Key Terms and Concepts

Routing metric   A method that routers use to determine the best path to a remote network, including hops, bandwidth, delay, load, MTU, path cost, and reliability, depending on the routing algorithm.

Syntax   The command string used from a command prompt to gather information or to configure a Cisco router.

Sample Questions

1. Which of the following commands will enable OSPF on a Cisco router?

   A. `router ospf 100`

   B. `router ospf id 100`

   C. `router 100 ospf`

   D. `ospf 100`

   Answer: A—`router ospf` *process-id* is the correct syntax for configuring OSPF.

2. Which of these selections is true regarding the following OSPF configuration? (Choose all that apply.)

   ```
   router ospf 45
   network 172.16.10.0 0.0.0.255 0
   network 10.0.34.0 0.0.0.255 0
   ```

   A. 45 is the area ID for network 10

   B. 0 is the area ID for network 10

   C. 0 is the area ID for network 34

   D. 0 is the area ID for network 34

   Answer: B, D—Selection B has a network ID of 172.16, a subnet address of 10, with hosts being defined in the fourth octet between 1–254. Selection D is correct because 10 is the network 0, 34 is subnet, and the hosts would be 1–254 for each subnet.

Verify OSPF operation.

Since OSPF can be difficult to understand, verifying the configuration and monitoring the OSPF routers become just as important as configuring a router. OSPF is a great routing protocol when used in a large internetwork. However, if OSPF is not configured properly, you might have obscure or even intermittent problems that can be difficult to find. Understanding the command used to verify OSPF is as important as understanding OSPF configuration.

It is important that you can monitor as well as configure OSPF on a Cisco router. This will help you in a production environment as well as on the ACRC exam. Since there are many commands that you can use, this section shows you the most common commands.

One of the most important things to keep in mind when studying for your ACRC exam is how to monitor or check a configuration on a router. This objective section gives you the information you will need regarding OSPF operation.

Critical Information

You need to have the ability and the knowledge to properly monitor the operation of OSPF as a crucial part of your network's success. An essential requirement to network operation is the status of OSPF, thereby ensuring network availability for all users.

You can use the following commands to verify OSPF operation:

- `show ip osfp` displays general information about the OSPF routing process.

- `show ip ospf interface` allows you to verify that interfaces have been configured in the intended areas. You can also see the timer and hello intervals with this command.

- `show ip ospf border-routers` shows you the routing table entries that connect to an area border router and an autonomous system boundary router.

Necessary Procedures

This section helps you to work through the commands for show ip ospf, show ip ospf interface, and show ip border-routers.

The *show ip ospf* Command

The show ip ospf command shows you general information about OSPF running on a router. This includes how many times the shortest path first algorithm has been run and the link-state update timer, which tells you how often hello messages are sent to neighbor routers. The following is an example of this command's output:

```
ROUTERA> show ip ospf
Routing Process "ospf 100" with ID 10.20.16.6
Supports only single TOS (TOS0) routes
It is an area border and autonomous system boundary
router
Summary Link update interval is 00:30:00 and the
update due in 00:00:54
External Link update interval is 00:30:00 and the
update due in 00:02:43
Redistributing External Routes from,
    connected with metric mapped to 100, includes
subnets in redistribution
    bgp 5754 with metric mapped to 50, includes subnets
in redistribution
SPF schedule delay 5 secs, Hold time between two SPFs
10 secs
Number of areas in this router is 2. 2 normal 0 stub
    Area BACKBONE(0)
        Number of interfaces in this area is 3
        Area has no authentication
        SPF algorithm executed 9778 times
        Area ranges are
            10.25.16.0/24 Active(1)
        Link State Update Interval is 00:30:00 and due
in 00:02:43
```

Link State Age Interval is 00:20:00 and due in 00:02:43

Area 14

Number of interfaces in this area is 2

Area has no authentication

SPF algorithm executed 30 times

Area ranges are

Link State Update Interval is 00:30:00 and due in 00:00:50

Link State Age Interval is 00:20:00 and due in 00:00:43

The *show ip ospf interface* Command

The show ip ospf command allows you to verify that interfaces have been configured in the intended areas. You can also see the timer and hello intervals with this command. You can gather information on interfaces or on a specific interface, as indicated by the following output:

```
ROUTERA# show ip ospf interface s1/0.1
Serial1/0.1 is up, line protocol is up
  Internet Address 10.16.16.65/27, Area 0
  Process ID 5774, Router ID 10.16.16.1, Network Type
BROADCAST, Cost: 64
  Transmit Delay is 1 sec, State DROTHER, Priority 10
  Designated Router (ID) 10.25.16.8, Interface address
10.16.16.72
  Backup Designated router (ID) 10.16.16.9, Interface
address 10.25.16.73
  Timer intervals configured, Hello 10, Dead 40, Wait
40, Retransmit 5
    Hello due in 00:00:09
  Neighbor Count is 8, Adjacent neighbor count is 2
    Adjacent with neighbor 10.16.16.8  (Designated
Router)
    Adjacent with neighbor 10.16.16.9  (Backup
Designated Router)
```

The *show ip ospf border-routers* Command

The ip ospf border-routers command shows you the routing table entries that connect to an area border router and an autonomous system boundary router. This command also shows you if it is an intra-area or inter-area router. The following is an example of the show ip ospf border-routers command:

```
ROUTERA#show ip ospf border-routers
OSPF Process 5774 internal Routing Table
Codes: i - Intra-area route, I - Inter-area route
i 10.25.18.5 [64] via 10.25.18.1, Serial3/0.1, ASBR,
Area 5, SPF 1020
I 10.25.18.97 [128] via 10.25.16.40, Serial1/0.1, ASBR,
Area 0, SPF 9819
I 10.25.18.97 [128] via 10.25.16.72, Serial2/0.1, ASBR,
Area 0, SPF 9819
I 10.25.18.97 [128] via 10.25.16.41, Serial1/0.1, ASBR,
Area 0, SPF 9819
I 10.25.18.97 [128] via 10.25.16.73, Serial2/0.1, ASBR,
Area 0, SPF 9819
I 10.25.18.96 [128] via 10.25.16.40, Serial1/0.1, ASBR,
Area 0, SPF 9819
```

Exam Essentials

Remember what each of the three commands are used for. Become familiar with and practice running the show ip ospf, show ip ospf interface, and show ip ospf border-routers commands.

Remember to use your help screens. There are many commands that you can use to monitor and verify OSPF. By using the help screens on Cisco routers, you can easily gather the information you need. Test this by typing *show ip ospf ?* This will supply you with all of the commands that you can use to verify OSPF operation on your router.

Key Terms and Concepts

Link-state routing protocol   Based on a routing algorithm that can use both broadcasts and multicasts to all routers in an internetwork. Since link-state routers get a larger view of the network, they are not prone to routing loops. More CPU and memory in each router are required.

Show command   Used in Cisco routers to gather information about the router or the internetwork.

Sample Questions

1. Which of the following commands will show you information about the routing process within OSPF?

   A. show ip ospf

   B. show ip ospf interface

   C. show ip ospf router

   D. show ip ospf border-routers

   Answer: A—The show ip ospf command displays a variety of general information about the routing process.

2. Which of the following commands will show you what interfaces are configured for an area?

   A. show ip ospf

   B. show ip ospf interface

   C. show ip ospf router

   D. show ip ospf border-routers

   Answer: B—You can use this command to verify that interfaces have been configured in the intended areas.

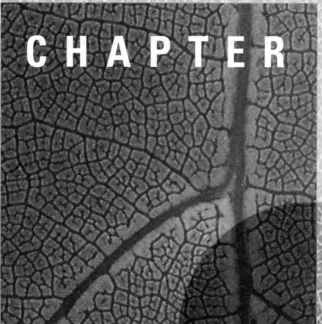

CHAPTER

8

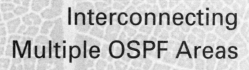

Interconnecting
Multiple OSPF Areas

Cisco ACRC Exam Objectives Covered in This Chapter:

▶ **Describe the issues with interconnecting multiple areas and how OSPF addresses.** *(pages 166 – 170)*

▶ **Explain the differences between the possible types of areas, routers, and LSAs.** *(pages 170 – 175)*

▶ **Configure a multiarea OSPF network.** *(pages 176 – 181)*

▶ **Verify OSPF operation.** *(pages 181 – 184)*

This chapter resumes discussion exactly where the Chapter 7 objectives conclude it. Chapter 7 explains how to configure a Cisco router with only a single area. This chapter will not only present how to configure Cisco routers in an internetwork but will also explain the different ways to configure a Cisco router within an area. This is a little more complicated than configuring a single Open Shortest Path First (OSPF) area because there are more new terms to learn.

Just like with Chapter 7, you must learn this chapter and its corresponding objectives if you are going to be successful—not only in a production environment but also on the ACRC exam. The absolute best way to study this chapter is to include hands-on experience with routers. However, if that is not possible, practice writing out the chapter's commands on paper.

Describe the issues with interconnecting multiple areas and how OSPF addresses.

The basic configuration of a Cisco router with multiple configurations is the same as with a single area. However, you need to determine the types of areas and how your router is going to fit into this area. It is important to remember that if you have an internetwork with multiple areas you will need to have a connection between each area and area zero (the backbone).

This objective covers the issues that exist when multiple areas are present on an internetwork. This is important information that you will need for the remainder of this chapter.

Critical Information

Areas are used within OSPF to define a group of routers and networks belonging to the same OSPF session. As demonstrated in Chapter 7, it is very simple to configure a router for one OSPF area. However, what happens when you consider adding several hundred routers into a single area? Quite simply, the benefits gained through OSPF are lost as the following problems begin occurring:

- Frequent SPF calculations

- Very large routing tables

- Large link-state database

- Increased router CPU utilization, reducing effectiveness

In order to compensate for these factors, OSPF has the capacity for creating multiple areas. It is important to note that the first area that should be created in any OSPF network is *area 0,* also referred to as the backbone area. The creation of area 0 is a requirement of proper OSPF operation and configuration.

The use of multiple OSPF areas is known as *hierarchical routing.* Through the use of multiple areas, you can reduce a large network into smaller, more manageable areas. Fortunately, the details of keeping the link-state database and the routing table are not shared between areas, thus restoring the many benefits of OSPF. This design technique allows for routing to occur between multiple OSPF areas, which is referred to as *inter-area routing.* OSPF also performs *intra-area routing,* which describes routing that occurs within an OSPF area. Multiple areas require OSPF to use routers as specific types, depending on their required function. The different types of routers are briefly described in the following list:

Internal router   All of its interfaces are within the same area.

Backbone router   Connects to the OSPF backbone, area 0.

Area border router (ABR)   Its interfaces are in multiple OSPF areas.

Autonomous system boundary router (ASBR)   It has at least one interface connected to an external internetwork, such as the Internet.

In addition to the listed responsibilities, a router can also be assigned additional responsibilities. These additions are assumed when a router is assigned the role of designated router (DR) or backup designated router (BDR). Designated routers can speak for all the routers in an area, so you can think of a DR as sort of a "router congressman."

NOTE   It is possible for a router to be more than one router type at a time. For example, if a router is connected to the Internet and OSPF area 1, it is both an ASBR and an ABR.

Exam Essentials

Remember the different types of OSPF routers that can be defined.   These router types include internal router, backbone router, area border router, and autonomous system boundary router.

Remember the difference between inter-area routing and intra-area routing.   Inter-area routing allows routing to occur between multiple OSPF areas. OSPF also performs intra-area routing, which is routing that occurs within an OSPF area.

Understand that the process ID is only administrative and can be any value.   The process ID, when configuring OSPF, is only for assigning an administrative ID to the OSPF routing process.

Key Terms and Concepts

ABR (area border router)   A router that has interfaces in multiple OSPF areas.

ASBR (autonomous system boundary router)   A router that has at least one interface connected to an external internetwork, such as the Internet.

Backbone router   A router that is connected to the OSPF backbone, area 0.

Hierarchical routing   Enables routing efficiency by logically separating a large internetwork into smaller areas.

Inter-area routing   Routing occurs between OSPF areas.

Internal router   A router that has all of its interfaces within the same area.

Intra-area routing: Routing that occurs within an OSPF area.

Sample Questions

1. Which type of OSPF router can be connected to multiple OSPF areas?

   A. Internal

   B. Backbone

   C. ABR

   D. ASBR

   Answer: C—Area system routers are used to connect multiple areas.

2. Which of the following describes routing that occurs between different routing processes?

   A. Intra-area

   B. Inter-area

    C. LSA

    D. OSPF

    Answer: B—Routers contained within one area that communicate routing information between each other are inter-area routers.

Explain the differences between the possible types of areas, routers, and LSAs.

This objective section covers the different types of routers that you can configure when configuring Cisco routers. It is important that you know exactly where your routers are placed in an internetwork. You can ascertain this information by creating or looking at a map of your network, noting where each router is situated. Once this is determined, you can configure your routers with OSPF area information.

It is important for you to understand this objective both when configuring Cisco routers and when taking the ACRC exam. Practice this chapter on Cisco routers or with pencil and paper.

Critical Information

OSPF allows and uses different area types. When deploying OSPF, there must be a backbone area. Standard and stub areas connect to the backbone area. The following list briefly introduces each router type and a short description of the area type:

    Backbone area   Accepts all LSAs, is used to connect multiple areas, and is known as area 0.

    Standard area   The normal OSPF area, which accepts internal and external LSAs and summary information.

Stub area   Will not accept any external routing updates but will accept summary LSAs; relies upon a default to route traffic outside of the area.

Totally stub area   Not allowed to accept external or summary advertisements.

Not-so-stubby area (NSSA)   Used to connect to ISPs. It accepts all LSA types except type 5.

Backbone Area

The backbone area is a transit area from one area to another and is always the central area within an OSPF internetwork. All other areas must connect to this area in order to properly exchange routing information and data. It is configured with the area 0 or area 0.0.0.0 commands, which are the same thing.

Standard Area

The standard OSPF area that processes all OSPF link updates and route summaries. It connects to the backbone, and all routers in this area have the same link-state database.

Stub Area

When the size of route tables and link-state databases grows too large and can't be remedied with route summarization alone, the area may be configured as a stub or totally stub area.

The difference between a stub area and a normal area is that intra-area and inter-area routes are the only routes allowed inside the stub area. To communicate with networks that are not present in the route table, the stub area relies on a default route of 0.0.0.0. This means that when a router does not have a route to the destination address it will forward the packet to the ABR from which it learned the default network 0.0.0.0. The ABR will then do the route lookup and forward the packet accordingly.

A stub area contains all routes from its area and other areas that are connected via the backbone and ABRs. It does not contain any external routes.

Totally Stub Area

A totally stub area contains an even smaller route table because the only routes it knows are the routes from within its own area. To contact networks outside of the area, the default route 0.0.0.0 is used as well. The ABR is responsible for forwarding packets to the correct destination. This type of area does not accept summary LSAs from any other area, nor does it accept any external summary LSAs from a different AS. The only way out is through the default route.

Not-So-Stubby Area

Full communication within the autonomous system results from the default route. However, no information about the Internet will be communicated into the area. NSSA routers propagate a type 7 LSA within the area to communicate with other routers, but not with routers outside the area. The border router will translate the type 7 LSA into a type 5 LSA to propagate the information to other areas.

Configuring Stub and Totally Stub Areas

Now that stub and totally stub areas have been explained, it is important for you to learn how to configure each of them. To configure a stub area, the following command should be implemented on an internal router that is not an ASBR and not connected to the backbone. It is also important to issue this command on every router within the stub or totally stub area.

```
area area-id stub
```

The command is self-explanatory—the area-id simply defines the stub area.

To make an area become totally stub, the same command is used, but with one modification; it must be issued on the ABR for the area. Note the following example:

```
area area-id stub no-summary
```

NOTE You cannot configure routers as stub routers if they belong to the backbone. An area cannot be defined as a stub area if an ASBR is part of the area.

Link-State Advertisements

Link-state advertisements (LSAs) are the heart of OSPF's information exchange process. Since OSPF does not send complete routing tables, it uses LSAs to provide changes in link-state information, thereby reducing routing updates. When a router receives an LSA, it checks its link-state database. If the LSA is new, the router floods the LSA out to its neighbors. After the new LSA is added to the LSA database, the router will rerun the shortest path first (SPF) algorithm. This recalculation by the SPF algorithm is absolutely essential to preserving accurate routing tables. The SPF algorithm is responsible for calculating the routing table, and any LSA change might also cause a change in the routing table. Different types of LSAs represent different types of route information. All of the LSA types are summarized in Table 8.1.

T A B L E 8.1: OSPF LSA Types

LSA Type	Description
1—Router LSA	This LSA is broadcasted only within its defined area. The LSA contains all of the default link-state information.
2—Network LSA	This LSA is multicasted to all area routers by the DR. This update contains network-specific information.
3 & 4—Summary LSA	Type 3 LSAs are generated by an ABR and contain route information for internal networks. They are sent to backbone routers so routes can be aggregated.
	Type 4 LSAs are also generated by an ABR, and they contain information about links to ASBRs. Summary information is multicasted by the ABR, and the information reaches all backbone routers.

TABLE 8.1: OSPF LSA Types *(continued)*

LSA Type	Description
5—Autonomous System LSA	As the name indicates, these LSAs originate from an ASBR. These packets contain information about external networks. They will be flooded to every OSPF area except stub areas.

Different LSA types represent the type of route that is being advertised, and they assist in restricting the number and type of routes that are accepted within a given area.

Exam Essentials

You must remember the different types of areas and be able to configure this on a router. The backbone area accepts all LSAs, is used to connect multiple areas, and is known as area 0. The standard area is the normal OSPF area and accepts internal and external LSAs and summary information. The stub area does not accept any external routing updates but will accept summary LSAs. The routers in the stub area rely upon a default to route traffic outside of the area. The totally stub area does not accept external or summary advertisements.

Understand the different LSA types. Remember that type 1 LSAs are router LSAs, type 2 LSAs are network LSAs, and type 3 and type 4 LSAs are summary LSAs.

You need to be able to configure a network as totally stub. To configure a network as totally stub, use the `area` area-id `stub no-summary` command.

Key Terms and Concepts

LSA (link-state advertisement)   Used to provide link-state updates to neighbor routers.

Standard area The normal OSPF area, which accepts internal and external LSAs and summary information.

Stub area Will not accept any external routing updates but will accept summary LSAs; uses a default route to get packets out of an area.

Totally stub area Does not accept external or summary advertisements.

Sample Questions

1. Which LSA type is generated by an ASBR?

    A. 1

    B. 2

    C. 3

    D. 4

    E. 5

    Answer: E—Type 4 LSAs are used to send information from an ASBR to an ABR.

2. What are type 3 and type 4 LSAs?

    A. Router

    B. Summary

    C. Network

    D. AS

    Answer: B—Type 3 LSAs are used to send information about networks within an area to the backbone and between ABRs. Type 4 is used to send information from an ASBR to an ABR.

Configure a multiarea OSPF network.

Configuration for multiple-area routers is the same as it is for internal routers. The different types of routers are defined by the area assignment of the connected networks. For example, if a router has two networks, with one assigned to area 10 and the other assigned to area 30, by default the router becomes an area border router. A similar example may be given with a backbone router; if an interface or network is assigned to area zero, it becomes a backbone router.

This objective section shows you the configuration commands used in a multiarea OSPF network. This is an important chapter to understand because you may currently be working in a production environment—or may end up working in a production environment—using OSPF with multiareas. Try practicing the commands discussed in this objective on routers. If you cannot do that, then be sure to practice writing the commands out on paper.

Critical Information

Many aspects need to be considered when you configure multiple areas on a Cisco OSPF router. When you configure OSPF with multiareas, the following configurations are necessary:

- The network command and wildcard masking
- Route Summarization
- Configuration of a stub area
- Configuration of a totally stub area
- Configuration for the cost of a default route propagated into the area

Each of these configurations is detailed in the following sections.

The *network* Command and Wildcard Masking

Using the network command and wildcard masking can get complicated really fast. It is important to understand the networks your router is attached to before attempting this configuration. To emphasize this, consider the following sample router configuration using the network command with a wildcard mask.

The sample router has three interfaces. Interface Ethernet 0 is connected to 172.16.10.0/24, area 0. Serial 0 is connected to 172.16.4.0/22, and serial 1 is connected to 172.16.8.0/22; both of these interfaces are connected to area 1. Notice that a different mask is being used for the WANs than is being used for the LANs. This is a benefit of using OSPF; it allows variable-length subnet masks (VLSMs). The router configuration should then look like this:

```
Router ospf 1
Network 172.16.10.0 0.0.0.255 area 0
Network 172.16.4.0 0.0.3.255 area 1
Network 172.16.8.0 0.0.3.255 area 1
```

Notice that you first define the backbone connection. The wildcard mask is simple since you specify a whole subnet. To figure out a wildcard mask, use all 1s minus the network mask. Here is an example:

```
255.255.255.255  (all 1s)
255.255.255.0  (the mask)
0  .0  .0  .255 (the answer)
```

For the serial interfaces connected to area 1, remember that the mask was not 24 bits, but 22 bits. The mask would then be:

```
255.255.255.255  (all 1s)
255.255.252.0  (the mask)
0  .0  .3  .255  (the answer)
```

Route Summarization

Route summarization in OSPF is used for the same reasons that other routing protocols use it. When a route table becomes large, it taxes the router in multiple ways: CPU utilization, and bandwidth and memory consumption. OSPF supports two types of route summarization: inter-area and external. As with many inter-area functions, the ABR is in charge of summarizing area routes. External summarization is exactly that; only external routes are summarized by the autonomous system border router.

The summarization commands must be issued on the respective routers. Inter-area summarization must be configured on the ABR with the following command within the OSPF routing session:

```
area area-id range address mask
```

The *area-id* is the OSPF area number. The *address* and *mask* define the range of IP addresses that will be summarized for the specified area. To configure external summarization, the following command must be entered within the OSPF routing session on the ASBR:

```
summary-address address mask
```

Notice that the area ID was not used in the command. This is because only external routes will be summarized. The address and mask define the range of external IP addresses that will be summarized. Remember that external routers are routes that are discovered via redistribution.

Stub Area Configuration

When route tables and link-state databases grow too large and can't be remedied with route summarization alone, the area may be configured as either a stub area or a totally stub area.

The difference between a stub area and a normal area is that intra-area and inter-area routes are the only routes allowed inside the stub area. To communicate with networks that are not present in the route table, the stub area relies on a default route of 0.0.0.0. This means that when a router does not have a route to the destination address it will forward the packet to the ABR from which it learned the default network 0.0.0.0. The ABR will then do the route lookup and forward the packet accordingly.

A stub area contains all routes from its area and other areas that are connected via the backbone and ABRs. It does not contain any external routes.

To configure a stub area, the following command should be implemented on an internal router that is not an ASBR and not connected to the backbone. It is also important to issue this command on every router within the stub area (or also the totally stub area).

```
area area-id stub
```

The command is self-explanatory; the *area-id* simply defines the stub area.

NOTE   You cannot configure a router as a stub router if it belongs to the backbone. And an area cannot be defined as a stub area if an ASBR is part of the area.

Configuring Totally Stubby Areas

To further shrink a route table for an area, you can make the route table totally stub. A totally stub area contains an even smaller route table because the only routes it knows are the routes from within its own area. To contact networks outside the area, the default route 0.0.0.0 is used as well. The ABR is responsible for forwarding packets to the correct destination.

To make a totally stub area, the same command is used, with one modification. It must be issued on the ABR for the area:

```
area area-id stub no-summary
```

Configuring the Default Route Cost

In a totally stub area, there are no routes defined to other networks. To reach these other networks and hosts in an internetwork outside of the router's defined area, a default route needs to be used. On an

ABR router, you can set the default cost of this route that will be advertised within the area. The configuration is as follows:

Area *area-id* default-cost *cost*

Exam Essentials

Remember where you can summarize. OSPF supports two types of route summarization: inter-area and external. As with many inter-area functions, the ABR is in charge of summarizing area routes. External summarization is exactly that; only external routes are summarized by the ASBR.

Understand how to create a wildcard mask. By using all 1s minus the mask, you can find your wildcard mask. For example:

255.255.255.255 (all 1s)
255.255.248.0 (the mask)
0.0.7.255 (the answer)

Remember how to create a stub network. To configure a stub area, the following command should be implemented on an internal router that is not an ASBR and not connected to the backbone. It is also important to issue this command on every router within the stub area or totally stub area.

area *area-id* stub

Key Terms and Concepts

Backbone area Accepts all LSAs, is used to connect multiple areas, and is known as area 0.

Stub area Will not accept any external routing updates but will accept summary LSAs; uses a default route to get packets out of an area.

Totally stub area Does not accept external or summary advertisements.

Sample Questions

1. Which wildcard mask should you use when configuring the following network?

> 172.16.16.0/20

A. 0.0.0.0

B. 0.0.255.255

C. 0.0.3.255

D. 0.0.15.255

E. 0.0.31.255

Answer: D—To figure out the wildcard mask, minus all 1s from the mask. In this case it is:

> 255.255.255.255 (all 1s)
> 255.255.240.0 (the mask)
> 0.0.15.255 (the answer)

2. Which of the following commands is used to create a totally stub network?

A. area *area-id* stub-total

B. area *area-id* totally-stub

C. area *area-id* stub no-summary

D. area *area-id* stub

Answer: C—The area *area-id* stub no-summary command is used to create a totally stub area.

▶ Verify OSPF operation.

Just as explained in all chapters and objectives in this book, if you configure something on a Cisco router, you must know how to verify your configuration. This objective shows you how to verify OSPF configuration on a Cisco router.

This is an important objective because it shows you the commands for verifying your configuration in both a single OSPF area as well as a multiarea OSPF network. Practice these commands on a router if possible.

Critical Information

It is very important to be able to verify your OSPF configuration on a Cisco router. The commands to verify can also be used to troubleshoot your internetwork in case of routing problems. The following commands are used to verify configuration of OSPF on a Cisco router:

- `show ip protocol` displays the IP routing protocols running on your Cisco router. It displays information about timers, as well as redistribution information. This is an excellent command to use when troubleshooting or verifying your routing configuration.

- `show ip route` shows you the IP routing table on a Cisco router. It shows you all the networks the routing process knows about as well as the default route, if configured. This is a great command to use to troubleshoot and verify your configuration of OSPF since it can show you all the routes it knows about.

- `show ip ospf interface` shows you the OSPF configuration on an interface level. It also gives you statistics on how it is running on an interface. It shows you the IP address, process ID, and area information associated with that particular interface.

- `show ip ospf` shows you the OSPF process and the details associated with the process. It also gives you the router ID (RID), which is the highest IP address configured on the router, unless a loopback interface has been configured; then the loopback interface IP address will automatically become the RID.

- `show ip ospf neighbor` gives you all the information about the relationships that the OSPF process has built with its neighbors. You can use the command in a more granular fashion by only typing in an interface or a neighboring RID. By typing the `show ip ospf neighbor detail` command, you will see all neighbor information in great detail.

- `show ospf database` shows you the topological database of all routes in the internetwork that is built by OSPF routers. After the topological database, the OSPF process builds a routing table based on the best cost to each network. (The topological database will keep up to six routes to a given network, and only the best route will be used in the routing table.) This command also shows you the different LSAs that are used to build the table.

To verify multiarea configurations, use the following commands in conjunction with the preceding commands:

- `show ip ospf border-routers` shows you the OSPF area border routers. This is a great command for troubleshooting configuration errors and understanding who the router is communicating with about the internetwork routes.

- `show ip ospf virtual-links` is used to verify virtual links, which are used when it is not possible, mainly due to bad design, to connect all areas to the backbone, area 0. The `show ip ospf neighbors` command is used in conjunction with this command to verify the virtual link.

Exam Essentials

Remember how to view the topological database created by the OSPF process. The `show ospf database` command shows you the topological database. It also shows you the different LSAs that are used to build the table.

Remember how to verify your virtual links. The `show ip ospf virtual-links` command is used to verify this simple configuration.

Remember how to see what routers you directly communicate with. The show ip ospf neighbor command gives you all the information about the relationships that the OSPF process has built with its neighbors.

Key Terms and Concepts

Backbone area   Accepts all LSAs, is used to connect multiple areas, and is known as area 0.

LSA (link-state advertisement)   Used to provide link-state updates to neighbor routers.

Virtual-link   Link made between two routers when one router is not connected to area 0.

Sample Questions

1. Which command shows you the topological database?

A. show ip ospf neighbors

B. show ip ospf database

C. show ip ospf topological

D. show ip ospf interface

Answer: B—The show ip ospf database command shows you the topological database. It also shows you the different LSAs that are used to build the table.

2. Which command displays the RID?

A. show ip ospf

B. show ip ospf rid

C. show ip neighbors

D. show ip ospf database

Answer: A—show ip ospf shows you the OSPF process and the details associated with the process. It also gives you the router ID.

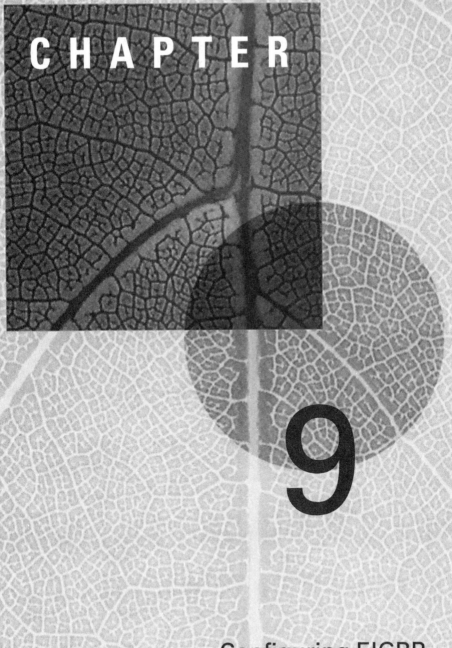

CHAPTER

9

Configuring EIGRP

Cisco ACRC Exam Objectives Covered in This Chapter:

▶ **Describe Enhanced IGRP features and operation.**
(pages 187 – 193)

▶ **Configure Enhanced IGRP.** *(pages 194 – 197)*

▶ **Verify Enhanced IGRP operation.** *(pages 197 – 200)*

As the objectives indicate, this chapter is all about
Enhanced Interior Gateway Routing Protocol (EIGRP)—what it is,
how to configure it, and how to verify and monitor EIGRP once it is
running on your router. To begin with, EIGRP is a hybrid routing
algorithm. This means that it uses the best features of both distance-
vector and link-state routing. EIGRP is used in a lot of internetworks,
but only if they are exclusively running Cisco routers. EIGRP is a proprietary Cisco routing algorithm, and it works very well.

Enhanced IGRP was created to resolve some of IGRP's problems.
These problems included that the entire route table is sent when
changes are made in the network and that formal neighbor relationships with connected routers are lacking. EIGRP allows for equal-
cost load balancing, incremental routing updates, and formal neighbor relationships, overcoming the limitations of IGRP. This enhanced
version uses the same distance-vector information as IGRP but with
a different algorithm. EIGRP uses diffused update algorithm (DUAL)
for metric calculation. EIGRP was created as a hybrid of both link-
state and distance-vector routing algorithms, which brings the best of
both worlds together.

EIGRP is configured the same as IGRP, which means that you configure a network process and autonomous system (AS). This chapter
shows you how to configure EIGRP on Cisco routers. As with all
chapters in this book that show configurations of any type, this chapter also shows you how to verify the configuration and route status
when running EIGRP on Cisco routers.

These objectives are really important for you to understand since they are designed to teach you about how EIGRP creates neighbor relationships and how to configure and verify EIGRP running on a Cisco router. When studying for the ACRC exam, you should remember that hybrid and link-state routing algorithms are a big part of the Cisco authorized training course and material.

Describe Enhanced IGRP features and operation.

This first objective concentrates on EIGRP and why it is used. EIGRP is a popular routing algorithm for good reason. It has better features than RIP and IGRP, and it is easier to configure than OSPF. EIGRP's outstanding features make it a stable and scalable protocol, and just as IGRP is a Cisco proprietary protocol, so is EIGRP.

It is important to understand EIGRP before you learn how to configure and administrate EIGRP running on your routers. When studying for your ACRC exam, you should try to practice all commands in this book. However, routing algorithms and their configurations are very important to understand and should be understood completely.

Critical Information

The EIGRP topology database stores all routes and metrics that become known to it via adjacent routers. Six routes can be stored for each destination network. From these six routes, the router must select a primary and a backup route. (The primary route is added to the route table.) While the best route is being chosen for a destination, the route is considered to be in an *active* state; after the route has been chosen, the route status changes to a *passive* state.

Through the use of existing metric information, such as bandwidth and the delay from both the local and adjacent routers, a composite metric is calculated. The local router adds its cost to the cost advertised by the adjacent router. (*Cost* is another word for metric.) The route with the best metric (lower is better) is chosen as the primary route. The route with the second-lowest metric becomes the backup route—assuming that one is available. Primary routes are moved to the route table after selection. (It is possible to have more than one primary route in order to perform load balancing.)

EIGRP also has link-state properties. One of these properties is that it propagates only the changes in the route table instead of sending an entire new route table to its neighbors. As you probably recall, when changes occur in the network, a regular distance-vector protocol will send the entire route table to neighboring routers; but less bandwidth is consumed when this is avoided. Neighboring routers don't have to re-initialize the entire route table, causing convergence issues; they just have to insert the new route changes. This is one of the big enhancements over IGRP.

Establishing Neighbor Relationships

EIGRP uses the Hello protocol to establish and maintain peering relationships with directly connected routers. Hello packets are sent between EIGRP routers to determine the state of the connection between them. Once the neighbor relationship is established via the Hello protocol, the routers can exchange route information.

Each router establishes a neighbor table in which it stores important information regarding its directly connected neighbors. The information consists of the neighbor's IP address, hold time interval, smooth round trip timer (SRTT), and queue information. These data are used to help determine when the link state changes.

When two routers initialize communication, their entire route tables are shared. Thereafter, only changes to the route table are propagated. These changes are shared with all directly connected EIGRP-speaking routers. The following list summarizes each of these steps:

- Hello packets are multicasted out of all of the router's interfaces.

- Replies to the hello packets include all routes in the neighboring router's topology database (also including the metrics). Routes that are learned from the originating router are not included in the reply.

- The originating router acknowledges the update to each neighbor via an Ack packet.

- The topology database is then updated with the newly received information.

- Once the topology database has been updated, the originating router advertises its entire table to all of the new neighbors.

- Neighboring routers acknowledge the receipt of the route information from the originating router by sending back an Ack packet.

EIGRP Updates

Updates can follow two paths. If a route update contains a better metric or a new route, the routers simply exchange the information. If the update contains information that a network is unavailable or the metric is worse than before, an alternate path must be found. The flow chart in Figure 9.1 on the next page describes the steps that must be taken to choose a new route.

The router first searches the topology database for feasible successors. If no feasible successors are found, a multicast request is sent to all adjacent routers. Each router will then respond to the query. Depending on how the router answers, different paths will be taken. After the intermediate steps are taken, two final actions can occur. If route information is eventually found, the route is added to the route table, and an update is sent. If the responses from the adjacent routers do not contain any route information, the route is removed from the topology and route tables. After the route table has been updated, the new information is sent to all adjacent routers via a multicast.

FIGURE 9.1: Handling route changes

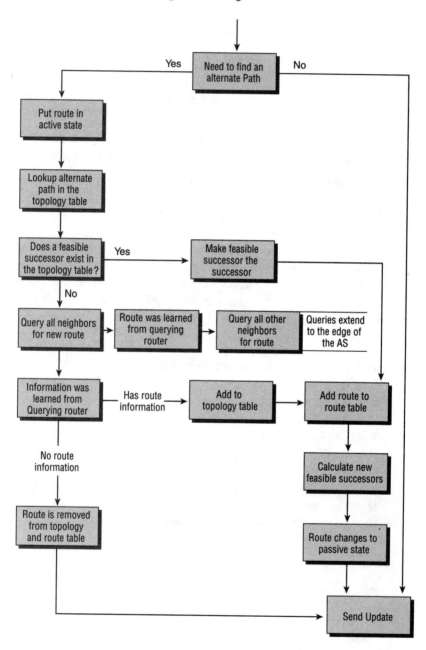

As has been previously mentioned, EIGRP allows for equal-cost load balancing, incremental routing updates, and formal neighbor relationships, overcoming the limitations of IGRP. This enhanced version uses the same distance-vector information as IGRP but with a different algorithm. Table 9.1 summarizes EIGRP's distinguishing features.

T A B L E 9.1: EIGRP Features

Feature	Description
Route tagging	Distinguishes routes learned via different EIGRP sessions.
Formal neighbor relationships	Uses the Hello protocol to establish peering.
Incremental routing updates	Only changes are advertised, instead of the entire route table.
Classless routing	Supports subnet and VLSM information.
Configurable metrics	Metric information can be set through configuration commands.
Equal-cost load balancing	Allows traffic to be sent equally across multiple connections.

NOTE EIGRP uses the same vector information as IGRP: bandwidth, delay, reliability, load, and MTU. Bandwidth and delay are the two metrics used by default; the others can be configured manually. When you configure reliability, load and MTU can cause the topology table to be calculated more often.

To aid in the calculation of the best route and load sharing, EIGRP utilizes several databases of information. These databases are as follows:

- The route database (where the best routes are stored)

- The topology database (where all route information resides)

- A neighbor table (where information concerning other EIGRP neighbors is housed)

Each of these databases exists for IP-EIGRP, IPX-EIGRP, and AT-EIGRP. Therefore, it is possible for EIGRP to have nine active databases when all three protocols are configured on the router.

Exam Essentials

Remember how EIGRP finds the best route to a remote network. EIGRP uses bandwidth (or speed of line) and delay of the line to determine the best route to a remote network.

Remember what DUAL is. Diffused update algorithm is used to calculate the best path to a remote network and has a great convergence time compared to distance-vector routing.

Understand how EIGRP creates neighbor relationships. EIGRP uses link-state properties to create neighbor relationships. Hello packets are sent every 5 seconds to neighboring routers to verify that they are alive.

Key Terms and Concepts

DUAL (diffused update algorithm) Used by EIGRP for metric calculation. (The higher the metric associated with a route, the less desirable the route is.)

Route tagging EIGRP functions within defined autonomous systems on a router. It is possible for multiple sessions of EIGRP to run on a single router. Each session is distinguished by the autonomous system (AS) number assigned to it. Routers that have Enhanced IGRP sessions running under the same AS number speak to each other and share routing information.

Neighbor relationships Established and maintained by EIGRP through its link-state properties. When a router finds a neighbor, it will communicate with this router. After they have updated each other about each other's directly attached links, they are then considered adjacent.

Route calculation and updates Because EIGRP uses distance-vector and link-state information when calculating routes using the DUAL algorithm, convergence is much faster than with IGRP. The trick behind the convergence speed is that EIGRP calculates new routes only when a change in the network directly affects the routes contained in its route table.

Sample Questions

1. True or false: The EIGRP topology database stores all routes and metrics that have become known via adjacent routers?

   A. True

   B. False

   Answer: A—The topology database keeps all routes to a remote network. The EIGRP protocol then chooses the best routers from this table and inserts them into the route table.

2. How many routes may be stored for each destination network?

   A. 1

   B. 2

   C. 6

   D. Unlimited

   Answer: C—Up to six routes can be stored in the topology table.

Configure Enhanced IGRP.

 EIGRP supports several different protocols, each of which has specific commands that are used to enable EIGRP. EIGRP can be configured for IP, IPX, and AppleTalk. This objective section presents the logistics of implementing and configuring EIGRP in Cisco internetworks.

It is important for you to be able to configure EIGRP in an internetwork. It is very popular, and you are likely to run across the EIGRP routing algorithm in a network somewhere. Also, when studying for your ACRC exam, EIGRP is an important piece to remember.

Critical Information

Cisco routers assume that serial connections use T1 speeds. However, it is possible to have slower links, such as 56Kbps or other values, connected to a serial interface. As has been previously stated, bandwidth is one of the two default metrics used to calculate a route's metric. If the bandwidth is slower than T1 speeds, EIGRP will still assign a metric value equivalent to that of a T1. To avoid this confusion, the bandwidth assigned to that interface should be changed. To do this, issue the following command within the Interface Configuration mode:

bandwidth *bandwidth*

- *bandwidth* is an integer value between 1 and 10,000,000 that defines the kilobits of bandwidth.

You can stop routing updates from exiting the router via specified interfaces by flagging them as passive interfaces from within the EIGRP session. Following is the command for doing this:

passive-interface *interface-type interface-number*

- *interface-type* defines the type of interface.
- *interface-number* defines the number of the interface.

If all that you want to do is to allow only certain networks to be advertised, use the `distribute-list` command. This command was previously discussed in Chapter 3, but it is reviewed here as well. The command is issued within the EIGRP session, and the following is an example of it:

```
distribute-list access-list-number [in | out]
interface-type interface-number
```

- *access-list-number* is the number of a predefined access list.

Necessary Procedures

An autonomous system must be defined for each EIGRP session on a router. To start an EIGRP session on a router, use the following command:

```
router eigrp autonomous-system-number
```

After the session has been started, networks that belong to that session need to be added. The networks need to be directly connected. The *autonomous-system-number* allows you to tell the router which routers it is allowed to communicate with.

The command to enter the networks must be entered within the EIGRP session configuration. The command and an example follow.

```
network network-number
```

- *network-number* is the IP address of a network connected to the router.

```
Router_B#config t
Enter configuration commands, one per line.  End with
    CNTL/Z.
Router_B(config)#router eigrp 200
Router_B(config-router)#network 172.16.0.0
Router_B(config-router)#network 10.0.0.0
Router_B(config-router)#^Z
Router_B#
```

Exam Essentials

Understand what an AS number is. Autonomous system numbers allow you to create smaller routing broadcast areas. Without an AS, you would have to broadcast all subnets in your entire network. You may or may not want to broadcast all subnets, so AS numbers give you that flexibility, which RIP will not.

Remember the general syntax for an EIGRP configuration. To configure EIGRP on a Cisco router, it is no different than IGRP.

```
network network-number
passive-interface interface-type interface-number
distribute-list access-list-number [in | out]
interface-type interface-number
```

Use the router eigrp command to initialize EIGRP on the router, and then add the AS number that the router will communicate with.

Key Terms and Concepts

Autonomous system   A group of routers that participate by sharing information about their topology via EIGRP.

EIGRP distribution list   An access list that can be used to filter specific routes from being received or sent on a specific interface.

EIGRP network   A network that is included in a particular autonomous system.

EIGRP passive interface   An interface that does not participate in the EIGRP routing process.

Interface bandwidth   A value between 1 and 10,000,000, defining the kilobits of bandwidth.

Sample Questions

1. How do you configure the bandwidth for an interface when using EIGRP?

   A. From interface configuration mode, bandwidth kilobytes-per-second

   B. From interface configuration mode, cost kilobytes-per-second

   C. From EIGRP configuration mode, bandwidth interface kilo-bytes-per-second

   D. From EIGRP configuration mode, cost interface kilobytes-per-second

   Answer: A—By using the bandwidth command on a serial interface.

2. Which of the following commands can you use to filter which routes are allowed to enter and leave a router?

   A. access-list

   B. passive interface

   C. distribute-list

   D. D. access-class

   Answer: C—By using the distribute-list command, you can filter which routes are advertised out a router.

Verify Enhanced IGRP operation.

Every Cisco router that you configure must also be monitored, and you must be able to verify the router's configuration and the changes that you make. Cisco routers can perform a lot of different functions; because of this, monitoring these functions becomes as important as the initial configuration.

You can use the commands listed in this objective section to gain a clearer understanding of the information discussed in this section as well as to diagnose a network problem. Troubleshooting skills are obtained after you work through many network problems. Each situation may call for a different method, and the following descriptions are intended solely to illustrate a general method; by no means should troubleshooting be restricted to the information provided in this section.

The commands that you can use to verify and monitor the EIGRP configuration on a Cisco router are important when working in a production environment and also when studying for your ACRC exam.

Critical Information

Cisco offers several commands to aid in troubleshooting EIGRP functionality. The following list contains all of the commands that are used in conjunction with verifying EIGRP operation. These commands can be used to see the different types of tables created and used by EIGRP.

- `show ip route eigrp` shows EIGRP entries in the route table. If all neighbors are present, verify the routes learned. By executing the `show ip route eigrp` command, you can gain a quick picture of the routes in the route table. If the route does not appear in the route table, verify the source of the route. If the source is functioning properly, check the topology table.

- `show ip eigrp neighbors` shows all EIGRP neighbors. When troubleshooting an EIGRP problem, it is always a good idea to get a picture of the network. The most relevant picture is provided by the `show ip eigrp neighbors` command. This command shows all adjacent routers that share route information within a given autonomous system. If neighbors are missing, check the configuration and link status on both routers to verify that the protocol has been configured correctly.

- `show ip eigrp topology` displays the topology table. If the route is in the topology table, it is safe to assume that there is a problem between the topology database and the route table. (There must be a reason why the topology database is not injecting the route into the route table.)

- `show ip eigrp traffic` shows the packet count for EIGRP packets sent and received and can be used to see if updates are being sent. If the counters for EIGRP input and output packets don't increase, no EIGRP information is being sent between peers.

- `show ip protocols` shows information about the active routing protocol sessions.

- `show ip eigrp events` shows a log of EIGRP events (e.g., routes being added or removed from the route table) and is an undocumented command. This command displays a log of every EIGRP event—when routes are injected and removed from the route table and when EIGRP adjacencies reset or fail. This information can be used to see if there are routing instabilities in the network.

Exam Essentials

Remember each command that can be used to verify and monitor EIGRP running on your router.   The commands listed and described in the preceding Critical Information section can be used to verify EIGRP on your router.

Know the difference between routed and routing protocols. Routed protocols, such as IP and IPX, transmit user data. Routing protocols, such as RIP and OSPF, are used to update routing tables between routers. By typing **sh ip protocol**, you can get routing information running on your router. By typing **sh protocol**, you can get routed information, including addresses.

Remember that the *show ip eigrp* events command is an undocumented command.   The show ip eigrp events command displays a log of every EIGRP event. This information can be used to see if there are routing instabilities in the network.

Key Terms and Concepts

EIGRP events command   A log of every EIGRP event, such as routes being injected and removed from the routing table, and whether EIGRP adjacencies reset or fail.

EIGRP neighbors command   All adjacent routers that share route information within a given autonomous system.

EIGRP topology command   The EIGRP topology database stores all routes and metrics that have become known via adjacent routers. (Six routes can be stored for each destination network.)

EIGRP traffic command   The counters for EIGRP input and output packets.

Sample Questions

1. How many routes can be stored for each remote network?

   A. 1

   B. 2

   C. 6

   D. Unlimited

   Answer: C—Each router's topology table can have up to six routes to a destination network.

2. Which of the following commands will display all routes learned from EIGRP?

   A. show ip eigrp topology

   B. show ip eigrp neighbors

   C. show ip eigrp neighbors detail

   D. show ip route eigrp

   Answer: D—You can use show ip route or show ip route eigrp to gather only EIGRP-found routes.

CHAPTER

10

Optimizing Routing
Update Operation

Cisco ACRC Exam Objectives Covered in This Chapter:

▸ **Select and configure the different ways to control route update traffic.** *(pages 203 – 206)*

▸ **Configure route redistribution in a network that does not have redundant paths between dissimilar routing processes.** *(pages 206 – 209)*

▸ **Configure route redistribution in a network that has redundant paths between dissimilar routing processes.** *(pages 210 – 215)*

▸ **Resolve path selection problems that result in a redistributed network.** *(pages 215 – 219)*

▸ **Verify route redistribution.** *(pages 220 – 222)*

I n this chapter, you learn how to optimize a router when running dynamic routing algorithms. Some routing algorithms use route tagging to automatically optimize the updates and give the administrator some control. Route tagging is implemented by EIGRP, OSPF, BGP, and many other routing protocols. It allows a routing protocol to define autonomous systems on a router, and each session is distinguished by the autonomous system (AS) number assigned to it. Routers that have sessions running under the same AS number and protocol speak to each other and share routing information. Routes learned via other routers within the AS are considered to be internal routes. It is also possible for one AS session to learn routes from a different AS session or protocol through redistribution. When this occurs, the routes are tagged as being derived from an external session. Each type of route is assigned its own administrative distance value.

This chapter presents more ways to control routing updates. You are shown how to configure your router to not send updates out of a specific interface, and also how to send only needed routes with a regular update message. You are shown how to configure routing algorithms when you have multiple paths to a destination but have dissimilar routing processes. And you also learn about route distribution and how to verify how the routes in your internetwork are being distributed.

This is an important chapter for you to understand if you work, or plan to work, in an internetwork environment. You must be able to understand how routers update other routes and how to control these updates. When studying for the exam, understanding routing updates is crucial for success.

Select and configure the different ways to control route update traffic.

Understanding how routers update each other with routing protocols is very important. Each routing protocol sends updates a little differently than the other routing protocols. This objective section shows you how to use two different commands to stop a router from updating a network or other routers.

Controlling route update traffic is important to understand because of security and bandwidth issues. By stopping broadcasts from going out of a certain interface on a router, you can essentially stop some routers from receiving updates and knowing about remote networks. Also, you can stop unnecessary routing updates from traversing a WAN, which can save precious bandwidth. This is an important objective to know both for the ACRC exam and when working in a production environment.

Critical Information

You can stop routing updates from exiting the router via specified interfaces by flagging them as passive interfaces. The following are the commands for any routing protocol:

```
passive-interface interface-type interface-number
```

- *interface-type* defines the type of interface.

- *interface-number* defines the number of the interface.

If all that you want to do is to allow only certain networks to be advertised, use the distribute-list command, an example of which follows:

```
distribute-list access-list-number [in | out]
interface-type interface-number
```

- *access-list-number* is the number of a predefined access list.

Normal methods of route filtering performed by distribution lists are effective when filtering route information. The most effective method of filtering OSPF is by implementing the filters on the ASBR as outbound filters. Inbound filters are effective in filtering routes, but, since they are inbound filters, LSA packets are still propagated. Cisco recommends that you filter within other routing protocols and that you don't filter OSPF if possible. This is done by implementing outbound filters on other routing protocols, which keeps unwanted networks from even entering the OSPF area.

Exam Essentials

Remember the command to stop a router from broadcasting a route update out of one interface. You can stop routing updates from exiting the router via specified interfaces by flagging them as passive interfaces. For example:

```
Config t
Router rip
Network 172.16.0.0
Passive s0
```

Remember the command to stop a router from broadcasting a known route. If all that you want to do is to allow only certain networks to be advertised, use the distribute-list command.

Key Terms and Concepts

Administrative distance Associated with the protocol type of all routing protocols. If multiple protocols are running on one router, the administrative distance value helps the router to decide which path is best; the protocol with the lower administrative distance will be chosen.

Autonomous system (AS) A specific instance of a routing process. Allows you to choose a smaller amount of routers that share a routing process.

Routing table Created by an administrator or routing protocol and tells the router the path to a remote network.

Route tagging Allows a routing protocol to define autonomous systems on a router. Each session is distinguished by the AS number assigned to it.

Sample Questions

1. Which of the following techniques never allows a route to be sent back through the interface from which it arrived?

   A. Holddown

   B. Poison reverse

   C. Split horizons

   D. Feedback

   Answer: C—Poison Reverse stops network loops by not allowing updates to be sent back to an originating router.

2. Which of the following commands will disable the propagation of RIP on an Ethernet interface?

   A. From RIP configuration, `no e 0`

   B. From RIP configuration, `passive-interface e 0`

   C. From RIP configuration, `disable-interface e 0`

D. From interface configuration, no `rip`

Answer: B—The passive command stops routing updates from being sent out of a router interface.

Configure route redistribution in a network that does not have redundant paths between dissimilar routing processes.

$\mathbf{A}$s an enterprise network grows, it is possible that more than one protocol will run on the router. An example of this is when a company acquires another company and needs to merge the two existing networks. The problem with this scenario surfaces when the routes of the purchasing company need to be advertised to the newly acquired company. The new company might, for example, run RIP to support their Unix routers, while your company is using EIGRP. This problem can be solved with route redistribution. Route redistribution allows you to actually change the routing update packet into the routing protocol used on that network.

This is an important objective to understand if you have multiple connections between buildings or if you are planning to install multiple connections between buildings. It is important to be able to provide route redistribution between dissimilar routing protocols, both when working in a production environment and when studying for the ACRC exam.

Critical Information

In addition to running disparate routing protocols, a router may have both multiple protocol sessions and configurations. Sessions are defined by the autonomous system number that is used when the routing protocol is implemented, which is true for EIGRP, IGRP,

OSPF, and BGP. With all of the different protocols and sessions running on a router, it is important that the information learned by each session can be shared among the other protocols and sessions. Route redistribution is the feature that allows for the exchange of route information among both multiple protocols and sessions.

Since different protocols calculate metrics distinctly, adjustments must be made when redistributing protocols. These adjustments cause some limitations in how the redistribution works, and they are made with the `default-metric` command.

Each routing table contains both internal and external routes. When routes from one protocol or session are injected or redistributed into another protocol or session, the routes are tagged as being external routes. Whenever redistribution is configured to a higher-level routing protocol (i.e., one with a higher administrative distance), new metrics must be assigned to route the information that is injected into the session. The command for doing this is much simpler than the command that is used when assigning metrics for EIGRP or IGRP; it is almost the same, but only one metric is assigned. Note in the following that the value of the metric is the cost, or hops, for the route:

```
default-metric cost
```

While redistribution allows multiple protocols to share routing information, it can also cause routing loops, slow convergence, and inconsistent route information. This is caused by the different algorithms and methods that are used by each protocol. It is not a good practice to redistribute bidirectionally. If, for example, you have both IGRP 100 and EIGRP 200 routing sessions running on your router, bidirectional redistribution would occur if you entered redistribution commands under each protocol session. Fortunately, you can reset metrics to help alleviate this problem, which is done by using the following `default-metric` command:

```
default-metric bandwidth delay reliability load MTU
```

This command takes the metrics for the protocol that is being injected into EIGRP and converts them directly to values that EIGRP can use. The *bandwidth* is the capacity of the link; *delay* is the time in microseconds; *reliability* and *load* are values from one to 255; and *MTU* is the maximum transmission unit, in bytes.

Finally, you can also change the administrative distance values that are assigned to EIGRP (90 for internal routes; 170 for external routes). The distance value tells the router which protocol to believe. The lower the distance value, the more believable the protocol. The distance values for EIGRP are changed with the following command from within the EIGRP session:

```
distance eigrp internal-distance external-distance
```

- *internal-distance* and *external-distance* have a range of values from one to 255.

Remember that a value of 255 tells the router to ignore the route. So, unless you want the routes from the protocol to be ignored, never use a value of 255.

Exam Essentials

Understand how to read the route table when running EIGRP. In EIGRP, external routes are flagged with EX, whereas the internal routes have no flag. Flagging with a D (dual) represents an EIGRP-learned route.

Understand what an ASBR is. In OSPF, the router where multiple protocols or sessions meet is called the autonomous system boundary router (ASBR).

Remember how route distribution is used. When a route from RIP, IGRP, or OSPF is injected into EIGRP, the route loses its identity, and its metrics are converted from the original format to EIGRP's format. The same applies for redistribution with other routing protocols. This can cause confusion within the router.

Key Terms and Concepts

Administrative distance   Associated with the protocol type of all routing protocols. If multiple protocols are running on one router, the administrative distance value helps the router to decide which path is best; the protocol with the lower administrative distance will be chosen.

Default-metric command   Allows you to tune routes that are learned from another routing protocol by affecting how reliably the router is regarded.

Route redistribution   The feature that allows for the exchange of route information among multiple protocols and multiple sessions.

Sample Questions

1. Which technique must be employed in order to share information between two dissimilar routing protocols?

   A. Redistribution

   B. Sharing

   C. Defaulting

   D. Diffusion

   Answer: A—Redistribution of network protocols allows dissimilar routing protocols to communicate.

2. When accepting information from a different routing protocol, which command would you use to let the router know how reliable the information is?

   A. hop-count

   B. cost-count

   C. default-metric

   D. preferred-protocol

   Answer: C—The default-metric command changes the default administrative distance.

Configure route redistribution in a network that has redundant paths between dissimilar routing processes.

When a router receives multiple routes for a specific network, one of the routes must be chosen as the best route from all of the advertisements. The router still knows that it is possible to get to a given network over multiple interfaces, yet all data defaults to the best route. This objective shows you how to configure your Cisco routers to redistribute dissimilar routing algorithms between sites with redundant links.

The information in this objective is important if you are building or maintaining an internetwork that has redundant paths and different routing protocols between sites. When studying for the exam, you need to understand how redistribution works, and this objective will show you how it works over redundant paths.

Critical Information

EIGRP has the ability to select more than one primary route or successor. For every destination, EIGRP can have up to six routes that can be stored in the topology database. By using multiple LAN or WAN connections from one router to another, multiple routes can exist to the next-hop address. When the links are symmetrical (i.e., they have the same circuit type and the same bandwidth capacity), the same local cost is assigned to each link. Since both links have the same feasible distance, the metrics for destinations accessible via the links will be equal. As EIGRP chooses the successor for a route, it looks for the route with the lowest cost. When EIGRP sees multiple routes with the same metric, it selects them all as successors. EIGRP then shares traffic loads across each of the multiple links. This is called *load balancing*.

The metrics associated with OSPF are different from those that are associated with IGRP and EIGRP. OSPF uses bandwidth as the main metric in selecting a route. The cost is calculated by using the bandwidth for the link. The equation is 10^8 divided by the bandwidth. You may change the bandwidth on the individual interface.

Configuring Different Cost Links

You will encounter situations where there are multiple links to a given destination but the links have different next-hops. The metrics for these links will not likely be the same even though each link may have a different cost assigned to it. In this situation, both EIGRP and IGRP allow for unequal-cost load balancing, which is achieved by using the following variance command:

```
variance multiplier
```

For the variance command, the multiplier can be an integer value from one to 128. The default setting for the multiplier is one. This command must be used inside the protocol configuration.

Changing the Default Metrics

If necessary when using EIGRP, you can adjust metrics within the router configuration interface. Metrics are tuned in order to change the manner in which routes are calculated. After you enable EIGRP on a router, you can change metric weights by using the following command:

```
metric weights tos K1 K2 K3 K4 K5
```

Each constant is used to assign a weight to a specific variable. This means that when the metric is calculated the algorithm will assign a greater importance to the specified metric. By assigning a weight, you are able to specify what is most important. If bandwidth is of greatest concern to a network administrator, for instance, a greater weight is assigned to K1. If delay is unacceptable, for example, the K2 constant should be assigned a greater weight. The tos variable is the type of service. Table 10.1 shows the relationship between the constant and the metric it affects.

TABLE 10.1: Metric Association of K Values

Constant	Metric
K1	Bandwidth (B_e)
K2	Delay (D_c)
K3	Reliability (r)
K4	Load (utilization on path)
K5	MTU

You can configure the OSPF distance with the following command:

```
distance ospf [external | Intra-area | Inter-area]
distance
```

This command allows the distance metric to be defined for external OSPF and either intra-area or inter-area routes. Distance values range from one to 255, and the lower the distance the better.

Configuring the OSPF Priority

Other values that are important to OSPF's operation are not actually metrics but can be configured as well. Values such as the router ID and the router priority are important in both router initialization and DR and BDR selection. You can change these values with some minor configuration changes. To change the router priority, use the following command on the desired interface:

```
ip ospf priority number
```

The *number* can range from zero to 255. (The higher value indicates a higher priority when choosing the DR and BDR for the area.) Each router's priority defaults to one, and if you change the priority to zero, the router will never become a DR or BDR.

Adding a Loopback Interface

A loopback interface must be added to the router in order to change the router ID. The IP address of the loopback can be a private address or a fake address. If the IP address is to be announced, a private IP address should be used. To implement a loopback interface on the router, use the following command:

```
interface loopback number
ip address A.B.C.D mask
```

IGRP and EIGRP have the capacity for unequal-cost load balancing by using the `variance` command to assign a weight to each feasible successor. As long as the secondary route conforms to the following three criteria, an unequal-cost load balancing session may be established:

- A limit of four feasible successors may be used.

- The feasible successor's metric must fall within the specified variance of the local metric.

- The local metric must be greater than the metric for the next-hop router.

Cisco's implementation of OSPF bases link cost on bandwidth. Other vendors may use other metrics to calculate the link's cost. When connecting links between routers from different vendors, you may have to adjust the cost to match the other routers. Both routers must assign the same cost to the link in order for OSPF to work. When using OSPF, the cost is manipulated by changing the value to a number within the range of one to 65,535. Since the cost is assigned to each link, the value must be changed on each interface; the following is the command to do this:

```
ip ospf cost
```

Exam Essentials

Remember how to assign unequal cost links with IGRP and EIGRP. To configure unequal costs routes, remember that both EIGRP and IGRP allow for unequal-cost load balancing. This is achieved by using the `variance` command.

Remember how to change an OSPF router's priority. To change the router's priority, use the `ip ospf priority` *number* command on the desired interface.

Remember how to change the cost of a link in OSPF. Since the cost is assigned to each link, the value must be changed on each interface. Use the `ip ospf` *cost* command to do this.

Key Terms and Concepts

Administrative distance Associated with the protocol type of all routing protocols. If multiple protocols are running on one router, the administrative distance value helps the router to decide which path is best; the protocol with the lower administrative distance will be chosen.

Bandwidth The rated throughput capacity of a given network medium or protocol.

Load balancing Using multiple paths to reach a single destination in order to gain improved performance by sharing the required bandwidth across all paths rather than only using the best path.

Sample Questions

1. Which of the following describes load balancing?

A. Providing multiple connections for redundancy

B. Providing a single path through the network

C. Using the added performance of multiple connections

D. Utilizing the best path through the network

Answer: C—The best answer if using the performance of multiple connections.

2. Which EIGRP command allows you to use multiple paths with different hop counts?

   A. `variance`

   B. `shared-paths`

   C. `no single-path`

   D. `default-metric`

Answer: D—If you have unequal cost links and want to use both links to combine bandwidth, change the default metric.

Resolve path selection problems that result in a redistributed network.

The number-one cause of problems in a network that is running disparate routing protocols is caused by a problem known as feedback. As you know, each routing protocol has an associated administrative distance that allows it to determine which routing protocol to listen to in the event that differing information is offered by two routing protocols. (The one with the lowest administrative distance is preferred.)

This objective can help you to overcome problems in a redistributed network, which is especially important in a large internetwork. This section shows you the different default administrative distances used in the routing protocols supported by Cisco routers. This is very important to understand when configuring and designing an internetwork and when studying for the ACRC exam.

Critical Information

IGRP has a default administrative distance of 100. The tuning of this value is accomplished with the following `distance` command:

```
distance 1-255
```

Valid values for the administrative distance range from one to 255. Again, the lower the value the better.

Metrics may be set when redistributing static routes or other protocol types within IGRP by using the following default-metric command:

default-metric *bandwidth delay reliability load MTU*

Bandwidth and delay have a range of values: from zero to 4,294,967,295 in kilobytes per second, or from zero to 4,294,967,295 in 10-microsecond units. Reliability ranges from zero to 255, with 255 being the most reliable. Load ranges from zero to 255; however, 255 means that the link is completely loaded. Finally, the value of the MTU has the same range as the bandwidth variable: zero to 4,294,967,295 (also in 10-microsecond units).

Assigning administrative distances is a problem unique to each network and is done in response to the greatest perceived threats to the connected network. Even when general guidelines exist, the network manager must ultimately determine a reasonable matrix of administrative distances for the network as a whole. Table 10.2 lists the default administrative distance of each routing protocol.

T A B L E 10.2: Default Administrative Distances

Route Source	Default Distance
Connected interface	0
Static route	1
External BGP	20
EIGRP	90
IGRP	100
OSPF	110
IS-IS	115
RIP	120

T A B L E 10.2: Default Administrative Distances *(continued)*

Route Source	Default Distance
EGP	140
Internal BGP	200
Unknown	255

Necessary Procedures

In the following example, the IGRP global-router-configuration command sets up IGRP routing in autonomous system 109. The network-router-configuration commands specify IGRP routing on networks 192.31.7.0 and 128.88.0.0. The first distance-router-configuration command sets the default administrative distance to 255, which instructs the router to ignore all routing updates from routers for which an explicit distance has not been set. The second distance-router-configuration command sets the administrative distance to 90 for all routers on the Class C network 192.31.7.0. And the third distance-router-configuration command sets the administrative distance to 120 for the router with the address 128.88.1.3.

```
router(config)#router igrp 109
router(config-router)#network 192.31.7.0
router(config-router)#network 128.88.0.0
router(config-router)#distance 255
router(config-router)#distance 90 192.31.7.0 0.0.0.255
router(config-router)#distance 120 128.88.1.3 0.0.0.0
```

Exam Essentials

Remember what causes feedback.   Feedback is caused if you increase the administrative distance in order to prefer one routing protocol over another.

Remember the way to resolve feedback. You can solve the feedback problem by changing the default administrative distance of a routing protocol.

Remember the ways to configure the administrative distance with IGRP. IGRP has a default administrative distance of 100. This value is tuned with the `distance` command.

Key Terms and Concepts

Administrative distance   A rating of the trustworthiness of a routing information source, which is set by the router's administrator. In Cisco routers, administrative distance is a number between zero and 255 (the higher the value, the less trustworthy the source).

Feedback   A state encountered when invalid information from a lower-level routing protocol, such as RIP, overrides a higher-level routing protocol, such as OSPF.

Sample Questions

1. True or false: The lower the administrative distance, the more preferred a routing protocol is?

   A. True

   B. False

   Answer: A—Administrative distance is used to weigh or assign the cost to a remote network.

2. Which of the following protocols has the lowest (i.e., best) administrative distance?

   A. RIP

   B. OSPF

   C. EIGRP

   D. Static routes

Answer: D—Directly connected routes have the best administrative distance by default (zero), and RIP has one of the highest at 120.

3. Which of the following has the highest (i.e., worst) administrative distance?

   A. Connected interfaces

   B. Static routes

   C. IGRP

   D. RIP

   Answer: D. Directly connected routes have the best administrative distance by default (zero), and RIP has one of the highest at 120.

4. What can occur when you modify the administrative distance of a less intelligent routing protocol, such as RIP, to be preferred over a more intelligent routing protocol, such as OSPF?

   A. Talkback

   B. Feedback

   C. Redistribution

   D. Flapping

   Answer: B—When the administrative distance of a less intelligent routing protocol is changed by an administrator, feedback can occur.

5. Which of the following group of protocols is listed in order of administrative distance, starting with zero?

   A. Connected interface, static route, EBGP, EIGRP, IGRP, RIP, OSPF

   B. Static route, connected interface, EBGP, EIGRP, OSPF, IGRP, RIP

   C. Connected interface, static route, EBGP, EIGRP, IGRP, OSPF, RIP

   D. Static route, connected interface, RIP, OSPF, EIGRP, IGRP, EBGP

   Answer: C—Directly connected routes have the lowest administrative distance, with RIP being one of the lowest.

Verify route redistribution.

Verifying route distribution is not a difficult process. However, it should be one of the first things you do after configuration. By understanding the commands used in verifying route distribution, you can possibly save yourself problems later.

This objective is important because you need to understand how your router understands the path to a remote network. By understanding the paths a router can use to find a remote network, you can create a more efficient routing table.

Critical Information

The best way to verify route redistribution is to simply take a look at your routing tables and verify that external routes are appearing with the proper metrics. You can tell where routes originate by viewing the routing table by protocol. Table 10.3 contains a list of commands that will enable you to do just that.

T A B L E 10.3: Commands to View Routing Table by Protocol

Command	Protocol
show ip route rip	Shows RIP entries in the routing table.
show ip route ospf	Shows OSPF entries in the routing table; optionally, you may specify the AS.
show ip route eigrp	Shows EIGRP entries in the route table; optionally, you may specify the AS.

Exam Essentials

Remember what a routing table does. A routing table is used in a router the same way a car driver uses a map; it tells the router how to send a packet to a remote network.

Understand what happens if a route entry is not in the routing table. If a route to a remote network is not in the table, the router will drop the packet and send an ICMP unreachable message to the sender.

Key Terms and Concepts

AS (autonomous system)   A specific instance of a routing process in which a group of networks under mutual administration share the same routing methodology. Autonomous systems are subdivided by areas and must be assigned up to an individual 16-bit number.

Routing table   Created by an administrator or routing protocol and tells the router the path to a remote network.

Sample Questions

1. Which of the following commands shows RIP entries in the routing table?

   A. show routing table rip

   B. show rip route

   C. show ip rip route

   D. show ip route rip

   Answer: D—The command show ip route shows the complete routing table. The command show ip route rip shows only the RIP inserted routes in the routing table.

2. When using redistribution with EIGRP, which of the following appears beside external routes?

   A. EX

   B. XE

   C. X

   D. E

   Answer: A—EIGRP uses DUAL to find routes. It will place a *D* by any EIGRP found routes. However, if a route is redistributed from one type of routing protocol into EIGRP, you will see an *EX*, for external route.

3. True or false: Bidirectional redistribution is a good idea and should be performed whenever possible?

   A. True

   B. False

   Answer: B—Redistributing in two directions is not a good idea.

CHAPTER

11

Connecting Enterprises to an
Internet Service Provider

Cisco ACRC Exam Objectives Covered in This Chapter:

▶ **Describe when to use BGP to connect to an ISP.**
(pages 224 – 227)

▶ **Describe methods to connect to an ISP using static and default routes, and BGP.** *(pages 228 – 234)*

T his chapter is dedicated to discussing how to connect Border Gateway Protocol (BGP) to an Internet Service Provider (ISP). This book contains chapters that discuss other protocols like RIP, EIGRP, and OSPF, but this chapter centers on issues directly related to BGP. In fact, as the objectives indicate, this chapter focuses on connecting an enterprise network to an ISP using BGP and configuring static and default routes as they relate to BGP implementation.

BGP is used mostly on the Internet by ISPs and is not too widely implemented in private organizations. BGP is known as an IP exterior routing protocol and is used to enable an interdomain routing system that guarantees loop-free exchange of routing information between autonomous systems (AS). (An AS is defined as a group of routes that shares the same policies.)

This chapter is important when discussing network design plans that include connecting to your network to the Internet.

Describe when to use BGP to connect to an ISP.

F ortunately, there are not too many reasons why you would want to connect your network to an ISP using BGP. Good for you if you can get by without using BGP. BGP can be complicated to configure, and if you can connect with a different type of protocol, the ISP then would take the brunt of the BGP configuration. This is worth the money you spend for your ISP alone.

This objective helps you to learn about BGP and when to use it to connect to your ISP. This is important to understand both when discussing plans for your internetwork growth and when studying for the ACRC exam.

Critical Information

BGP is one of the hardest routing protocols to configure. It is important to understand when you should use BGP. The following scenarios are examples of when BGP should be used:

- When you are multi-homing (an enterprise network connects to multiple ISPs)

- When you have different policy requirements than the ISP

- When you are connecting two or more ISPs and forming a network access point (NAP)—also known as an exchange point

Outside of these scenarios, static or default routes may be used in certain situations, especially where the complexity of BGP is not needed. One example of this would be when an enterprise network is connected to multiple ISPs but the second connection is used only as a backup. And another example would be when a campus network is not worried about receiving exterior routes; any route that was not included in its routing table (anything not local) will be sent to the ISP.

NOTE To gather more information about BGP, please read Chapter 6 of the Sybex *ACRC Study Guide* (ISBN 2403-8) and RFC 1163.

The two types of BGP are internal BGP (iBGP) and external BGP (eBGP). There are several differences between the two. Primarily, iBGP is used to share BGP information with routers within the same autonomous system, while eBGP is used to share route information between two different autonomous systems.

Exam Essentials

Remember when to use BGP to connect to an ISP. You should use BGP to connect to an ISP when you have different policy requirements than the ISP. You should also use it when you are multi-homing or have connections to more than one ISP.

Remember the types of BGP. The two types of BGP are iBGP and eBGP. iBGP is internal and used to share BGP information with routers within the same autonomous system; eBGP is external and used when you are connecting to different autonomous systems.

Understand that BGP is to be used as a last resort. If you can use static or default routing and avoid having to configure BGP, you will save CPU cycles and possibly prevent a headache.

Key Terms and Concepts

AS (autonomous system) A collection of networks under a common administration sharing a common routing strategy.

BGP (Border Gateway Protocol) Used as an interdomain dynamic routing protocol.

Default route Administratively assigned routing table entry that is used to direct packets to a next-hop router.

Dynamic routing Adjusts automatically to network topology or traffic changes.

Static route Administratively assigned route that is configured and entered into the routing table. By default, static routes take precedence over routes found by dynamic routing protocols.

Sample Questions

1. When should you use BGP to connect to an ISP?

   A. When your ISP supports BGP

   B. Only when you have different policy requirements than the ISP

   C. Only when your ISP uses BGP to connect to the Internet

   D. When you use BGP as your internal routing protocol

   Answer: B—If you have multiple connections to different ISPs, different policy routing than your ISP, or a multi-homed router, then BGP is a good routing algorithm for you.

2. What are the two types of BGP?

   A. iBGP

   B. sBGP

   C. eBGP

   D. fBGP

   Answer: A, C—iBGP is used internally and with the same AS, and eBGP is used when communicating externally or with a different AS.

3. Networks using BGP are segmented into sections called _____? (Fill in the blank.)

   A. *Domains*

   B. *Autonomous systems*

   C. *Access points*

   D. *Districts*

   Answer: B—ASs are used to create routing groups.

Describe methods to connect to an ISP using static and default routes, and BGP.

This objective discusses connecting to an ISP with static routes, default routes, and BGP. You should always try to connect to an ISP using static or default routes, but use BGP if different policies must be used.

This objective reviews static and default routing and then discusses how to use BGP to connect your network to an ISP. It is important, when studying BGP, to understand the reason you'd use BGP and why static routes can be the preferred routes in most networks.

Critical Information

This section reviews static routing and how to configure it on a Cisco router. It also discusses the different default routing that is available and then proceeds to cover BGP configuration when connecting an ISP.

Static Routing

You can create static routes on your Cisco router that will be used in your routing table to help IP make routing decisions. Static routing has a high administrative distance by default, which is one. The only default administrative distance that is higher that is also directly connected to networks is zero. To get an idea of how a router uses trustworthiness ratings, RIP has a default administrative distance of 120. The closer to zero the better. (A floating static route is a term used when you have established an alternate connection to an ISP.)

Static routes are created using the ip route command, an example of which follows:

```
Ip route [destination network] [mask] [next hop] [admin distance]
```

- **Ip route** is a command used to set a static or default route.

- **destination network** is the remote network that you want to place in your router's routing table.

- **mask** is the subnet mask used on the network.

- **next hop** is where to send packets designated for remote or destination networks.

- **administrative distance** is set by an administrator as a weight or trustworthiness setting.

Default Routing

Default routing is really static routing that uses wildcards to pass unknown packets to a next-hop router. The next-hop router must have the remote network listed in its routing table; otherwise, the packet will be dropped.

To create a default route, you use zeros in place of the network number. This tells the router to forward any unknown packets to the specified interface or to the next hop address. Following is the command string:

```
Ip route 0.0.0.0 0.0.0.0 [next hop address] [admin
distance]
```

Or you can use the following interface to send the packets out:

```
Ip route 0.0.0.0 0.0.0.0 [router interface] [admin
distance]
```

BGP Routing

Setting up BGP routing is not unlike setting up IGRP or EIGRP. BGP uses autonomous systems. Following is the command string:

```
Router bgp [as]
network number
neighbor [ip address] remote-as [as]
```

- **Router bgp** activates the BGP protocol on your Cisco router.

- as identifies the local autonomous system.

- network number identifies the network number that is to be advertised by BGP.

- neighbor [ip address] remote-as [as] identifies the autonomous system of the neighbor or peer router.

Necessary Procedures

This section demonstrates using the help screens on a Cisco router, including how to set a static, default, and BGP configuration.

Static Routing

By using the ip route command, you can create static routes. The following output shows the ip route command used with the help command:

```
Router(config)#ip route ?
  A.B.C.D  Destination prefix


Router(config)#ip route 172.16.10.0 ?
  A.B.C.D  Destination prefix mask


Router(config)#ip route 172.16.10.0 255.255.255.0 ?
  A.B.C.D    Forwarding router's address
  Ethernet   IEEE 802.3
  Null       Null interface
  Serial     Serial


Router(config)#ip route 172.16.10.0 255.255.255.0
172.16.20.2 ?
  <1-255>    Distance metric for this route
  permanent  permanent route
  tag        Set tag for this route
  <cr>


Router(config)#ip route 172.16.10.0 255.255.255.0
172.16.20.2 150
```

Default Routing

The following output is a default route example. The route 0.0.0.0 with a mask of 0.0.0.0 is a default route in the routing table. They tell the router that if there is no matching route for the destination IP address in the packet, the 0.0.0.0 will match and the packet will be routed to the next hop address.

```
Router(config)#ip route 0.0.0.0 0.0.0.0 ?
  A.B.C.D    Forwarding router's address
  Ethernet   IEEE 802.3
  Null       Null interface
  Serial     Serial


Router(config)#ip route 0.0.0.0 0.0.0.0 172.16.20.1 ?
  <1-255>    Distance metric for this route
  permanent  permanent route
  tag        Set tag for this route
  <cr>


Router(config)#ip route 0.0.0.0 0.0.0.0 172.16.20.1 150
```

The following command shows how to set an interface to be the destination for an unknown packet. It has the same effect as the preceding example.

```
Router(config)#ip route 0.0.0.0 0.0.0.0 ?
  A.B.C.D    Forwarding router's address
  Ethernet   IEEE 802.3
  Null       Null interface
  Serial     Serial


Router(config)#ip route 0.0.0.0 0.0.0.0 serial 0 ?
  <1-255>    Distance metric for this route
  A.B.C.D    Forwarding router's address
  permanent  permanent route
  tag        Set tag for this route
  <cr>
```

BGP Routing

This section presents how to configure a simple BGP routing configuration. First, you should select BGP routing and the AS number. The next line tells the BGP routing algorithm which network number(s) to advertise. And the last command tells the router the neighbor router's identity and what the autonomous system is.

```
Router(config)#router ?
  bgp       Border Gateway Protocol (BGP)
  egp       Exterior Gateway Protocol (EGP)
  eigrp     Enhanced Interior Gateway Routing Protocol
(EIGRP)
  igrp      Interior Gateway Routing Protocol (IGRP)
  isis      ISO IS-IS
  iso-igrp  IGRP for OSI networks
  mobile    Mobile routes
  ospf      Open Shortest Path First (OSPF)
  rip       Routing Information Protocol (RIP)
  static    Static routes


Router(config)#router bgp ?
  <1-65535>  Autonomous system number


Router(config)#router bgp 100
Router(config-router)#network 172.16.0.0
Router(config-router)#neighbor 172.16.20.1 remote-as 200
```

Exam Essentials

Understand the differences between static, default, and BGP routing. Static routing is when the administrator creates a route to a remote network. Default routing is when the administrator creates a type of default gateway. And BGP is used as a dynamic routing algorithm.

Remember how to create a static route.   The command string to create a static route is as follows:

```
Ip route [destination network] [mask] [next hop] [admin
distance]
```

Remember how to configure a default route.   The command string to create a default route is as follows:

```
Ip route 0.0.0.0 0.0.0.0 [next hop address] [admin
distance]
```

Or you can use the following interface to send the packets out:

```
Ip route 0.0.0.0 0.0.0.0 [router interface] [admin
distance]
```

Remember how to configure a simple BGP network.   The commands to configure a simple BGP network algorithm are as follows:

```
Router bgp [as]
network number
neighbor [ip address] remote-as [as]
```

Key Terms and Concepts

AS (autonomous system)   A collection of networks under a common administration sharing a common routing strategy.

BGP (Border Gateway Protocol)   Used as an interdomain dynamic routing protocol.

Default route   Administratively assigned routing table entry that is used to direct frames to a next-hop router.

Dynamic routing   Adjusts automatically to network topology or traffic changes.

Static route   Administratively assigned route that is configured and entered into the routing table. By default, static routes take precedence over routes found by dynamic routing protocols.

Sample Questions

1. Which of the following is a valid static route?

   A. `route ip 10.10.2.0 255.255.0.0 10.3.0`

   B. `ip route 255.255.0.0 172.16.0.0 43`

   C. `ip route 10.10.2.0 255.255.0.0 10.10.3.0 43`

   D. `ip route 10.10.2.0 43 255.255.0.0 10.10.3.0`

   Answer: C—`ip route [dest. Net] [mask] [next hop] [admin dist]` is the correct syntax.

2. What does the 150 represent in the following command?

   `Ip route 172.16.30.0 255.255.255.0 172.16.40.2 150`

   A. Administrative distance

   B. Ticks

   C. Hops

   D. Nothing; it is invalid in this command

   Answer: A—The administrative distance is a measurement ranging from 0–255, where 0 is the highest or most trusted.

3. Which of the following commands can be used as a default route?

   A. A. `ip route 172.16.30.0 0.0.0.0 172.16.30.2`

   B. `ip route 0.0.0.0 255.255.255.0 172.16.30.2`

   C. `route ip 0.0.0.0 0.0.0.0 172.16.30.2`

   D. `ip route 0.0.0.0 0.0.0.0 172.16.30.2`

   Answer: D—You use zeros instead of an address and mask to create a default route.

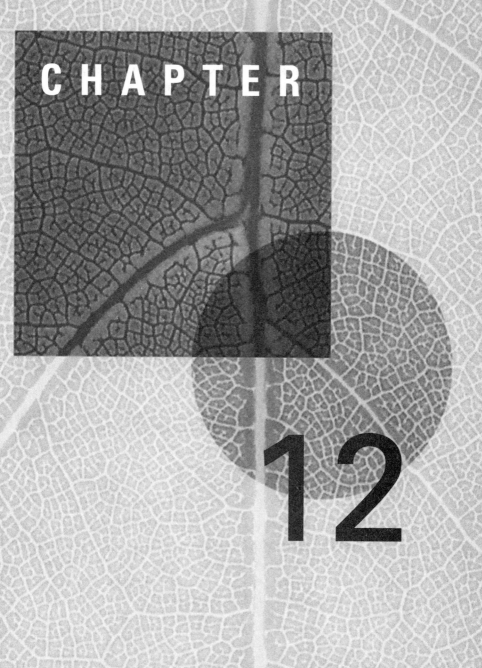

CHAPTER

12

WAN Connectivity Overview

Cisco ACRC Exam Objectives Covered in This Chapter:

▶ Compare the differences between WAN connection types: dedicated, asynchronous dial-in, dial-on-demand, and packet switched services. *(pages 237 – 241)*

▶ Determine when to use PPP, HDLC, LAPB, and IETF encapsulation types. *(pages 241 – 246)*

▶ List at least four common issues to be considered when evaluating WAN services. *(pages 247 – 250)*

As you can see by reviewing the objectives, this chapter discusses different WAN connection types, encapsulation types, and the services available with Cisco routers. This chapter gives you the information you need to understand the Cisco WAN support available through their routers. It is important that you come to understand all of the WAN services and how they work so you can make clear, concise decisions when deciding upon a WAN solution for your company.

As an example of what you need to understand about the different WAN services, consider that High-Level Data Link Control (HDLC) is a Cisco proprietary WAN service used between point-to-point networks. And if you want to connect a Cisco router with a different brand of router on a point-to-point link, you need to use something like Point-to-Point Protocol (PPP), which is an industry standard and works with all routers.

Since WAN services are so popular and available almost everywhere, knowing the different types of encapsulations is also very important. When studying for the ACRC exam, make sure you don't skip the WAN support chapters in this book, including this one.

Compare the differences between WAN connection types: dedicated, asynchronous dial-in, dial-on-demand, and packet switched services.

This first objective section details the differences between WAN connection types. Encapsulation methods are not discussed in this section because it is intended as an overview of how routers connect to a DCE network, including the different ways to physically connect with a WAN.

For the exam, you must remember the different types of connections available for supporting WANs on Cisco routers. It very important to understand connection types and issues before moving on to the next few objectives.

Critical Information

Cisco provides many options for meeting internetworking business requirements. These Cisco services are presented in the following list and are detailed in the paragraphs that follow.

- Dedicated-leased lines
- Dial-in modems
- Dial-up connections using Cisco routers
- Packet-switched services

Dedicated Links

Point-to-point serial links are dedicated links that provide full-time connectivity. Cisco-router serial ports are used to gain access at a rate of up to 45Mbps if you use the correct adapters provided by your reseller. They connect into a channel service unit/data service unit (CSU/DSU), which then plugs into the demarc that is provided by the telephone company. Figure 12.1 shows how point-to-point connections can be made between remote offices and a corporate office.

FIGURE 12.1: Point-to-point connections between branches and a corporate office

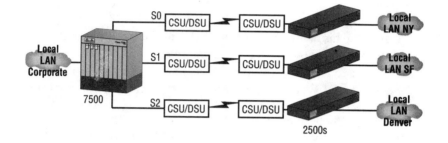

If the established business requirements dictate that constant connections and steady data flow must prevail, a dedicated point-to-point connection can be an optimal solution. Even so, this approach does have a disadvantage, which is that tariffs must be paid for point-to-point connections, even when a connection is in an idle state with no data being transmitted.

Asynchronous Dial-In Products

Any user with an asynchronous modem can make connections to an internetwork using the Public Switched Telephone Network (PSTN), and there are many common situations requiring this type of access. For instance, users who are traveling can dial in to check e-mail or to update a database, while others may dial in from home to finish projects, send and retrieve e-mail, and even print documents to be available for them when they arrive at work the next day.

Cisco answers the need for remote services by providing a variety of asynchronous dial-in products, such as the AS5200 access server. This device provides up to 48 asynchronous modems for both dial-in and dial-out services, and it runs the Cisco IOS, so it can also perform routing, authentication, and security-related tasks. If demands don't dictate the need for as many as 48 ports, there are Cisco products that offer a lower port density.

Dial-on-Demand Routing

Dial-on-demand routing (DDR) allows wide area links to be used selectively. With DDR, the administrator can define "interesting" traffic on the router and then initiate WAN links based upon that traffic. Access lists also define interesting traffic, so there's a great deal of flexibility given to the administrator. For instance, an expensive ISDN connection to the Internet can be initiated to retrieve e-mail, but not for a WWW request. DDR is an effective tool in situations where WAN access is charged in some time interval, and it's best to use it in situations where WAN access is infrequent.

Dial-on-demand routing provides the missing software ingredient for creating a fully functional backup system. Versatile DDR can be used over several different types of connections and is supported in Cisco IOS version 9 and later. It supports the following networking protocols: IP, IPX, AppleTalk, and others. But DDR's flexibility is even more extensive. For instance, it can be used over several different types of interfaces, synchronous and asynchronous serial interfaces, as well as ISDN.

Packet-Switched Services

Packet-switched services are usually run over a publicly maintained network, such as PSTN, but, if necessary, a large organization can build a private packet switched network (PSN). PSN data delivery can take place within frames, packets, or cells, and it occurs transparently to end users. Frame Relay, X.25, SMDS, and ATM are some of the topologies that employ packet-switching technology.

Exam Essentials

Remember the different types of WAN connections. The different WAN connection types are dedicated-leased lines, dial-in modems, dial-up connections using Cisco routers, and packet-switched services.

Understand when you would use dial-in connections. If you use less than two or three hours a day on the Internet or dial-up line, then a dial-up connection should be cost effective for you. However, if you need to transmit over two to three hours of data each day, a dial-up connection would not be the solution; you would want a point-to-point dedicated link.

Understand when you would use packet switching services. If you need to transmit bursty data, then a packet-switched network is a good solution.

Key Terms and Concepts

DDR (dial-on-demand routing) Used to auto-dial a network connection whenever "interesting" packets are discovered by the router. Interesting packets are defined with the use of access lists by the adminstrator.

ISDN (Integrated Services Digital Network) A communication protocol that is offered by telephone companies and can carry data, voice, and other source traffic.

PSN (packet switched networks) Used to transmit bursty traffic across DCE (data communications equipment).

Sample Questions

1. Which type of WAN connection should you use if you have five to six hours of bursty traffic that need to cross a WAN every day?

   A. ISDN

   B. PSN

   C. DDR

   D. Modems

   Answer: B—Packet switched networks are best used for bursty traffic throughout the day.

2. Which type of WAN connection should you use if you need to have your router make a connection whenever e-mail traffic is needed to cross the WAN?

    A. ISDN

    B. PSN

    C. DDR

    D. Sync

    Answer: C—Dial-on-demand routing is used to dial up whenever interesting packets are detected.

Determine when to use PPP, HDLC, LAPB, and IETF encapsulation types.

As you have probably already noticed, this objective covers Point-to-Point Protocol; High-Level Data Link Control; Link Access Procedure, Balanced (LABP); and Frame Relay's Internet Engineering Task Force (IETF). It is imperative that you come to understand the differences between all of these encapsulation methods.

PPP, HDLC, LAPB, and IETF are all used when connecting Cisco routers, but you can only use each type during certain circumstances. For example, IETF is only used when connecting a Cisco router to a non-Cisco router between a Frame Relay network. HDLC is the default encapsulation method on serial links, but it can only be used when connecting two Cisco routers with a point-to-point circuit. Point-to-Point Protocol is used when you need to make a point-to-point connection but is typically only used when you need to connect between non-Cisco boxes, ISDN, or if you need authentication. LAPB is used when you are using X.25 or when you need the extra error checking that it provides.

If you can understand and explain the differences between these methods, you will be able to both make smarter business decisions and do well on the exam.

Critical Information

The PPP, HDLC, LAPB and IETF encapsulation methods are presented in detail in the following paragraphs. By coming to understand these methods of encapsulations available on Cisco routers, you can determine the best times to use each of them.

Point-to-Point Protocol

PPP is a data-link protocol that can be used over either asynchronous (dial-up) or synchronous (ISDN) media, and it uses Link Control Protocol (LCP) to build and maintain data-link connections. LCP is packed with a number of features, including the following:

- Authentication using either PAP (Password Authentication Protocol) or CHAP (Challenge Handshake Authentication Protocol)

- Compression of data for transmission across media

These features weren't available in SLIP (Serial Line Internet Protocol), PPP's predecessor, so having them available now indicates progress.

Another new PPP feature is the support for multiple protocols. SLIP supported only IP, but through NCP (Network Control Protocol), PPP supports IP, IPX, AppleTalk, DECnet, OSI/CLNS, and transparent bridging. NCP is actually a family of protocols—one for each layer-three protocol supported by PPP. PPP specifies an authentication mechanism, while CHAP and PAP are typically used. It is extensible, so other companies (e.g., Microsoft) can implement their own security.

To configure PPP on a serial link, use the `encapsulation ppp` command. The `ppp authentication` subcommand allows you to specify the type of PPP authentication and the type of authentication protocol.

Multilink PPP

By using ISDN with PPP encapsulation, Cisco routers can support multiple connections over the same physical interface. This allows Cisco routers to use dial-up connections to establish more than one connection at a time to an access server. Why would you want a router to be able to do that? Because, if it can, you're granted twice the bandwidth of a single dial-up line.

The capacity to increase bandwidth between point-to-point dial-up connections by grouping interfaces and then splitting and recalculating packets to run over that group of interfaces is called *multilinking*. Before you can run multilink, you must define the "interesting" packets by using the dialer-list global command. This command directs the router to search for specific network protocols for making and keeping a link active. You can apply a dialer list to an interface by using the dialer-group subcommand.

You can also specify dynamic IP addressing of ISDN PPP hosts and PPP multilink hosts by using the peer default ip address subcommand. Doing this will assign a unique IP address to each individual ISDN interface from a pool of addresses. You can provide a DNS name server and WINS server to ISDN dial-up users as well by using the async-bootp dns-server and async-bootp nbns-server global commands.

High-Level Data Link Control

The HDLC protocol is a popular ISO-standard, bit-oriented, Data-Link-layer protocol that specifies an encapsulation method for data on synchronous serial data links. HDLC's development began when the International Standardization Organization (ISO) modified SDLC and came up with HDLC. Thereafter, the International Telecommunication Union Telecommunication Standardization Sector (ITU-T) tweaked HDLC a bit more and released Link Access Procedure (LAP), and then Link Access Procedure, Balanced (LAPB). After that, the Institute of Electrical and Electronic Engineers (IEEE) went to work on HDLC, and the result was the IEEE 802.2 specification.

HDLC is the default encapsulation method used by Cisco routers over synchronous serial links. Cisco's HDLC is proprietary; it won't communicate with any other vendor's HDLC implementation. But don't give Cisco grief for it because everyone's HDLC implementation is proprietary. When routers were covered in Chapter 5, they were using HDLC encapsulation on all serial links.

LAPB Protocol

LAPB encapsulation is great when you need to configure a simple, reliable serial connection. LAPB can be implemented if you have a private serial line or with X.25 encapsulation.

LAPB's job is to make sure that frames are error free and properly sequenced. It's a bit-oriented protocol, and the following are the three different LAPB frame types:

Information frames (I-frames) Transport upper-layer information and a bit (no pun intended) of control information. I-frames schlep both *send* and *receive* sequence numbers, and they relate to jobs such as sequencing, flow control, error detection, and recovery.

Supervisory frames (S-frames) Bearing control information, S-frames handle both requesting and suspending transmissions, plus they report on status and acknowledge that I-frames have been received. S-frames only receive sequence numbers.

Unnumbered frames (U-frames) Also bearing control information, U-frames handle things such as link setup and disconnection, and error reporting. U-frames don't schlep any sequence numbers.

Opting for LAPB instead of HDLC encapsulation is a good solution if you're experiencing noisy serial links and you're not running time-sensitive applications because, unlike HDLC, which expects the upper layers to be responsible for missing data, LAPB will retransmit missing frames. However, if your serial link is solid, HDLC encapsulation is the better choice because of its lower overhead.

Internet Engineering Task Force

Internet Engineering Task Force (IETF) is used when connecting a Cisco router to a different brand of router when running Frame Relay. There are only two encapsulation methods—one being IETF and the other being Cisco. When connecting between two Cisco routers running Frame Relay, Cisco is the default encapsulation.

Exam Essentials

Remember when you would use each type of encapsulation. PPP, HDLC, LAPB, and IETF are used when connecting Cisco routers, but only during certain circumstances can you use each type. For example, IETF is only used when connecting a Cisco router to a non-Cisco router between a Frame Relay network. HDLC is the default, but it can only be used when connecting two Cisco routers with a point-to-point circuit. Point-to-Point Protocol is used when you need to make a point-to-point connection, but typically only when you need to connect between non-Cisco boxes or if you need authentication. LAPB is used when you are using X.25 or need the extra error checking that it provides.

Understand when LAPB would be used over HDLC. LABP has error checking that can make up for poor line quality. However, this costs you efficiency and the overhead of router CPU and bandwidth.

Remember when to use PPP over HDLC. HDLC is proprietary, while PPP is an industry standard and works with all routers. If you need to connect to an off-brand router with a Cisco router, you need to use PPP instead of HDLC.

Key Terms and Concepts

HDLC (High-Level Data Link Control)   The default Cisco encapsulation method on point-to-point links.

IETF (Internet Engineering Task Force)   An industry standard encapsulation method for use on Frame Relay networks.

LAPB (Link Access Procedure, Balanced)   Typically used with X.25, this protocol can also be used to add error checking on a poor line.

PPP (Point-to-Point Protocol)   An industry standard protocol that runs on all routers. It has more features than HDLC, such as error checking and authentication.

Sample Questions

1. When would you use LAPB over HDLC?

   A. If you have one Cisco router and one other brand of router that needs to communicate

   B. Between two Cisco routers

   C. Whenever you can

   D. When you have a noisy line

   Answer: D—LAPB adds error checking that works well on poor lines.

2. When would you use IETF?

   A. Whenever you can

   B. When you have two Cisco routers

   C. When you need to connect a Cisco router to a non-Cisco router with Frame Relay encapsulation

   D. When you have a noisy line

   Answer: C—Internet Engineering Task Force is used as a Frame Relay encapsulation method when connecting disparate routers together.

List at least four common issues to be considered when evaluating WAN services.

There are more than four issues to be considered when deciding upon a type of WAN service for your network. It is imperative that you understand the different WAN services available so you can make informed business decisions.

This objective section lists the WAN issues you must consider, and this should then help you to determine the WAN service you can use to support your network. By understanding the issues that can come up when choosing a WAN service, you can be better prepared to meet any business requirement that comes up.

Critical Information

When a company grows, it is imperative that its internetwork grows with it. The network's administrator must not only understand the various user-group differences regarding their specialized needs for the mélange of LAN and WAN resources but they must find a way to meet or exceed these requirements while also planning for growth. The following paragraphs detail important factors to consider when defining and researching business requirements for the purposes of internetwork design or refinement.

Network Availability

Because networks are so heavily relied upon—they're ideally up and running 24 hours a day, 365 days a year—failures and downtime must be minimized. It's also vital that when a failure does occur it is easy to isolate so that the time needed to troubleshoot the problem is reduced.

Bandwidth Requirements

Accurately determining the actual and eventual bandwidth requirements with information gathered from both users and management is crucial. It can be advantageous to contract with a service provider to establish connectivity between remote sites. Bandwidth considerations are also an important element for the next consideration: cost.

Cost Considerations

In a perfect world, you could simply install nothing but Cisco Catalyst 5000 series switches that provide switched 100Mbps to each desktop with gigabit speeds between data closets and remote offices. However, since the world is not perfect, and because budget constraints often won't allow for doing that, Cisco offers an abundance of switches and routers tailored to many needs and wallet sizes. This is one very big reason why it's so important to accurately assess actual needs. A budget must be carefully delimited when designing an internetwork.

Ease of Management

Ramifications such as the degree of difficulty associated with creating network connections must be understood and carefully regarded. Factors associated with configuration management include analyses of both the initial configuration and the ongoing configuration tasks related to running and maintaining the entire internetwork. Traffic management issues—the ability to adjust to different traffic rates, especially in bursty networks—also apply here.

Type of Application Traffic

Application traffic can typically be comprised of small to very large packets, and the internetwork design must reflect and regard the typical traffic type in order to meet business requirements.

Routing Protocols

The characteristics of routing protocols can possibly cause some ugly problems and steal a lot of precious bandwidth in networks where they're either not understood or improperly configured.

Exam Essentials

Remember all of the reasons to consider when evaluating a WAN service. Even though the objective lists only four reasons, you need to remember all of the reasons to consider: availability, bandwidth, cost, ease of management, application traffic, and routing protocols.

Remember what a routing protocol is. Routing protocols are used to dynamically update routing tables.

Key Terms and Concepts

Bandwidth The rated throughput capacity of a given network medium.

Packet Used (as well as datagrams) to send data streams received from the Transport layer to remote networks through an internetwork.

Routing protocols Used to update routing tables on routers within an internetwork. Examples are RIP, IGRP, EIGRP, and OSPF.

Sample Questions

1. Which of the following are used to determine which WAN type to use?

   A. Ease of management

   B. Cost

   C. Number of users

   D. Bandwidth

   E. All of the above

   Answer: E—All of these selections need to be understood before a WAN type can be determined.

2. Which of the following can use excessive bandwidth if not carefully tuned?

   A. Routing algorithms

   B. Hub power outages

   C. Management

   D. Cost

   Answer: A—Even though selection C seems like a good answer, routing algorithms can use a huge amount of bandwidth if not carefully thought out.

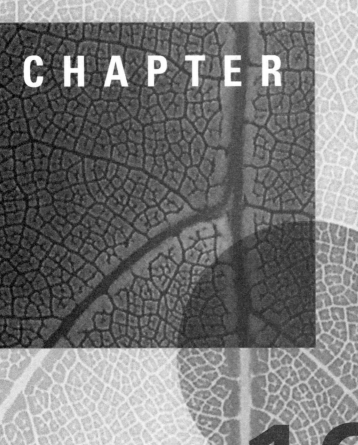

CHAPTER

13

Configuring
Dial-on-Demand Routing

Cisco ACRC Exam Objectives Covered in This Chapter:

▶ **Describe the components that make up ISDN connectivity.** *(pages 253 – 257)*

▶ **Configure ISDN BRI.** *(pages 257 – 260)*

▶ **Configure Legacy dial-on-demand routing (DDR).** *(pages 260 – 268)*

▶ **Configure dialer profiles.** *(pages 268 – 273)*

▶ **Verify DDR operation.** *(pages 274 – 276)*

ntegrated Services Digital Network (ISDN) is a digital service designed to run over existing telephone networks. (The ability to deliver a true digital service across your existing local loop is very cool indeed.) ISDN can support both data and voice—a telecommuter's dream. ISDN applications require bandwidth because typical ISDN applications and implementations include high-speed image applications (such as Group IV facsimile), high-speed file transfer, video conferencing, and multiple links into the homes of telecommuters.

This chapter describes ISDN's different components and then shows you how to configure ISDN on your Cisco routers. The focus, naturally, is configuration. However, before you learn how to configure ISDN, it is critical that you come to understand the components that make up ISDN connectivity. After learning about the ISDN configuration commands, dial-on-demand routing (DDR) is discussed, emphasizing DDR configuration options as well as how to use it with ISDN connectivity.

You will probably see ISDN in your professional carrier. It is imperative that you understand how ISDN is configured and used in an internetwork. When studying for your ACRC exam, do not skip the different configurations, protocols, and standards.

Describe the components that make up ISDN connectivity.

$\mathbf{A}$s the introduction indicates, this first objective focuses on the different components and protocols used to create ISDN connectivity. This section begins with the terminal types and reference points, discusses the different ISDN protocols, and also covers the command for setting the ISDN switch type that your router will connect to. The difference between BRI and PRI is also discussed.

You need to remember the different types of components that make up ISDN. This is important both when setting up an ISDN line and when studying for your ACRC exam.

Critical Information

ISDN is actually a set of communication protocols proposed by telephone companies that allows them to carry data, voice, etc. It provides a group of digital services that simultaneously conveys data, text, voice, music, graphics, and video to end users, and it was designed to offer these services over the existing telephone systems. ISDN is referenced by a suite of ITU-T standards encompassing the OSI model's Physical, Data Link, and Network layers.

ISDN Terminals

Devices connecting to the ISDN network are known as terminals, and the following describes the two types of terminals:

TE1 (terminal equipment type 1)   Terminals that understand ISDN standards.

TE2 (terminal equipment type 2)   Terminals that predate ISDN standards. (To use a TE2, you have to use a terminal adapter.)

ISDN Reference Points

The following list describes ISDN's four reference points and defines logical interfaces:

R reference point The reference point between non-ISDN equipment and a terminal adapter (TA).

S reference point The reference point between user terminals and an NT2.

T reference point The reference point between NT1 and NT2 devices.

U reference point The reference point between NT1 devices and line-termination equipment in a carrier network. (This occurs only in North American locations where the NT1 function isn't provided by the carrier network.)

ISDN Protocols

ISDN protocols are defined by the ITU. The following list will help you to understand the different series of protocols and the diverse issues they deal with:

- Protocols beginning with the letter *E* deal with using ISDN on the existing telephone network.

- Protocols beginning with the letter *I* deal with concepts, terminology, and services.

- Protocols beginning with the letter *Q* deal with switching and signaling.

ISDN Switch Types

AT&T and NorTel are credited with producing the majority of the ISDN switches in place today, but additional companies also make them. Table 13.1 lists the key words you need to use, along with the isdn switch-type command, in order to configure a router for the variety of switches to which it's going to connect. If you don't know which switch your provider is using at their central office, simply call them to find out.

T A B L E 13.1: ISDN Switch Types

Switch Type	Key Word
AT&T basic-rate switch	basic-5ess
NorTel DMS-100 basic-rate switch	basic-dms100
National ISDN-1 switch	basic-ni1
AT&T 4ESS (ISDN PRI only)	primary-4ess
AT&T 5ESS (ISDN PRI only)	primary-5ess
NorTel DMS-100 (ISDN PRI only)	primary-dms100

The following is an example of configuring your router ISDN inter-face to communicate with an AT&T basic-rate switch:

```
RouterA#config t
RouterA(config)#isdn switch-type basic-5ess
```

Basic Rate Interface

ISDN Basic Rate Interface (BRI) service provides two B channels and one D channel. The BRI B-channel service operates at 64Kbps and carries data, while the BRI D-channel service operates at 16Kbps and usually carries control and signaling information. The D-channel sig-naling protocol spans the OSI reference model's Physical, Data Link, and Network layers. BRI also provides framing control for a total bit rate of up to 144Kbps.

When configuring ISDN BRI, you'll need to obtain service profile identifiers (SPIDs), and you should have one SPID for each B channel (i.e., two for BRI). You can think of SPIDs as the telephone number of each B channel. The ISDN device gives the SPID to the ISDN switch, which then allows the device to access the network for BRI or PRI service. Without an SPID, many ISDN switches don't allow an ISDN device to place a call on the network. Not all configurations require unique SPIDs, however. Some are autosensed. To be sure, ask your Internet Service Provider.

Primary Rate Interface

The ISDN Primary Rate Interface (PRI) service delivers 23 B channels and one 64Kbps D channel in North America and Japan for a total bit rate of up to 1.544Mbps. In Europe, Australia, and other parts of the world, ISDN provides 30 B channels and one 64Kbps D channel for a total bit rate of up to 2.048Mbps.

Exam Essentials

Remember the ISDN protocols. The Q protocol is used for switching and signaling. The E protocol is used for existing telephone service, and the I protocol is used for concepts, terminology, and services.

Remember the ISDN switch types and how to configure them. Basic-5ess is typically used in America. (You need to check with your ISP.) You can configure the switch type with the isdn switch-type command.

Understand what a BRI is. A Basic Rate Interface consists of two 64Kbps B channels and one 16Kbps D channel. B channels are used for data and voice, and the D channel is for signaling and clocking.

Understand what a PRI is. A Primary Rate Interface delivers 23 64Kbp B channels and one 64Kbp D channel. B channels are used for data and voice, and the D channel is for signaling and clocking.

Key Terms and Concepts

ISDN (Integrated Services Digital Network) A communication protocol that allows telephone networks to carry data and voice.

BRI (Basic Rate Interface) ISDN interface composed of two B channels and one D channel for voice, video, and data-circuit-switched communication.

PRI (Primary Rate Interface) Consists of a single 64Kbps D channel plus 23 (T1) or 30 (E1) B channels for voice or data.

Switch-type command   Used to set the ISDN switch type in a Cisco ISDN router.

Sample Questions

1. Which ISDN protocol is responsible for switching?

A. E

B. BRI

C. Q

D. I

Answer: C—The ISDN Q protocol is responsible for signaling and switching.

2. What is the command for setting your ISDN router to connect to a basic-5ess switch? (Type in your answer.)

Answer: `isdn switch-type basic-5ess`

Configure ISDN BRI.

Accessing ISDN with a Cisco router means that you will need to purchase either a Network Termination 1 (NT1) or an ISDN modem. If your router has a BRI interface, you're ready to rock. Otherwise, you can use one of your router's serial interfaces—if you can obtain a TA. A router with a BRI interface is called a TE1 (terminal end-point 1), and one that requires a terminal adapter is called a TE2 (terminal end-point 2).

ISDN supports virtually every upper-layer network protocol (IP, IPX, AppleTalk, you name it), and you can choose PPP, HDLC, or LAPD as your encapsulation protocol.

This section discusses only the very basics of configuring a BRI. More complicated and advanced configurations are discussed later in this chapter. Understanding how to configure a BRI is fundamental in ISDN. You need to know this information before going on to the advanced objectives. All ISDN information is heavily tested on the exam.

Critical Information

When configuring ISDN, a few commands are necessary and some are not. You can configure ISDN a few different ways, but this objective focuses on configuring a BRI port. The first command, which follows, is to choose your interface by using the BRI command:

```
config t
interface bri0
  ip address 172.16.10.1 255.255.255.0
  encapsulation ppp
  dialer rotary-group 1
  isdn switch-type basic-ni
  isdn spid1 0835866101 8358661
  isdn spid2 0835866301 8358663
```

Notice that you are to choose the interface bri0 and then set an IP address. These instructions tell the interface to use PPP encapsulation and then to use dialer rotary-group 1 to dial.

The following list explains the preceding commands:

- The switch-type command can be used as a global or interface command.

- The last command is the spid command. Several ISDN service providers use central-office switches that require dial-in numbers called service profile identifiers. The SPIDs are used to authenticate that call requests are within contract specifications.

SPIDs are only used in the United States and are typically not required for ISDN data communications applications. The local SPID number is supplied by the service provider. A SPID is usually a seven-digit telephone number with some optional numbers. However, service providers may use different numbering schemes. For the DMS-100 switch type, two SPIDs are assigned—one for each B channel. Once your service provider has assigned you SPIDs, you must define these SPIDs on the router so that when access to the switch is attempted the router has the valid information available.

Exam Essentials

Remember the basic BRI configuration. You will need to be able to configure a BRI interface with an IP address, encapsulation, and SPIDs, as shown in the Critical Information section.

Remember what a SPID is used for. A service profile identifier is a numbering scheme that some service providers use to define the services to which an ISDN device subscribes.

Remember how to configure the ISDN switch type. Use the `isdn switch-type` *type* command to configure the switch type.

Key Terms and Concepts

ISDN (Integrated Services Digital Network) A digital subscriber line offered by telephone companies that permits telephone networks to carry data, voice, and other source traffic.

SPID (service profile identifier) A numbering scheme that some service providers use to define the services to which an ISDN device subscribes.

BRI (Basic Rate Interface) Composed of two B channels and one D channel that can transmit voice, video, and data.

Sample Questions

1. To set the type of ISDN switch on your Cisco router, which of the following commands is valid?

    A. `switch-type`

B. switch isdn-type

C. isdn switch-type

D. isdn-switch type

Answer: C—Use the isdn switch-type command when connecting to an ISP switch.

2. Which is true regarding SPIDs?

A. They are used to authenticate that Frame Relay requests are within contract specifications.

B. They are used to authenticate that call requests are within contract specifications.

C. LDNs are a required parameter.

D. They are mandatory in America and Europe.

Answer: B—Several ISDN service providers use central-office switches that require service profile identifiers, which are used to authenticate that call requests are within contract specifications.

Configure Legacy dial-on-demand routing (DDR).

Sometimes it just isn't worth the cost to install expensive, dedicated WAN circuits. Why pay for continuous connectivity when all you really need is about four to five hours per week? This type of scenario is where DDR really shines. Basically, any situation where only occasional connectivity is needed screams for DDR.

With DDR, the branch office routers will initiate connections with the headquarter's router only when necessary (as with a typical dial-up solution). However, with DDR in place, the routers will initiate, maintain, and close this connection without requiring user intervention—*not* a typical dial-up solution.

As you can see, this objective covers DDR configuration. This is a great objective because you will not only use this information at work and on the ACRC exam but also at home when connecting your home LAN to an ISDN network through your ISP.

Critical Information

From the user's perspective, DDR network operation is no different than operating with dedicated WAN links. DDR users access the WAN whenever they want to; they don't have to do anything to set it up. However, when the time comes to pay the bill for these WAN services, the statement covers only the actual time spent rather than all of the extra time accrued by dedicated circuits. So you get fully functional WAN services at dial-up prices. What a deal! What more could you want?

While DDR is a truly awesome solution for many situations, it's not for every WAN situation. However, here are some situations where DDR really excels:

- Low bandwidth requirements

- Infrequent usage

- Periodic, rather than continuous, traffic patterns

- ISDN or PSTN (dial-up, circuit-switched WAN services)

In these situations, DDR can provide most of the functionality of a traditional WAN, and it frequently does so at significant savings over traditional WAN costs.

Whenever DDR is configured, the administrator can define which types of traffic will trigger calls.

Now suppose you don't want to connect for WWW requests, but you do want to connect to upload sales orders and for e-mail traffic. You can do this by defining what Cisco calls interesting traffic. As the administrator, you can control whether calls are made for every request or only when certain types of requests are made. As you'll see, the tool used for this definition is an access list. Plus, as the administrator, you can also specify exactly how long to remain connected after last seeing interesting traffic. By configuring a *dialer idle timeout*, you can mandate the connection to be closed after being connected for *x* period of time without seeing any sales orders or e-mail traffic.

DDR Configuration Steps

Before doing any actual configurations, you need to be familiar with the steps by which DDR operates. A few of the steps are common to all DDR implementations, but the following list describes, in order, all of the necessary configuration steps:

1. Upon receiving traffic, the router will check its routing table to see if it knows of a route to the specified destination network. If it finds one, the router then checks to see if the outbound interface uses DDR. If it does, the router finally checks to see if the traffic is defined as interesting, because only interesting packets can initiate DDR connections.

2. After determining that there is indeed a route to the destination network, the next-hop router is located, and the router determines dialing instructions for the interface.

3. The router will then check to see if the interface is currently connected. If not, the router will initiate the call (assuming that the traffic has been deemed interesting). If the interface is currently connected, the traffic will be sent. If the traffic was defined as interesting, the dialer idle timeout will be reset.

4. The connection is maintained, and all traffic is routed until the idle timeout expires. Once the timeout expires, the call is terminated.

Once the link is up, the router will transmit both interesting and uninteresting traffic. However, unless interesting traffic is continuous (more frequent than the dialer idle timeout setting), the link will close. So uninteresting traffic can only take advantage of a call that's been established and maintained by interesting traffic; uninteresting traffic can't keep a call it establishes by itself.

Static Routing

Obviously, routing updates between routers can't be sent over a link that doesn't exist or is inactive. In most networks, routers build routing tables by using dynamic routing algorithms such as RIP, IGRP, or EIGRP. However, since routing updates are not sent over DDR inactive links, the administrator of the network (that means you!) will usually configure static routes in each router so that hosts can still find network services when the DDR link is inactive. After all, having routing updates initiate calls at regular intervals may very well negate any gains afforded by DDR over a leased line. In these situations, static routing is generally preferable to any form of dynamic routing. Consider the following listing:

```
RouterC#config t
Enter configuration commands, one per line. End with
    CNTL/Z.
RouterC(config)#ip route 172.16.50.0 255.255.255.0 bri0
RouterC(config)#^Z
RouterC#
```

This example defines that any traffic destined for the 172.16.50.0 network is to be sent via BRI 0. If you want to create a static route, you use the ip route command, but you might not have known that you can then distribute these static routes to the other routers in your internetwork with the redistribute command. This is shown in the following example:

```
Router(config)#router igrp 109
Router(config-router)#network 131.108.0.0
Router(config-router)#redistribute static ?
  metric     Metric for redistributed routes
  route-map  Route map reference
  <cr>
Router(config-router)#redistribute static metric ?
  <1-4294967295>  Bandwidth metric in Kbits per second
```

You don't need to set the metric for the static route, but you can use this to weight the link higher than a directly connected T1 link, which can be really helpful in dial-backup situations.

If you don't have dynamic or static routes in place to all networks, your routers won't be able to find them. However, creating a default route on your routers will cause them to forward unknown packets to the default networks. You can effect this with the `ip default-network` command. Also, you can use the `passive` command to stop broadcasts from routing protocols from triggering a DDR link. This command tells the router not to transmit routing information on the specified interface. The use of both the `ip default-network` and the `passive` commands is demonstrated in the following example:

```
Router#config t
Enter configuration commands, one per line. End with
    CNTL/Z.
Router(config)#ip default-network ?
    A.B.C.D  IP address of default network

Router(config)#ip default-network 172.16.50.0
Router(config)#router rip
Router(config-router)#network 172.16.50.0
Router(config-router)#passive s0
```

Legacy DDR

Legacy DDR is the router's ability to make a call and establish a connection when appropriate. As an administrator, by defining interesting traffic, you control what is or is not an appropriate criterion for placing a call. Following are the four steps involved in configuring legacy DDR:

1. Specify interesting traffic (what kind of traffic is required to bring up the link).

2. Assign interesting-traffic definition to the ISDN interface.

3. Define destination (teach the router how to get to a destination).

4. Define call parameters (the number to call; how to place the call).

Necessary Procedures

Interesting traffic is specified using the `dialer-list` command. A dialer list is created much like an access list is, and the syntax is similar as well.

Suppose you want IP traffic but not IPX or AppleTalk traffic to be able to initiate a call. You can proceed as follows:

```
RouterC#config t
Enter configuration commands, one per line. End with
  CNTL/Z.
RouterC(config)#dialer-list 5 protocol ip permit
RouterC(config)#dialer-list 5 protocol ipx deny
RouterC(config)#dialer-list 5 protocol appletalk deny
RouterC(config)#^Z
RouterC#
```

After entering Configuration mode, use the `dialer-list` command, followed by a dialer-group number, the `protocol` keyword, and then `permit` or `deny`. By default, all traffic is defined as interesting and will initiate a connection. As with access lists, there's an implicit deny at the end of each dialer list. The `dialer-list 5` above and `dialer-list 6` below are equivalent.

```
RouterC#config t
Enter configuration commands, one per line. End with
  CNTL/Z.
RouterC(config)#dialer-list 6 protocol ip permit
RouterC(config)#^Z
RouterC#
```

Also as with access lists, as the following example demonstrates, the context-sensitive help can be extremely useful when you're wading through the syntax:

```
RouterC#config t
Enter configuration commands, one per line. End with
  CNTL/Z.
RouterC(config)#dialer-list ?
  <1-10>  Dialer group number

RouterC(config)#dialer-list 6 ?
  protocol  Permit or Deny based on protocols

RouterC(config)#dialer-list 6 protocol ip ?
  deny    Deny specified protocol
```

```
list     Add access list to dialer list
permit   Permit specified protocol
```

`RouterC(config)#dialer-list 6 protocol ip permit ?`
`<cr>`

`RouterC(config)#dialer-list 6 protocol ip permit`
`RouterC(config)#^Z`
`RouterC#`

You can see that you have the ability to decide which protocols will be defined as interesting, but what if, as in the earlier example, you want to define some traffic within a protocol stack as interesting and other traffic within the same protocol stack as uninteresting? The answer lies in using access lists. Note the following lines from the preceding help example:

`RouterC(config)#dialer-list 6 protocol ip ?`
```
deny     Deny specified protocol
list     Add access list to dialer list
permit   Permit specified protocol
```

`RouterC(config)#dialer-list 6 protocol ip ?`

You can, of course, permit or deny based on protocol, or you can use the list keyword and specify an access list to define interesting traffic. If you need more granular control than just specifying an entire protocol stack to define interesting traffic, you can use this option and then build extremely detailed access lists to define the type of interesting traffic that you need. Note the following example:

`RouterC#configure term`
`Enter configuration commands, one per line.  End with CNTL/Z.`
`RouterC(config)#access-list 101 permit tcp any any eq smtp`
`RouterC(config)#access-list 101 permit tcp any any eq pop3`
`RouterC(config)#access-list 101 deny ip any any`
`RouterC(config)#dialer-list 7 protocol ip list 101`
`RouterC(config)#^Z`
`RouterC#`

With access-list 101, it was specified that both checking and sending e-mail should be allowed but that all other IP traffic is denied. So, in dialer-list 7, it was stated that access-list 101 is to be used as a criterion for testing whether traffic is interesting.

NOTE access-list 101 will not actually permit or deny any packets unless it's applied to an interface with an access-group command. It will be used only to decide if the packets are interesting. Even though IP packets other than e-mail are not interesting, they will still be routed (assuming that the link is up).

In the example, it is possible to have entered IPX or AppleTalk access lists and used those as well as the IP access list in dialer-list 7. Also, only one access list per protocol is allowed in a dialer list, just as with interface configurations.

Exam Essentials

Remember when to use the *redistribute* command.   Allows routing information discovered through one routing protocol to be distributed in the update messages of another routing protocol.

Remember what Internetwork Packet Exchange is for and when it is used.   IPX is a protocol suite made popular by Novell after it was derived from Xerox. IPX is a protocol used to transfer packets on an internetwork and is similar to IP.

Key Terms and Concepts

SPID (service profile identifier)   A numbering scheme that some service providers use to define the services to which an ISDN device subscribes.

BRI (Basic Rate Interface)   Composed of two B channels and one D channel that can transmit voice, video, and data.

Sample Questions

1. Interesting traffic is specified by using the _____ command? (Fill in the blank.)

   A. dialer list

   B. dialer

   C. dialer-list

   D. dialer-interesting

   Answer: C—Use the dialer-list command to set up interesting traffic.

2. What is the correct order of the following steps when setting up interesting traffic?

   1. Define destination.

   2. Define interesting traffic.

   3. Assign interesting-traffic definition to ISDN interface.

   4. Define call parameters.

   A. 2, 3, 1, 4

   B. 1, 2, 3, 4

   C. 2, 3, 4, 1

   D. 3, 4, 1, 2

   Answer: A—The correct order is to define interesting traffic, assign the interesting-traffic definition to the ISDN interface, define the destination, and then define the call parameters.

Configure dialer profiles.

There is one major problem with the legacy DDR configuration that was reviewed in the preceding section. When the interface was configured there, it actually configured the physical interface with parameters such as network address, encapsulation, etc. However, what if you want to use that same interface to dial a different number and to use different parameters when establishing that connection? With legacy DDR, the interface configuration is statically assigned. Fortunately, dialer profiles alleviate this problem.

To help you understand how to solve the problems that can happen with legacy DDR, this objective teaches you how to configure your Cisco ISDN routers with dialer profiles. This is important if you need to dial more than one location and have different parameters.

It's imperative that you know all of the DDR configuration types, and dialer profiles.

Critical Information

Once you've selected the dialer interface to be configured, you must complete the following steps:

- Configure a network address for the interface.

- Configure an encapsulation type.

- Configure the dialer group (interesting traffic).

- Configure the dialer map (destination).

- Configure the dialer idle timeout (optional).

Dialer profiles allow you to create multiple virtual interfaces (called dialer interfaces) that have different configurations for different circumstances. All physical interfaces are placed in a *dialer pool* and can be used by any dialer interface that has access to that pool. This abstraction separates the physical interface from the configuration, so it allows multiple configurations to be used on the same physical interface. Dialer profiles are a relatively new feature; they were introduced in IOS version 11.2.

The steps for creating a dialer profile are similar to the steps used in legacy DDR:

1. Specify interesting traffic. (What kind of traffic is required to bring up the link?)

2. Define the static routes. (Direct the router to get to a destination.)

3. Configure the dialer interface. (The configuration goes here, not on the physical interface.)

4. Configure the physical interface. (Make it a member of a dialer pool.)

Necessary Information

This section describes how to configure a dialer interface and dialer profile. Following is an example of these configurations on the BRI 0 interface:

```
RouterC#config t
Enter configuration commands, one per line. End with
    CNTL/Z.
RouterC(config)#int bri0
RouterC(config-if)#ip address 172.16.20.1 255.255.255.0
RouterC(config-if)#encapsulation ppp
RouterC(config-if)#dialer-group 5
RouterC(config-if)#dialer map ip 172.16.20.2 name
    RouterC 5556677
RouterC(config-if)#dialer idle-timeout 300
RouterC(config-if)#^Z
RouterC#
```

Since DDR isn't an encapsulation method, you will need to run it with an encapsulation method that Cisco supports. One of the following data link encapsulations will do:

- Cisco recommends Point-to-Point Protocol because it can be used with asynchronous, synchronous, and ISDN interfaces, it has multi-protocol support, and it provides authentication security via CHAP and PAP.

- High-Level Data Link Control supports multiple protocols but can only be run on synchronous and ISDN interfaces. It also doesn't provide for any authentication.

- Serial Line Interface Protocol (SLIP) is an older protocol that can run on only asynchronous interfaces. It can't use multiple protocols (IP only) and has no provision for authentication.

- X.25 can be run on ISDN and synchronous interfaces.

The `dialer-group` interface command assigns the DDR interface to a dialer access group. The group number (a value between 1 and 10) specifies which group the DDR interface belongs to, and this number must match the value of the dialer list. This command connects the DDR interface to access-list statements, which identify interesting packets. The `dialer map` interface command defines the phone numbers (one or multiple) for a DDR interface connecting to the DCE device. The `dialer map` and `dialer-group` commands work together to initiate dialing by associating interesting packets. You choose specific protocols (IP, IPX, or AppleTalk) with the `protocol` keyword. The `dialer idle-timeout` interface command specifies how long a link stays active after the last interesting packet was passed. (The default is 120 seconds.)

Dialer Profiles

The following example was used for the legacy DDR configuration:

```
RouterC#config t
Enter configuration commands, one per line. End with
    CNTL/Z.
RouterC(config)#int bri0
RouterC(config-if)#ip address 172.16.20.1 255.255.255.0
RouterC(config-if)#encapsulation ppp
RouterC(config-if)#dialer-group 5
RouterC(config-if)#dialer map ip 172.16.20.2 name
    RouterC  5556677
RouterC(config-if)#dialer idle-timeout 300
RouterC(config-if)#^Z
RouterC#
```

Now take a look at how the following illustrates the same configuration using a dialer profile:

```
RouterC#config t
Enter configuration commands, one per line. End with
    CNTL/Z.
```

```
RouterC(config)#interface dialer1
RouterC(config-if)#ip address 172.16.20.1 255.255.255.0
RouterC(config-if)#encapsulation ppp
RouterC(config-if)#dialer remote-name RouterC
RouterC(config-if)#dialer string 5556677
RouterC(config-if)#dialer-group 5
RouterC(config-if)#dialer pool 10
RouterC(config-if)#dialer idle-timeout 300
RouterC(config-if)#exit
RouterC(config)#int bri0
RouterC(config-if)#no ip address
RouterC(config-if)#dialer pool-member 10
RouterC(config-if)#^Z
RouterC#
```

Notice that the entire configuration is now on the dialer1 interface and that the actual physical interface (BRI 0) is just a member of dialer pool 10. At this point, you can configure additional dialer interfaces with distinct parameters and also use dialer pool 10 (and thus use BRI 0).

Exam Essentials

Remember how to create a dialer interface. By specifying the command dialer and a number, you can create a dialer interface.

Understand why PPP is the ISDN encapsulation of choice. PPP is preferable because it can be used with asynchronous, synchronous, and ISDN interfaces, it has multi-protocol support, and it provides authentication security via CHAP and PAP.

Key Terms and Concepts

ISDN (Integrated Services Digital Network) A digital subscriber line offered by telephone companies that permits telephone networks to carry data, voice, and other source traffic.

BRI (Basic Rate Interface) Composed of two B channels and one D channel that can transmit voice, video, and data.

Sample Questions

1. What encapsulation method can be used with asynchronous, synchronous, and ISDN interfaces?

    A. HDLC

    B. ISDN

    C. PPP

    D. LAPB

    Answer: C—PPP has multi-protocol support and provides authentication security via CHAP and PAP.

2. List, in order, the following steps for creating a dialer profile.

    1. Configure the dialer interface.

    2. Configure the physical interface.

    3. Define the static routes.

    4. Specify interesting traffic.

    A. 1, 2, 3, 4

    B. 2, 4, 3, 1

    C. 3, 2, 1, 4

    D. 4, 3, 1, 2

    Answer: D—To create a dialer profile, you need to specify the interesting traffic, define the static routes, configure the dialer interface, and then configure the physical interface.

Verify DDR operation.

Verifying and monitoring your ISDN connection is as important as configuring your router. To verify and monitor ISDN connections, you can use many different commands. Some commands can be used to troubleshoot by using the different layers of the OSI reference model. By following the layers of the OSI Reference model, you can logically find where a configuration or switch problem occurs.

This objective helps you to learn how to verify your ISDN configuration as well as how to monitor and troubleshoot. This is important when configuring an ISDN line and when studying for your exam.

Critical Information

Once you've completed the steps for configuring legacy DDR, you're ready to verify and test your configuration. The following commands are useful when testing legacy DDR configuration:

- show interface bri shows the first B channel on the BRI. When you have configured for ISDN, you can check the interface to see evidence of your configuration and also some of the resulting call-setup details.

- show interface bri 0 displays information about the BRI interface D channel only.

- show interface bri 1 2 displays both B channels (first and last). If the command is entered without the parameters 1 and 2, only D-channel status is shown.

- show controllers bri 1 checks layer one, the Physical layer, of the BRI.

- show dialer and debug dialer gather information about the DDR configuration or functions used by ISDN.

- show isdn status provides the output from the logical-link layers one, two, and three—memory, timers, and status of PRI channels.

- `show ppp multilink` displays bundle information on a rotary group in the packet-multiplexing section, including the number of members in a bundle and the bundle to which a link belongs.

- `debug dialer` indicates whether the multilink is up after authentication and also shows when the overload occurs that brings up the second BRI link.

- `debug isdn q921` shows the layer-two procedures that are taking place on the D channel of the ISDN interface. This command is useful when you want to observe signaling events between the access router and the ISDN switch. (This debug information does not include data transmitted over the B channels that are also part of the router's ISDN interface.)

- `debug isdn q931` shows the layer-three call setup and teardown of the ISDN network connections. The router tracks only activities that occur on the user side, not the network side, of the network connection.

Exam Essentials

Remember which commands can check the different OSI layers.   For the Physical layer, use the `show controllers` command. For the Data Link layer, use the `debug isdn q921` command. And for the Network layer, use the `debug isdn q931` command.

Remember the command to view your B channel.   Use the `show interface bri` command to view the first B channel on the BRI.

Remember the command to view your D channel.   To see information about the BRI interface D channel only, use the `show interface bri 0` command.

Key Terms and Concepts

ISDN (Integrated Service Digital Network)   A digital-subscriber network that works over the existing telephone company network.

Debug command   Router command that is used to debug what is happening in the router.

Layer one   The Physical layer of the OSI reference model. Its main functions are physical topology, bit signaling, and synchronization.

Layer two   The Data Link layer of the OSI reference model. Its main functions are to provide framing and media access.

Layer three   The Network layer of the OSI Reference model. Its main functions are routing packets through an internetwork and network addressing.

Sample Questions

1. Which of the following commands will show you the call setup and teardown of the ISDN user side of the network?

   A. show controllers

   B. debug isdn q921

   C. debug isdn q931

   D. show interface

   Answer: C—debug isdn q931 shows the third-layer call setup and teardown of the ISDN network connections.

2. Which of the following commands will let you observe signaling events between the access router and the ISDN switch?

   A. show controllers

   B. debug isdn q921

   C. debug isdn q931

   D. show interface

   Answer: B—The debug isdn q92 command is useful when you want to observe signaling events between the access router and the ISDN switch.

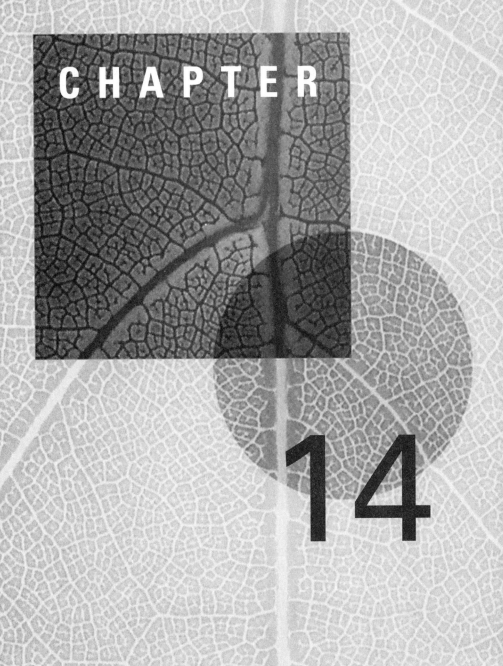

CHAPTER

14

Customizing DDR Operation

Cisco ACRC Exam Objectives Covered in This Chapter:

▶ **Configure dial backup.** *(pages 279 – 283)*

▶ **Verify dial backup operation.** *(pages 283 – 291)*

▶ **Configure MultiLink PPP operation.** *(pages 291 – 294)*

▶ **Verify MultiLink PPP operation.** *(pages 295 – 301)*

▶ **Configure snapshot routing.** *(pages 302 – 306)*

▶ **Configure IPX spoofing.** *(pages 306 – 310)*

T his chapter discusses the different reasons for setting up a dial-on-demand routing (DDR) link. It shows you how to configure dial backup both when a primary link goes down and when a primary link gets saturated. This chapter also shows you how to verify your configuration, which is an important part of every chapter in this book. Multilink is covered as well, and you are shown how to use multilink in an ISDN environment. Both snapshot and IPX spoofing are discussed, as well as their configuration.

These are important objectives because they can save your dialup link from having to come up every time a network change takes place. The idea of a backup link is to have a redundant link in case of failure, to add bandwidth to a saturated primary link, or to call a site periodically when intermittent data needs to be transmitted.

When studying for the exam, the best thing you can do is to practice on a real BRI interface. If you cannot obtain access to a router that has a BRI interface, bear in mind that the chapter shows you all of the commands that you will need to know in order to configure dial backup. This is important if you need to configure dial backup.

Configure dial backup.

This first objective section shows you how to configure a simple DDR dial-backup link. To have a backup link, you need to have a BRI interface or async port(s) that your router can use to dial and make a connection to another location. This objective discusses using a BRI configuration.

This is an important objective if you work at an internetwork that needs backup links. When studying for the ACRC exam, hands-on is the best way to prepare for this objective.

Critical Information

Dial backup allows you to use a DDR connection to back up a regular primary connection, which means that if a primary connection fails the DDR connection will come to life and continue to pass traffic.

Failure can be defined in two ways: either the loss of connectivity or the saturation of bandwidth. The first definition is obvious; when your T1 goes down, that's failure. However, the second definition isn't quite so apparent. For example, when your T1 reaches 90% utilization and a user needs to download a mega-file from the Internet, the link is as good as down as far as your user is concerned. In this case, dial backup can sense that the bandwidth utilization is high and use DDR to provide an additional path for traffic to follow, thus responding to peak demand.

You should take note of the following two commands:

- `backup delay` tells the BRI 0 interface to wait an administratively assigned number of seconds after the failure of a primary link before starting up and, if the ISDN connection is established, to wait another administratively assigned number of seconds after the primary link recovers before tearing it down.

- **backup load** specifies that the ISDN call not be placed until an administratively assigned percentage of the primary link's available bandwidth is in use and that it remain available until the primary link's bandwidth use is less than another administratively assigned percentage of bandwidth.

Necessary Procedures

This section shows you how to configure a BRI interface for both a primary-link failure and a saturated-link failure.

Primary-Link Failure

In this scenario, a DDR link is configured to back up a failed primary link. Consider the following configuration:

```
RouterC#configure term
Enter configuration commands, one per line. End with
    CNTL/Z.
RouterC(config)#int s0
RouterC(config-if)#backup interface bri0
RouterC(config-if)#backup delay 5 60
RouterC(config-if)#^Z
RouterC#
```

Interface BRI 0 is configured to back up interface serial 0. The **backup delay** command tells the BRI 0 interface to wait 5 seconds after the failure of serial 0 before starting up and, if the ISDN connection is established, to wait 60 seconds after serial 0 recovers before tearing it down. So now, when your frame's away, your users can still play—using ISDN, of course.

Primary-Link Bandwidth Saturation

In this scenario, a DDR link will back up a saturated primary link. Note the configuration at the top of the next page.

```
RouterC#configure term
Enter configuration commands, one per line. End with
    CNTL/Z.
RouterC(config)#int s0
RouterC(config-if)#backup interface bri0
RouterC(config-if)#backup load 80 30
RouterC(config-if)#^Z
RouterC#
```

In this scenario, BRI 0 comes alive and helps to interface serial 0 when it becomes too busy. When the backup load command is entered, it specifies that the ISDN call not be placed until 80% of serial 0's available bandwidth is in use and that it remains available until serial 0's bandwidth use is less than 30%.

Exam Essentials

Remember how to set an interface to be a backup.   Use backup interface bri(number) to set a primary serial link to use a BRI port if the link becomes unavailable or over saturated.

Remember how to configure a router to bring up a BRI port when a primary link fails.   The backup delay command is used on a serial interface to set the amount of time until the backup link comes up and then goes down when the primary link fails.

Remember how to configure your router to handle over-saturation of bandwidth.   Use the backup load command on a primary interface to configure the router to bring up and then down a backup dialup port when the bandwidth of the primary link is over saturated.

Key Terms and Concepts

Bandwidth   The rated throughput capacity of a given network medium or protocol.

BRI (Basic Rate Interface) A standard ISDN interface on a router that can be configured and plugged directly into an ISDN network. It can send data and voice with a bandwidth of 128K.

Primary link Main link on a point-to-point WAN.

Saturation When bandwidth is oversubscribed and data throughput is deteriorated.

Sample Questions

1. What does the following command mean?

`RouterC(config-if)#`**`backup delay 5 60`**

A. Wait five seconds before bringing down the backup link, and wait 60 seconds before bringing up the backup link after the primary link is restored.

B. Wait five milliseconds before bringing up the backup link, and wait 60 milliseconds before bringing down the backup link after the primary link is back up.

C. Wait five seconds before bringing up the backup link, and wait 60 seconds before bringing down the backup link after the primary link is back up.

D. Wait five minutes before bringing up the backup link, and wait 60 minutes before bringing down the backup link after the primary link is back up.

Answer: C—The command `backup delay 5 60` means that the BRI 0 interface is to wait 5 seconds after the failure of serial 0 before starting up and, if the ISDN connection is established, to wait 60 seconds after serial 0 recovers before tearing it down.

2. What does the following command mean?

`RouterC(config-if)#`**`backup load 80 30`**

A. When the primary link reaches 80% utilization, bring up the secondary link until the primary link is below 30% utilization.

B. When the primary link reaches 30% utilization, bring up the secondary link until the primary link is below 80% utilization.

C. When the link is up for 80 minutes, make 30% of the backup link bandwidth available.

D. When the link is up for 30 minutes, make 80% of the backup link bandwidth available.

Answer: A—The command `backup load 80 30` means that the ISDN call will not be placed until 80% of serial 0's available bandwidth is in use and that it will remain available until serial 0's bandwidth use is less than 30%.

Verify dial backup operation.

The Cisco IOS provides a broad range of troubleshooting commands to assist administrators in the deployment and configuration of ISDN, including the common problems previously noted. Although many of these commands are common to other topologies and protocols (`ping`, for example), other commands are specific to ISDN, including `debug isdn q931`.

This objective is important when configuring dial backup. You must be able to verify your configuration.

Critical Information

The three steps for configuring legacy DDR are: specifying interesting traffic, setting up static routing, and configuring the dialer. Once you've completed these three steps, you're ready to verify and test your configuration. The following commands are useful when testing legacy DDR configuration:

- `ping` establishes a connection with a remote network (assuming that you defined it as interesting).

- show dialer gives the current status of a link. The show dialer command reports information regarding the DDR connections, including the number dialed, the success of the connection, the idle timers that control the duration of a DDR connection without data packets, and the number of calls that were screened or rejected due to administrative policy.

- show isdn status gives the status of ISDN connections. The show isdn status command is one of the more significant trouble-shooting commands because the output reports not only the status of the interface but a breakdown of each layer.

- debug q921 is for call setup and teardown. The q921 protocol addresses layer two of the OSI model and its relationship to ISDN. The D channel is always connected in ISDN, and the channel is used for signaling between the switch and the local ISDN device. Connections over the B channels cannot occur without signaling commands on the D channel.

- debug ppp negotiation provides real-time information about the establishment of a session when the router is configured for Point-to-Point Protocol.

- debug q931, specifically the q931 specification, addresses layer three of the OSI model for ISDN. (Events occurring at layer three may be monitored with the debug isdn q931 command.)

- debug dialer is for call setup and teardown, providing information regarding the cause of a dialing connection and the status of the connection.

Necessary Procedures

This section shows you the commands used in verifying ISDN DDR connectivity. It is imperative that you can configure ISDN DDR, but you must also be able to verify the connections once it is configured. This section shows you the commands used in an ISDN DDR environment.

The *ping* Command

As with non-DDR connections, the ping command is one of the most useful troubleshooting tools. Ping verifies routes and other connections; in DDR, the command triggers a call. The following shows you the ISDN DDR line coming up because of a ping command being generated:

```
Bottom#ping 10.1.1.1

Type escape sequence to abort.
Sending 5, 100-byte ICMP Echos to 10.1.1.1, timeout is
   2 seconds:
.
00:37:12: %LINK-3-UPDOWN: Interface BRI0:1, changed
   state to up
00:37:13: %LINEPROTO-5-UPDOWN: Line protocol on
   Interface BRI0:1, changed state to up.!!!
Success rate is 60 percent (3/5), round-trip min/avg/
   max = 32/38/48 ms
Bottom#
00:37:14: %LINK-3-UPDOWN: Interface BRI0:2, changed
   state to up
00:37:15: %LINEPROTO-5-UPDOWN: Line protocol on
   Interface BRI0:2, changed state to up
```

Note that the five pings generated by the router completed before the second B channel came up. The ping command is perhaps the most common troubleshooting tool in TCP/IP networks.

WARNING   It is quite common for the first three pings to fail in DDR ISDN connections. This is due to the two- to three-second delay in establishing the connection. It is usually not an indication of a problem.

The *show dialer* Command

This command is useful for verifying a previous connection or for checking the number called. Note that dialer map statements, which link network addresses to ISDN numbers, can be implemented incorrectly. For example, IP address one is linked to letter B instead of A. Although the router dials and the ISDN connection may succeed, it cannot pass packets due to layer-three mismatches. The following example shows you the output of the show dialer command:

```
Bottom#show dialer

BRIO - dialer type = ISDN

Dial String      Successes   Failures    Last called
    Last status
18008358661          2          0        00:02:49
successful
0 incoming call(s) have been screened.
0 incoming call(s) rejected for callback.

BRIO:1 - dialer type = ISDN
Idle timer (120 secs), Fast idle timer (20 secs)
Wait for carrier (30 secs), Re-enable (15 secs)
Dialer state is idle

BRIO:2 - dialer type = ISDN
Idle timer (120 secs), Fast idle timer (20 secs)
Wait for carrier (30 secs), Re-enable (15 secs)
Dialer state is idle
```

The *show isdn status* Command

The following display reports a correctly configured router and switch. Note that the SPIDs are confirmed and that all layers are active on both B channels.

```
Top#show isdn status
Global ISDN Switchtype = basic-ni
ISDN BRIO interface
    dsl 0, interface ISDN Switchtype = basic-ni
    Layer 1 Status:
    ACTIVE
    Layer 2 Status:
```

```
TEI = 83, Ces = 1, SAPI = 0, State =
MULTIPLE_FRAME_ESTABLISHED
TEI = 84, Ces = 2, SAPI = 0, State =
MULTIPLE_FRAME_ESTABLISHED
 Spid Status:
TEI 83, ces = 1, state = 5(init)
    spid1 configured, no LDN, spid1 sent, spid1 valid
    Endpoint ID Info: epsf = 0, usid = 1, tid = 1
TEI 84, ces = 2, state = 5(init)
    spid2 configured, no LDN, spid2 sent, spid2 valid
    Endpoint ID Info: epsf = 0, usid = 3, tid = 1
 Layer 3 Status:
 0 Active Layer 3 Call(s)
 Activated ds1 0 CCBs = 0
Total Allocated ISDN CCBs = 0
```

The *debug isdn q921* Command

Administrators use this command to monitor the proper flow of messages when calls do not connect. It is recommended that a baseline debug be performed and recorded to compare against suspected problem debug output. Following is the debug isdn q921 command:

```
Bottom#debug isdn q921
ISDN Q921 packets debugging is on
00:19:15: ISDN BR0: TX -> RRp sapi = 0  tei = 92 nr = 12
00:19:64424550400: ISDN BR0: RX <- RRf sapi = 0  tei = 92
    nr = 12
Bottom#ping 10.1.1.1

Type escape sequence to abort.
Sending 5, 100-byte ICMP Echos to 10.1.1.1, timeout is
    2 seconds:
    .
00:19:23: ISDN BR0: TX -> INFOc sapi = 0  tei = 92
    ns = 12  nr = 12  i = 0x080
10305040288901801832C0B31383030383333538363631
```

```
00:19:98789554100: ISDN BR0: RX <- INF0c sapi = 0
    tei = 92  ns = 12  nr = 13
i =
    0x08018302180189952A1B809402603D8307383335383636318E
    0B2054454C544F4E45203120
00:19:23: ISDN BR0: TX -> RRr sapi = 0  tei = 92  nr = 13
00:19:103079256064: ISDN BR0: RX <- INF0c sapi = 0
    tei = 92  ns = 13  nr = 13
(Output cut for berivity)
```

The *debug ppp negotiation* Command

This command is useful if connections are possible with the HDLC protocol and failures may occur with the PPP protocol. The debug ppp negotiation command is shown below:

```
Bottom#debug ppp negotiation
PPP protocol negotiation debugging is on
Bottom#ping 10.1.1.1

Type escape sequence to abort.
Sending 5, 100-byte ICMP Echos to 10.1.1.1, timeout is
    2 seconds:

00:22:28: %LINK-3-UPDOWN: Interface BRI0:1, changed state
    to up
00:22:28: BR0:1 PPP: Treating connection as a callout
00:22:28: BR0:1 PPP: Phase is ESTABLISHING, Active Open
00:22:28: BR0:1 LCP: O CONFREQ [Closed] id 3 len 10
00:22:28: BR0:1 LCP:    MagicNumber 0x50239604
    (0x050650239604)
(output cut for brevity)
```

The *debug isdn q931* Command

The output from this command, an example of which follows, is best compared to a baseline debug captured on a working connection. However, administrators may use the output to verify acknowledgments and messages without a complete understanding of the protocol.

```
Bottom#debug isdn q931
ISDN Q931 packets debugging is on
00:15:184683593728: ISDN BR0: RX <-  STATUS_ENQ pd = 8
   callref = 0x82
00:15:43: ISDN BR0: TX ->  STATUS pd = 8  callref = 0x02
00:15:43:          Cause i = 0x809E - Response to STATUS
   ENQUIRY or number unassigned
00:15:43:          Call State i = 0x0A
(output cut for berivty)
```

The *debug dialer* Command

Note in the following output that an IP packet has caused the dial to occur. This information, and its inverse, can provide assistance for tuning connections. Administrators frequently do this to limit the use of an ISDN circuit when charged on distance and per-minute tariffs.

```
Bottom#debug dialer
Dial on demand events debugging is on
Bottom#ping 10.1.1.1

Type escape sequence to abort.
Sending 5, 100-byte ICMP Echos to 10.1.1.1, timeout is
   2 seconds:

00:27:26: BRI0: Dialing cause ip (s=10.1.1.2, d=10.1.1.1)
00:27:26: BRI0: Attempting to dial 18008358661
00:27:27: %LINK-3-UPDOWN: Interface BRI0:1, changed
   state to up.
00:27:27: dialer Protocol up for BR0:1
00:27:28: %LINEPROTO-5-UPDOWN: Line protocol on Interface
   BRI0:1, changed state
to up
00:27:29: %LINK-3-UPDOWN: Interface BRI0:2, changed
   state to up.!!!
Success rate is 60 percent (3/5), round-trip min/avg/max =
   32/37/48 ms
Bottom#
```

```
00:27:29: dialer Protocol up for BRO:2
00:27:30: %LINEPROTO-5-UPDOWN: Line protocol on Interface
   BRI0:2, changed state
to up
```

Exam Essentials

Remember the different commands that are used to verify dialup connections. ping is always a good command to use to check IP connectivity across any link. The debug commands are great to use to see what the routers are seeing in real time. show dialer is good for understanding what the dialer interface is doing, and show isdn will give you ISDN information for all ISDN protocols.

Remember the different debug commands that are available. debug ppp negotiation is a good command to use to see PPP statistics and real time activity. q921 gives you layer-two events, and q931 gives you layer-three events. The debug dialer command shows you the setup and teardown of the connection.

Key Terms and Concepts

Q921 ISDN specification for the Data Link layer.

Q931 ISDN specification for the Network layer, which provides signaling to establish, maintain, and clear ISDN network connections.

Layer two Data Link layer of the OSI reference model; its primary purpose is to identify machines on a LAN and media access.

Layer three Network layer of the OSI reference model; its primary purpose is to route through an internetwork and network addressing.

ISDN (Integrated Services Digital Network) A telecommuter digital communication protocol that permits telephone networks to carry data, voice, and other traffic.

PPP (Point-to-Point Protocol)   Provides router-to-router and host-to-network connections over synchronous and asynchronous circuits.

Sample Questions

1. Which command would you use to see real-time activity of ISDN layer two?

   A. debug q921

   B. debug ppp negotiation

   C. debug q931

   D. show dialer

   Answer: A—q921 is the specification for layer-two ISDN activity.

2. Which command would you use to see layer-three ISDN activity?

   A. debug q921

   B. debug ppp negotiation

   C. debug q931

   D. show dialer

   Answer:C—q931 is the ISDN specification for layer three.

Configure MultiLink PPP operation.

Multilink PPP is the ability to aggregate several separate physical interfaces into a single virtual pipe. With multilink PPP, multiple ISDN channels can be combined to form a single, faster channel—at least virtually.

This chapter shows you the two commands that, in order to bring up both BRI lines together, must be added to the DDR configuration that was presented in the first objective. This is very important and must be configured in an ISDN environment. When setting up an ISDN section, multilink PPP is essential to configure and understand.

Critical Information

This section shows you how to configure multilink PPP. Multilink allows you to connect two routers with multiple separate channels. Although the routers are connected via two separate channels, the two channels will act as a single connection when using multilink PPP.

The following two commands are the only commands that are required when configuring multilink on your ISDN line:

- `ppp multilink` tells the BRI interface to combine both B (bearer) channels in an ISDN configuration. If you do not use this command, the router will only use one B channel and you can only achieve a maximum bandwidth of 64K.

- `dialer load-threshold` is used to tell the BRI when to bring up the second line. The parameters are:

```
dialer load-threshold [load]
    [outbound|inbound|either]
```

The load parameter represents the utilization percentage. It is an administratively assigned number between one and 255. (Note that 100% utilization is represented by 255.) The `outbound` command is used to calculate the load using outbound data only. The `inbound` command is for calculating bandwidth saturation using inbound traffic only. The `either` command is to calculate the load using both inbound and outbound loads. If you want both B channels to come up at the same time, set the threshold to 1 `either`.

Necessary Procedures

Configuration is relatively straightforward. Consider the following legacy DDR configuration:

```
RouterC#configure term
Enter configuration commands, one per line.  End with
  CNTL/Z.
RouterC(config)#int bri0
RouterC(config-if)#ppp multilink
RouterC(config-if)#dialer load-threshold 100 either
RouterC(config-if)#^Z
RouterC#
```

Assume that BRI 1 was already configured for legacy DDR. The ppp multilink is added, which enables multilink on both B channels. The dialer load-threshold command is used next to specify that once utilization exceeds 40%, either inbound or outbound, the additional link should be used.

Configuration is similar on dialer profile configurations, although with dialer profiles the modifications aren't made to the physical interface; they're applied to the dialer interface. Be aware that all physical interfaces included in the dialer pool are potential candidates to be added into the multilink bundle.

Exam Essentials

Understand why the *ppp multilink* command is necessary. If you do not use the ppp multilink command, only one B channel will be used and bandwidth can never exceed 64k.

Remember how to set the *dialer load–threshold* command. Use the dialer load-threshold [load] [outbound|inbound|either] command to tell the router when to bring up the second BRI line.

Key Terms and Concepts

BRI (Basic Rate Interface)   A standard ISDN interface on a router that can be configured and plugged directly into an ISDN network. It can send data and voice with a bandwidth of 128K.

Multilink   To aggregate several separate physical interfaces into a single virtual pipe.

PPP (Point-to-Point Protocol)   Provides router-to-router and host-to-network connections over synchronous and asynchronous circuits.

Sample Questions

1. Which command can combine multiple channels into one virtual channel?

   A. multichannel

   B. ppp multilink

   C. linkalot

   D. linkland2

   Answer: B—The PPP multilink allows the second B channel to be used.

2. Which command can be used to set a connection to use a second bearer channel?

   A. threshold load-dialer

   B. load dialer-threshold

   C. dialer load-threshold

   D. either bearer-load 50

   Answer: C—When using the PPP multilink command, you should also use the dialer load-threshold command to set the amount of bandwidth used before the second bearer channel is brought up.

Verify MultiLink PPP operation.

There are really only two primary commands that you need to remember for verifying multilink PPP operation: debug ppp multilink and show dialer. Some debug ppp commands were described in preceding sections. This objective section shows you the debug ppp fragments command, which is used when the Network-layer fragments packets because they are too large for layer-two encapsulation.

This chapter is important because you must be able to troubleshoot ISDN connection problems. When studying for the ACRC exam, try practicing all of these commands on a router and memorizing the output of each command.

Critical Information

The show dialer command was already explained earlier in this chapter, so this section describes and demonstrates only the debug ppp multilink command. However, this section still shows you all of the commands that you can use to verify connectivity with ISDN and multilink PPP.

- debug ppp multilink fragments displays information about individual multilink fragments and important multilink events.

- clear interface bri *n* resets the various counters that are available on the interface and terminates a connection on the interface. The *n* value should equal the port or the port and slot of the interface.

- show interface bri *n* makes information available regarding the ISDN BRI D channel.

- show interface bri *n* 1 2 displays a single B channel of the BRI interface.

- `show controller bri` is most useful for troubleshooting with Cisco's TAC, but some information can assist the administrator. Most importantly, the status of the interface, and the superframe error counter are available with this show command.

Necessary Procedures

This section demonstrates all of the commands listed in the preceding Critical Information section.

The *debug ppp multilink fragments* Command

You can get a fast sample by using the debug ppp multilink fragments command with the ping command. The debug output indicates that a multilink PPP packet on interface BRI 0 (on the B channel) is an input (I) or output (O) packet. The sequence number of each packet is shown along with the size of the fragment. The following output shows you the debug ppp multilink fragments command:

```
Router# debug ppp multilink fragments
Router# ping 172.16.10.1

Type escape sequence to abort.
Sending 5, 100-byte ICMP Echos to 172.16.10.1, timeout
    is 2 seconds:
!!!!!
Success rate is 100 percent (5/5), round-trip min/avg/
    max = 32/34/36 ms
Router#

2:00:28: MLP BRIO: B-Channel 1: O seq 80000000: size 58
2:00:28: MLP BRIO: B-Channel 2: O seq 40000001: size 59
2:00:28: MLP BRIO: B-Channel 2: I seq 40000001: size 59
2:00:28: MLP BRIO: B-Channel 1: I seq 80000000: size 58
2:00:28: MLP BRIO: B-Channel 1: O seq 80000002: size 58
2:00:28: MLP BRIO: B-Channel 2: O seq 40000003: size 59
2:00:28: MLP BRIO: B-Channel 2: I seq 40000003: size 59
2:00:28: MLP BRIO: B-Channel 1: I seq 80000002: size 58
```

```
2:00:28: MLP BRIO: B-Channel 1: O seq 80000004: size 58
2:00:28: MLP BRIO: B-Channel 2: O seq 40000005: size 59
2:00:28: MLP BRIO: B-Channel 2: I seq 40000005: size 59
2:00:28: MLP BRIO: B-Channel 1: I seq 80000004: size 58
2:00:28: MLP BRIO: B-Channel 1: O seq 80000006: size 58
2:00:28: MLP BRIO: B-Channel 2: O seq 40000007: size 59
2:00:28: MLP BRIO: B-Channel 2: I seq 40000007: size 59
2:00:28: MLP BRIO: B-Channel 1: I seq 80000006: size 58
2:00:28: MLP BRIO: B-Channel 1: O seq 80000008: size 58
2:00:28: MLP BRIO: B-Channel 2: O seq 40000009: size 59
2:00:28: MLP BRIO: B-Channel 2: I seq 40000009: size 59
2:00:28: MLP BRIO: B-Channel 1: I seq 80000008: size 58
```

The *clear interface bri*n Command

This command is most useful for clearing a call that was activated by a dialer map or some other catalyst, which may be desired when configuring and testing new access lists and other call triggers. The following output displays the clear int bri0 command:

```
Bottom#clear int bri0
Bottom#
00:26:158913789951: %ISDN-6-DISCONNECT: Interface BRIO:2
disconnected from 8358663 , call lasted 104 seconds
00:26:154624128828: %LINK-3-UPDOWN: Interface BRIO:2,
   changed state to down
00:26:36: %ISDN-6-LAYER2UP: Layer 2 for Interface BRO, TEI
   92 changed to up
00:26:36: %ISDN-6-LAYER2UP: Layer 2 for Interface BRO, TEI
   93 changed to up
00:26:37: %LINEPROTO-5-UPDOWN: Line protocol on Interface
   BRIO:2, changed state
to down
```

The *show interface bri*n Command

Note in the following example that the command reports the B channels' status, as well as spoofing on the interface. This is due to the dynamic nature of DDR connections; they are only up when necessary.

In addition, note that the interface was not configured for Point-to-Point Protocol but is using the default encapsulation of HDLC.

It is important for administrators to review the output of the show interface command, especially when researching user reports of slow performance. For example, the txload and rxload parameters provide a strong indication of bandwidth loads.

```
Bottom#show interface bri0
BRI0 is up, line protocol is up (spoofing)
   Hardware is BRI with U interface and POTS
   Internet address is 10.1.1.2/24
   MTU 1500 bytes, BW 64Kbit, DLY 20000 usec,
      reliablility 255/255, txload 1/255, rxload 1/255
   Encapsulation HDLC, loopback not set
   Last input 00:00:05, output 00:00:05, output hang
   never
   Last clearing of "show interface" counters never
   Input queue: 0/75/0 (size/max/drops); Total output
   drops: 0
   Queueing strategy: weighted fair
   Output queue: 0/1000/64/0 (size/max total/threshold/
   drops)
      Conversations  0/1/256 (active/max active/max
      total)
      Reserved Conversations 0/0 (allocated/max
      allocated)
   5 minute input rate 0 bits/sec, 0 packets/sec
   5 minute output rate 0 bits/sec, 0 packets/sec
      85 packets input, 791 bytes, 0 no buffer
      Received 4 broadcasts, 0 runts, 0 giants,
      0 throttles
      0 input errors, 0 CRC, 0 frame, 0 overrun,
      0 ignored, 0 abort
      92 packets output, 701 bytes, 0 underruns
      0 output errors, 0 collisions, 4 interface resets
```

0 output buffer failures, 0 output buffers
swapped out
1 carrier transitions

The *show interface bri* n *1 2* Command

Although this command can be important when isolating an individual B-channel problem, the show interface bri n 1 2 command usually suffices for the majority of troubleshooting processes. The following output displays the show interface bri0 1 command:

```
Bottom#show interface bri0 1
BRI0:1 is down, line protocol is down
  Hardware is BRI with U interface and POTS
  MTU 1500 bytes, BW 64Kbit, DLY 20000 usec,
      reliablility 255/255, txload 1/255, rxload 1/255
  Encapsulation PPP, loopback not set, keepalive set
  (10 sec)
  LCP Closed, multilink Closed
  Closed: BACP, CDPCP, IPCP
  Last input 00:02:09, output 00:02:09, output hang never
  Last clearing of "show interface" counters never
  Queueing strategy: fifo
  Output queue 0/40, 0 drops; input queue 0/75, 0 drops
  5 minute input rate 0 bits/sec, 0 packets/sec
  5 minute output rate 0 bits/sec, 0 packets/sec
      219 packets input, 3320 bytes, 0 no buffer
      Received 219 broadcasts, 0 runts, 0 giants,
  0 throttles
      146 input errors, 9 CRC, 59 frame, 0 overrun,
  0 ignored, 78 abort
      279 packets output, 16195 bytes, 0 underruns
      0 output errors, 0 collisions, 0 interface resets
      0 output buffer failures, 0 output buffers
  swapped out
      15 carrier transitions
```

The *show controller bri* Command

The interface hardware controller information is displayed with the show controller bri command. The following shows you the output of the show controller bri command:

```
Bottom#show controller bri
BRI unit 0:BRI unit 0 with U interface and POTS:
Layer 1 internal state is ACTIVATED

Layer 1 U interface is ACTIVATED.
ISDN Line Information:
    Current EOC commands:
        RTN - Return to normal
    Received overhead bits:
        AIB=1, UOA=1, SCO=1, DEA=1, ACT=1, M50=1, M51=1,
    M60=1, FEBE=1
    Errors:  [FEBE]=0, [NEBE]=0
    Errors:  [Superframe Sync Loss]=0, [IDL2 Data
    Transparency Loss]=0
        [M4 ACT 1 -> 0]=0
(output cut for berivity)
```

Exam Essentials

Remember the command to see layer-three fragmentation. The debug ppp multilink fragments command shows you the packets being fragmented on an ISDN network.

Remember the command to see an individual B channel. Use the show interface bri *n* 1 2 command to see information regarding the B channels on an ISDN network.

Remember how to see information about the ISDN BRI D channel. Use the show interface bri *n* command to see information regarding the D channel on an ISDN network.

Key Terms and Concepts

Bandwidth   The rated throughput capacity of a given network medium or protocol.

BRI (Basic Rate Interface)   A standard ISDN interface on a router that can be configured and plugged directly into an ISDN network. It can send data and voice with a bandwidth of 128K.

Multilink   To aggregate several separate physical interfaces into a single virtual pipe.

PPP (Point-to-Point Protocol)   Provides router-to-router and host-to-network connections over synchronous and asynchronous circuits.

Sample Questions

1. Which of the following commands can be used for verifying multi-link PPP?

   A. sh dialer-up

   B. sh mul ppp

   C. sh dial

   D. sh ppp mul

   Answer: C, D—show ppp multilink and show dialer are the two commands that you can use to verify PPP. However, the other commands listed in this objective can be used as well.

2. Which command can be used to view the interface hardware controller information?

   A. sh controller bri

   B. sh multilink ppp

   C. sh dialer

   D. sh dialer-up

   Answer: A—The interface hardware controller information is displayed with the show controller bri

Configure snapshot routing.

Snapshot routing is another method of controlling traffic across DDR links. As you already know, static or default routing should be used with DDR networks. The primary reason for avoiding dynamic routing is that routers running dynamic routing protocols have a nasty habit of trying to communicate at regular intervals. Even link-state routing protocols exchange hellos. If DDR links were to come up for every routing update, most of the benefits of DDR over dedicated links would be lost. If DDR links don't come up, routers will assume that remote networks have gone away and will eventually delete the associated routes from their routing tables.

This objective section gives you the information that you need in order to configure DDR and allow only interesting traffic that is assigned by you to bring up the line, while still running dynamic routing protocols. It is important to remember that although you can use Snapshot routing in place of static or default routing it is only supported with distance-vector routing algorithms. This is very important to know when configuring BRI. The ACRC exam hits this whole chapter very hard, and this objective is no exception.

Critical Information

Snapshot routing allows some dynamic routing protocols to be run across DDR links, thus saving administrators the burden of configuring and maintaining static routes. With snapshot routing, DDR links are not required to be up all of the time. Also, routers that are configured with snapshot routing will not expire the routes learned via the DDR links (as they normally would when the links go down). Snapshot routing works only with distance-vector routing protocols (IP RIP, IPX RIP, RTMP, and IGRP). Link-state protocols, including EIGRP, are not candidates for snapshot routing.

Snapshot routing works best in hub-and-spoke topologies. With meshed DDR networks, static routing is still a better option. Also, snapshot routing is not for every hub-and-spoke network. A small network that is not likely to have many changes would probably still be easier to manage using static routing. Snapshot routing is most useful in large, dynamic hub-and-spoke DDR networks.

Operation of snapshot routing is relatively straightforward and includes the following three main steps:

1. Client (spoke) routers are configured with a routing update interval. This determines how often the client will contact the server (hub) router to exchange routing information. The server router will wait for the client router to contact it to exchange routing information.

2. When the interval is reached, the client router connects with the server router and exchanges routing information.

3. After exchanging routing information, the client router takes a snapshot of the newly updated routing table and "freezes" it. No updates to the routing table take place until the next scheduled update (even if the DDR link comes up for interesting traffic).

While waiting for the next scheduled update, the server routers will broadcast route updates to the rest of the network at normal intervals as if they really were connected to the client routers. They will not expire routes.

Necessary Procedures

Configuration of snapshot routing is relatively simple; only two commands are required on both client and server routers. Both commands, brief descriptions of which follow, are entered in Interface Configuration mode (physical or dialer interface):

- `snapshot client` or `snapshot server` enable snapshot routing.

- `dialer map` defines a dialer map

In the example below, Router A is a client router and Router B is the server router. Both routers are already configured for DDR, and then you add the following snapshot routing commands:

```
RouterA#config t
RouterA(config)#int BRI0
RouterA(config-if)#snapshot client 5 480 dialer
RouterA(config-if)#dialer map snapshot 1 name RouterB
    5556677
RouterA(config-if)#^Z
```

```
RouterB#config t
RouterB(config)#int dialer1
RouterB(config-if)#snapshot server 5 dialer
RouterB(config-if)#dialer map snapshot 1 name RouterA
    5556688
RouterB(config-if)#^Z
RouterB#
```

On Router A, when the snapshot client command is entered, the 5 specifies the time in minutes that the routers will spend communicating once they connect to exchange routing information. (Notice that the same parameter is used on Router B .) On Router A, 480 is specified as the number of minutes between connections (six hours). As mentioned, the client router controls the connection interval, so, while both routers must know and agree on the amount of time that they will be connected, only the client needs to know the interval at which they will connect; the server does not receive this information. The dialer keyword is optional and is used to allow the client to dial the server if the DDR link is not already up.

Exam Essentials

Remember that you set up a client and a server. Since Snapshot routing is used over a dialup WAN connection, you need to define the router on each side of the link as either the client or the snapshot server.

Remember how to configure a client. Use the snapshot client active-time quiet-time command string to set up a snapshot client.

Remember how to configure a server. Use the snapshot server active-timer command string to configure a server to use snapshot routing.

Remember how to set up a dialer map for each side. Use the dialer map snapshot sequence-number name name dial-string command string on each side of the DDR connection.

Key Terms and Concepts

BRI (Basic Rate Interface) A standard ISDN interface on a router that can be configured and plugged directly into an ISDN network. It can send data and voice with a bandwidth of 128K.

Multilink To aggregate several separate physical interfaces into a single virtual pipe.

PPP (Point-to-Point Protocol) Provides router-to-router and host-to-network connections over synchronous and asynchronous circuits.

Sample Questions

1. Which of the following statements is true regarding snapshot routing?

   A. It can save you money by keeping your dialup line running 24 hours a day.

   B. It is used instead of routing tables in a router.

   C. Snapshot routing works only with distance-vector routing protocols.

   D. Snapshot routing works only with link-state routing protocols.

   Answer: C—Cisco has decided that link-state protocols cannot be used with Snap shot routing.

2. What does the 480 represent in the following command?

`snapshot client 5 480 dialer`

A. The number of seconds between connections

B. The number of minutes between connections

C. The number of hours between connections

D. The number of packets that can be passed when connected

Answer: B—The client router must be configured with an active time and a quiet time. This tells the routers how often to update their routing tables with each other.

Configure IPX spoofing.

IPX is a big consideration when configuring a DDR link. IPX uses something called *keepalive* packets to keep a client logged into a server. If the server does not hear from a client in a predetermined amount of time, it will log them out. This feature is designed to help with Novell's stringent licensing requirements.

In this objective section, you learn about the watchdog feature of Novell servers and how to keep these clients from timing out across a dialup network. This is done by *spoofing* the server into thinking the clients are alive by using the router to keep the session alive instead of the workstations. This allows you to use a dialup connection and still use IPX networking. This is important to understand because, if you just configure your router to use interesting IP and IPX packets, your clients will time out. It is important to study and write out the commands needed for IPX spoofing.

Critical Information

NetWare servers are good sheepdogs; they keep track of their clients. Under normal circumstances, the NetWare server will send an IPX watchdog packet to the workstation if it hasn't heard from the workstation in a while. This assures the server that the workstation is still alive and working but that it's just not currently using the server's resources. Figure 14.1 shows a sample internetwork using dialup and IPX networking.

FIGURE 14.1: IPX server watchdog on LAN

NetWare Client   NetWare Server

For Figure 14.1, suppose that the workstation is running an application, such as RCONSOLE, that requires that the server and workstation establish an SPX connection. In an effort to maintain its connection, SPX will send periodic keepalive packets between the two machines. No problem? Well, consider the same client and server in Figure 14.2.

FIGURE 14.2: IPX server watchdog across DDR

DDR Connection

NetWare Client   NetWare Server

The server and workstation have a DDR connection between them. (Remember that IPX doesn't care about your internetwork; it wants to work like it's on a huge LAN.) You have a problem; either you can have the DDR link up all the time or you can risk having your SPX and watchdog timers time out. However, there is a solution for this one, which involves fooling the IPX servers.

The trick is to have the router answer the watchdog request or SPX keepalive as if it were the actual workstation or server. In the preceding figure, if the router on the Ethernet segment local to the server can respond to the watchdog request destined for the workstation across the DDR link, the DDR link never has to be started. Likewise, if the router on the same Ethernet segment as the workstation can respond to any SPX keepalives destined for the server, you can again protect your DDR link from unnecessary usage.

Necessary Procedures

The configuration of these responses is called *spoofing* and is as follows:

```
RouterC#configure term
Enter configuration commands, one per line. End with
    CNTL/Z.
RouterC(config)#int bri0
RouterC(config-if)#no ipx route-cache
RouterC(config-if)#ipx spx-spoof
RouterC(config-if)#ipx watchdog-spoof
RouterC(config-if)#ipx spx-idle-time 240
RouterC(config-if)#^Z
RouterC#
```

The BRI 0 interface will spoof both the SPX keepalive and watchdog packets rather than initiate a call. The no ipx route-cache command is required before entering the spoof commands. Remember that you can't just define the keepalive and watchdog packets as uninteresting to protect your DDR link because, if you do that, you'll cause timeouts on servers and workstations. You have to set up the spoofs shown here to protect your DDR link and keep your NetWare servers and clients happy too.

Exam Essentials

Remember that the *no ipx route-cache* command should be entered first. The IPX route cache is turned on by default. It allows the interfaces to run a CRC and takes some processing load off the router's CPU. However, the router will not look at the header of a packet and determine if it should be spoofed or not. It is important to turn off the IPX route cache.

Memorize the four spoofing commands and be able to write them down. The no ipx route-cache, ipx spx-spoof, ipx watchdog-spoof, and ipx spx-idle-time commands are the four commands you enter to set up IPX spoofing.

Key Terms and Concepts

BRI (Basic Rate Interface)   A standard ISDN interface on a router that can be configured and plugged directly into an ISDN network. It can send data and voice with a bandwidth of 128K.

Keepalive   Message sent by one network device to inform another network device that the virtual circuit between the two is still active.

Sample Questions

1. In the spaces provided, write in the four commands needed to set up IPX spoofing.

   ```
   RouterC#configure term
   RouterC(config)#int bri0
   RouterC(config-if)# _____
   RouterC(config-if)# _____
   RouterC(config-if)# _____
   RouterC(config-if)# _____
   ```

Answer: no `ipx route-cache`, `ipx spx-spoof`, `ipx watchdog-spoof`, and `ipx spx-idle-time` 240 are, repectively, the four commands needed to set up IPX spoofing.

2. In the space provided below, enter the command that should be entered first before any other IPX spoofing commands.

_____

Answer: no `ipx route-cache`. If you do not enter this command first, the router will not look inside the packets to determine the contents. The router needs to look in the packet to know whether to spoof or not to spoof.

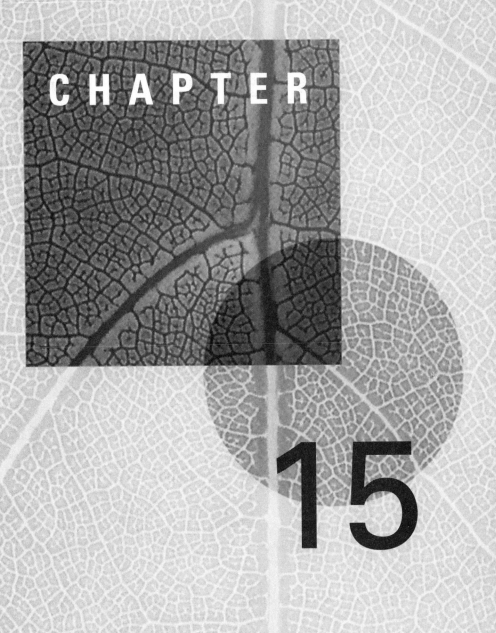

CHAPTER

15

Bridging Overview

Cisco ACRC Exam Objectives Covered in This Chapter:

▶ **Define routable and nonroutable protocols and give an example of each.** *(pages 313 – 316)*

▶ **Define various bridging types and describe when to use each type.** *(pages 317 – 320)*

Bridging is a method of connecting individual network segments so that they look like a single LAN. Bridging takes place at layer two of the OSI model, as opposed to routing, which takes place at layer three. See Figure 15.1.

FIGURE 15.1: OSI-model bridge routing

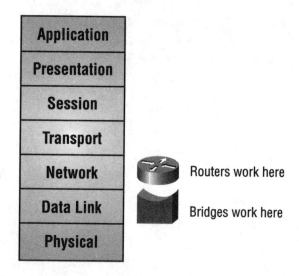

Application	
Presentation	
Session	
Transport	
Network	Routers work here
Data Link	Bridges work here
Physical	

Traffic must be bridged, rather than routed, for many reasons. For starters, some network protocols cannot be routed and must be bridged. (This chapter will take a look at several of those protocols.) With Ethernet networks, bridging is a common method of controlling collisions and reducing contention for the media. (If you haven't heard of Ethernet switches over the last few years, you must not have been paying attention, because they are everywhere!) Ethernet switches are really nothing more than multi-port bridges (on steroids, of course). Their operation is similar to that of the transparent bridges that will be discussed later.

This chapter also details the different types of bridging support available with Cisco routers. And Chapter 16 presents bridging configurations.

This is an important chapter to understand because of the background that is detailed throughout it. So, before moving on to Chapter 16, where you learn how to configure a Cisco router with bridging, you need to have a good understanding of the basics. This chapter gives you that.

When studying, be sure to understand the configurations in the chapter by practicing on routers. If you can't do that, practice printing out the commands on paper.

Define routable and nonroutable protocols and give an example of each.

A routable protocol is a protocol that has a logical Network-layer address. This address can be used to route packets through an internetwork and deliver them to remote networks. A nonroutable protocol does not have Network-layer information in its header and only uses Data-Link (layer two) addresses. These addresses can only be used on a local network and cannot be routed. This means that nonroutable protocols can only be transmitted and received on one broadcast domain, and they cannot pass through routers to another network.

This objective section shows you why configuring a Cisco router with both routing and bridging is important when business requirements dictate that both types of protocols must be used on your internetwork. To pass your ACRC exam, you must understand how both bridging and routing work, including how they work together.

Critical Information

Since bridges operate at layer two rather than layer three of the OSI model, they don't see all of the protocol-dependent things with which routers have to deal. For example, IP and IPX packets are really indistinguishable to a bridge. IP and IPX are layer-three specifications, and the bridge really doesn't care about their differences. The bridge simply focuses on the layer-two frames and avoids the hassle of looking any further.

Bridging creates a single, extended, Data-Link network. This is often referred to as a *flat* network. With Cisco IOS, all routable protocols can be bridged. However, don't think that this is an easy shortcut to avoid routing. Bridging creates its own special concerns. For example, bridges will forward broadcasts, while routers will block them, which means that while 1500 workstations will work nicely in a routed network they may melt the wire with broadcasts alone in a bridged one.

The following sections take a quick look at some situations where you have to bridge.

Routable and Non-Routable Protocols

Some protocols cannot be routed. In their specifications, they simply do not provide for layer-three network addressing. That means they must share a common Data-Link network (layer two) to communicate, which calls for bridging. These non-routable protocols are as follows:

- LAT (Local Area Transport)
- MOP (Maintenance Operation Protocol)
- NetBEUI

NetBIOS is the interface used in Windows and should not be confused with NetBEUI, which is a Data-Link-layer protocol created to work with NetBIOS. It carries address information that is not logical and, therefore, cannot be routed. Because of the popularity of

Microsoft Windows NT (which uses NetBIOS), some networks must be bridged.

With NT, you can configure IP or IPX as the default protocol. However, if you have machines on multiple segments using NetBEUI as the sole communications protocol, you will have to bridge between those segments so that those machines can communicate.

Exam Essentials

Understand where bridging is specified with the OSI Reference model. Bridging works by creating smaller collision domains and by filtering by the hardware (MAC) address of network devices. Since Bridges use MAC addresses for filtering a network, bridges are specified at the MAC sub-layer of the Data Link layer.

Be able to list some routable and nonroutable protocols. IP and IPX are examples of routable protocols. Examples of nonroutable protocols are LAT, MOP, and NetBEUI.

Remember why you would use bridging. If you have protocols that must be supported and you cannot change to a routable protocol, then, to allow network devices to communicate between network segments, you must enable bridging.

Remember that bridges do not create smaller broadcast domains. Bridges create smaller collision domains, but the network is still one large broadcast domain because bridges do not stop broadcasts from propagating throughout the network.

Key Terms and Concepts

Routable Protocols Can use layer-three logical information to send data packets to remote networks.

Nonroutable protocols Only use layer-two information to find a device. Cannot be transmitted through a router by default.

Sample Questions

1. Which of the following protocols cannot be routed?

   A. IP

   B. SPX

   C. NetBEUI

   D. LAT

   Answer: C, D—NetBEUI and LAT, as well as MOP, cannot be routed, and they only work at the Data Link layer.

2. Which of the following is a reason why you would enable bridging on your router?

   A. When you have devices on the same network segments that need to communicate with each other but they either cannot run a bridgeable protocol or refuse to add a bridgeable protocol

   B. When you have devices on separate network segments that need to communicate with each other but they either cannot run a bridgeable protocol or refuse to add a bridgeable protocol

   C. When you have devices on the same network segments that need to communicate with each other but they either cannot run a routable protocol or refuse to add a routable protocol

   D. When you have devices on separate network segments that need to communicate with each other but they either cannot run a routable protocol or refuse to add a routable protocol

   Answer: D—Bridging should be enabled when you have to communicate across a network segment but the devices cannot or will not install a routing protocol.

Define various bridging types and describe when to use each type.

This objective section teaches you about the different types of bridging support on Cisco routers, and Chapter 16 continues that by teaching you how to configure a few of the bridging types. It is important to understand the differences between the bridging types before you configure bridging.

When studying for your exam, this objective will be very helpful for a quick review of the different types of Cisco bridging support available.

Critical Information

This objective discusses the big picture of the different types of bridging support available on Cisco routers. The following are the four bridging types, and each of these are discussed in the following sections:

- Transparent bridging
- Source-route bridging
- Source-route transparent bridging
- Source-route translational bridging

Transparent Bridging

A transparent bridge can connect two or more network segments into a single Data-Link LAN. It is called a transparent bridge because the devices on the network are unaware that the bridge is even there. The bridge simply listens to frames and passes them along. It does not address, modify, or receive frames. It really is transparent to the devices on the network.

Transparent bridging is generally used with Ethernet. To be transparent to network devices, the bridge performs certain functions:

- Learning MAC addresses

- Forwarding packets

- Filtering packets

These functions allow the bridge to act transparently. Additionally, with multiple bridges, there is the possibility of an endless loop, so the bridge is required to perform a fourth function:

- Avoiding loops

Source-Route Bridging

IBM created source-route bridging (SRB) in the mid-1980s to connect corporate Token Rings to their IBM mainframes. With SRB, the source knows the entire route to a destination before any data are transmitted. It is called source-route bridging because the source device gets to choose the entire route to the destination device. SRB is part of the IEEE 802.5 Token Ring specification.

SRB was not designed for large internetworks. The specifications for IBM Token Ring define a maximum of eight rings and seven bridges. 802.5 defines up to 14 rings and 13 bridges.

Source-Route Transparent Bridging

Source-route transparent bridging (SRT) was introduced by IBM in 1990. With SRT, both SRB and transparent bridging occur within the same device. You can use SRT on Token Ring networks where some devices are doing SRB but some are not. SRT does not translate between two bridging domains; the SRB and transparent bridging systems do not communicate via the SRT. If the traffic arrives with SRB routing information, SRB is used. If not, transparent bridging is used. Token-Ring-to-Ethernet communication is not provided by SRT.

Source-Route Translational Bridging

Source-route translational bridging (SR/TLB) is used when bridging domains must be crossed. With SRT, it is possible to do both SRB and transparent bridging. With SR/TLB, SRB and transparent bridging domains can now communicate. With SRT, communication from Ethernet to Token Ring is not supported. With SR/TLB, that issue is addressed. SRB generally runs on a Token Ring network, while transparent bridging is generally associated with Ethernet. It should be noted that SR/TLB is a Cisco IOS feature and is not an industry standard.

Exam Essentials

Remember the four types of bridging support on Cisco routers. Transparent bridging, source-route bridging, source-route transparent bridging, and source-route translational bridging are the four types of Cisco bridging support.

Remember the four functions that transparent bridging provides. Transparent bridging provides for learning MAC addresses, forwarding packets, filtering packets, and avoiding network loops.

Understand how source-route bridging works. With SRB, the source knows the entire route to a destination before any data are transmitted.

Key Terms and Concepts

Source-route bridging A bridging protocol that works by having the source hosts know the entire route to a destination before any data are transmitted.

Transparent bridging A bridging protocol that can connect two or more network segments into a single Data-Link LAN. It is called a transparent bridge because the devices on the network are unaware that the bridge is even there.

Sample Questions

1. How does source-route bridging work?

   A. Application.

   B. Presentation.

   C. The destination knows the entire route to a source before any data are transmitted.

   D. The source knows the entire route to a destination before any data are transmitted.

   Answer: D—Created by IBM, each device knows the complete network route to get to a destination host before transmitting any data.

2. Transparent bridges perform what four functions?

   A. Routing packets

   B. Learning MAC addresses

   C. Learning the entire route to a destination before transmitting any data

   D. Forwarding packets

   E. Filtering packets

   F. Avoiding loops

   Answer: B, D, E, F—Transparent bridging is generally used with Ethernet. To be transparent to network devices, the bridge performs certain functions, as listed above.

CHAPTER

16

Configuring Transparent
Bridging and Integrated
Routing and Bridging

Cisco ACRC Exam Objectives Covered in This Chapter:

▶ **Configure transparent bridging.** *(pages 322 – 330)*

▶ **Configure integrated Routing and Bridging (IRB).**
(pages 330 – 336)

T his chapter further explores the concepts of bridging. Bridging is fundamentally different from routing in that it operates on a completely different level. As indicated by the objectives, transparent bridging is discussed first, and then the chapter moves on to cover configuring both integrated routing and bridging (IRB).

As you probably recall, a transparent bridge can connect two or more network segments into a single Data-Link LAN. It is called a transparent bridge because the devices on the network are unaware that the bridge is even there. The bridge simply listens to frames and passes them along. It does not address, modify, or receive frames. The bridge really is transparent to the devices on the network.

Integrated routing and bridging (IRB) is an IOS 11.2 feature that allows you to route and bridge the same protocol within a single router. Normally, you cannot have packets cross a single router between routed and bridged interfaces. However, with IRB, you can.

This chapter shows you how to configure both transparent bridging and integrated routing and bridging. These are important objectives because they are used so often on networks with NT devices. For the ACRC exam, you will need to be able to configure transparent bridging and integrated routing and bridging.

Configure transparent bridging.

A s you already can tell, this first objective shows you how to configure transparent bridging on Cisco routers. There is not a lot of work involved, but it can be confusing if you are not careful. Read this objective carefully and then practice on routers if you can.

This is an important objective because it allows you to both troubleshoot an existing Cisco bridging environment as well as configure a new Cisco bridging environment. Either practice the commands covered in this objective on a Cisco router or write them out on paper.

Critical Information

Configuration of transparent bridging is relatively simple. For example, suppose that you encounter the scenario shown in Figure 16.1.

F I G U R E 16.1: NT network

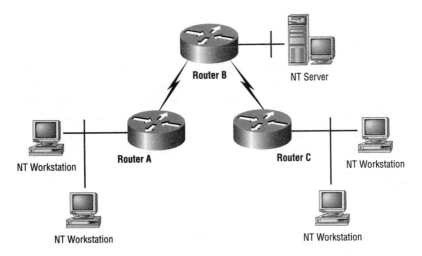

You have Windows NT workstations and servers on different segments. If you are running NetBEUI, you need to bridge so that these devices can communicate with each other. You need to start the configuration on each router by using the `bridge 1 protocol ieee` command. The 1 indicates the bridge-group number that is used on each individual interface. This command is not required; you could omit it to disable the Spanning Tree Protocol (STP).

On Router B, the `bridge 1 priority 0` command is used in Global Configuration mode. This sets the priority by setting the spanning tree root to zero on Router B, meaning that it will most likely become the root. You need to do this on only one router per bridge group. This command is also not required unless you wish to influence the root election process. Make sure to select a router near the center of your bridge-group network.

Finally, on each interface, after entering Interface Configuration mode, use the `bridge-group 1` command to make that interface a member of the bridge group. Any interfaces with this command applied will be part of the same bridged network. At this point, all five segments (three Ethernet, two serial) in the sample network are part of the same flat network. Your NT workstations running NetBEUI are now be able to communicate with the NT server without any problems.

Avoiding Loops

Redundant paths can be good or bad. When they work correctly, redundant paths provide fault tolerance for certain failures. However, when redundant paths do not work correctly, they can cause complete network failure. This is important to understand when configuring bridging because Cisco supports two protocols and you need to understand how they work. Consider the network shown in Figure 16.2.

F I G U R E   16.2:   Redundant bridges

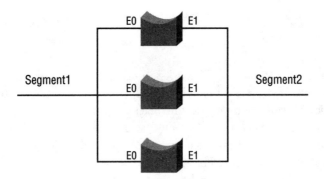

Three bridges connect Segment 1 and Segment 2. All three bridges hear all frames on each segment; all three bridges also build MAC address databases. However, what if all three bridges forward frames? Suppose that a frame on Segment 1 is destined for a device on Segment 2 and that all three bridges forward the frame. How will the destination device react when it receives three identical frames? It will probably be a bit confused.

There is, however, a worse case. Suppose that a *broadcast* is issued on Segment 1. All three bridges will pick it up and flood it to Segment 2. But now each bridge hears two broadcasts on Segment 2—one from each of the other two bridges. They are actually copies of the same broadcast, but, since these are transparent bridges, there is no way to know that. So each bridge floods the two broadcasts it receives on Segment 2 back to Segment 1. Now there are six frames on Segment 1, which become 12 frames on Segment 2, which becomes 24 frames on Segment 1, and so on. This is called a *broadcast storm*, and it is a real problem with topological loops and bridges. As this example shows, a single broadcast frame can cause a broadcast storm that will consume all available bandwidth in seconds.

This problem results from the transparent nature of the bridges. Routers tear apart and rebuild packets and, therefore, can address issues such as TTL, number of hops, etc. They also handle broadcasts much differently from bridges. However, transparent bridges by definition do not modify packets. They just filter, forward, or flood. Of course, there is a solution.

Spanning Tree Protocol

The Spanning Tree Protocol solves this problem. It allows multiple paths to exist for fault tolerance, yet it creates a loop-free topology to reduce the risk of broadcast storms. It does this by turning off (blocking) unnecessary interfaces until they are needed. For example, in the preceding example, you may end up with the situation that is illustrated in Figure 16.3 on the next page.

Spanning Tree Protocol will turn off (block) the interfaces, which will cause loops, and then re-enable the interfaces when necessary for fault tolerance (in case another active path fails, for example).

FIGURE 16.3: Spanning Tree implemented

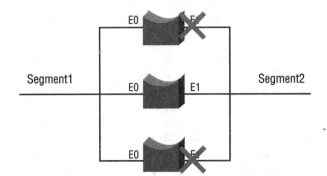

Cisco supports two Spanning Tree Protocols for transparent bridging. They are not compatible; they will not communicate with each other. They are as follows:

- DEC
- IEEE 802.1D

The IEEE protocol was actually derived from work done by DEC; nevertheless, they are not compatible.

Verifying Configurations

As with all configurations discussed in this book, verification of your configuration is just as important as the configuration itself. To verify your configuration, you can use the following two commands:

- `show bridge`
- `show span`

Necessary Procedures

This section shows you sample bridging configurations for three routers.

Router A

```
RouterA#config t
Enter configuration commands, one per line.  End with
    CNTL/Z.
RouterA(config)#bridge 1 protocol ieee
RouterA(config)#int s0
RouterA(config-if)#bridge-group 1
RouterA(config-if)#int e0
RouterA(config-if)#bridge-group 1
RouterA(config-if)#^Z
RouterA#
```

Router B

```
RouterB#config t
Enter configuration commands, one per line.  End with
    CNTL/Z.
RouterB(config)#bridge 1 protocol ieee
RouterB(config)#bridge 1 priority 0
RouterB(config)#int s0
RouterB(config-if)#bridge-group 1
RouterB(config-if)#int s1
RouterB(config-if)#bridge-group 1
RouterB(config-if)#int e0
RouterB(config-if)#bridge-group 1
RouterB(config-if)#^Z
RouterB#
```

Router C

```
RouterC#config t
Enter configuration commands, one per line.  End with
    CNTL/Z.
RouterC(config)#bridge 1 protocol ieee
RouterC(config)#int s0
RouterC(config-if)#bridge-group 1
RouterC(config-if)#int e0
RouterC(config-if)#bridge-group 1
RouterC(config-if)#^Z
RouterC#
```

Verification of Configurations

You can use a few commands to verify operation of your bridge. This section presents the show bridge and show span commands.

```
RouterC#show bridge

Total of 300 station blocks, 298 free
Codes: P - permanent, S - self

Bridge Group 1:

Address          Action      Interface      Age   RX count     TX count
0000.0c5d.6ec8   forward     Ethernet0      1     1            0
0000.0c3e.822a   forward     Ethernet0      4     1            0

RouterC#
```

The show bridge command displays the contents of the database of learned MAC addresses. The Total of 300 station blocks, 298 free line refers to the database entries. When the number of free blocks falls below 25, another block of 300 will be issued. The two entries are listed under bridge group 1. Their MAC address, action (discard or forward), interface where they are located, and age are displayed.

```
RouterC#show span

Bridge Group 1 is executing the IEEE compatible Spanning
  Tree protocol
  Bridge Identifier has priority 32768, address
    0000.0c3e.822a
  Configured hello time 2, max age 20, forward delay 15
  Current root has priority 0, address 0000.0c5d.6ec8
  Root port is 3 (Serial0), cost of root path is 17857
  Topology change flag not set, detected flag not set
  Times:  hold 1, topology change 30, notification 30
          hello 2, max age 20, forward delay 15,
            aging 300
  Timers: hello 0, topology change 0, notification 0
```

```
Port 2 (Ethernet0) of bridge group 1 is forwarding
    Port path cost 100, Port priority 128
    Designated root has priority 0, address 0000.0c5d.6ec8
    Designated bridge has priority 32768, address
        0000.0c3e.822a
    Designated port is 2, path cost 17857
    Timers: message age 0, forward delay 0, hold 1

Port 3 (Serial0) of bridge group 1 is forwarding
    Port path cost 17857, Port priority 128
    Designated root has priority 0, address 0000.0c5d.6ec8
    Designated bridge has priority 0, address
        0000.0c5d.6ec8
    Designated port is 3, path cost 0
    Timers: message age 1, forward delay 0, hold 0

RouterC#
```

The show span command will give you the output of the bridge and STP information configured on all interfaces.

Exam Essentials

It is essential that you understand how to configure transparent bridging. You need to configure the bridge by first using the global bridge 1 protocol command and then assigning that bridge group to an interface with the bridge-group command.

Understand how the Spanning Tree Protocol stops network loops. It allows multiple paths to exist for fault tolerance, yet it creates a loop-free topology to reduce the risk of broadcast storms.

Remember the two protocols that Cisco supports for bridging. Cisco supports two Spanning Tree Protocols for transparent bridging: DEC and IEEE 802.1D. They are not compatible, and they will not communicate with each other.

Key Terms and Concepts

STP (Spanning Tree Protocol)   Used in bridged environments to stop network loops.

Transparent bridge   Connects two or more network segments into a single data-link LAN. It is called a transparent bridge because the devices on the network are unaware that the bridge is even there.

Sample Questions

1. Type in the command to bridge the IEEE protocol for bridge group 1.

   Answer: `bridge 1 protocol ieee`

2. Which of the following is true about the STP?

   A. Used in both routing and bridging environments

   B. Used in stopping broadcast storms

   C. Finds redundant paths

   D. Stops routing loops

   Answer: C—The Spanning Tree Protocol is used to stop loops in networks that have redundant links.

Configure integrated Routing and Bridging (IRB).

Integrated routing and bridging is accomplished by creating a bridge-group virtual interface (BVI), which represents the bridge group in the routed environment. The interface number of the BVI must correspond to the bridge-group number you wish to include in

IRB. The BVI can then be configured and will act just like any other routed interface.

This is an important objective to understand and study. Careful study of the objective will allow you to understand how bridging and routing can work together both when you are troubleshooting an existing environment and when configuring a new IRB Cisco internetwork. As with the other objectives concerning configurations, you should either practice the commands in this objective on a Cisco router or be able to write them out on paper.

Critical Information

BVI configuration can be useful when you have to connect bridged and routed networks, or perhaps when you need to preserve network addresses (such as IP) and yet still route those protocols to a larger internetwork.

There are several steps to the configuration:

- Use the `bridge irb` command to enable IRB.

- Use the `interface bvi1` command to create the BVI with the appropriate bridge-group number.

- Configure the BVI. (It's given an IP address.)

- Back in Global Configuration mode, enter the `bridge 1 route ip` command. (This allows the BVI to accept IP packets from bridge group 1 and route them.)

- Enter the `no bridge 1 bridge ip` command to tell the BVI *not* to bridge IP packets. (It's already been told not to route them. By default, it will bridge them unless you route them.)

After you configure the IRB, you may use the following couple of commands—explained in the Necessary Procedures section—to verify your configuration:

- `show int bvi 1`

- `show int s0 irb`

Necessary Procedures

Consider Figure 16.4, supposing that you need to bridge from Router A to Router C, but you want to route to the Ethernet interface on Router B. You can then configure IRB on Router B.

FIGURE 16.4: IRB example

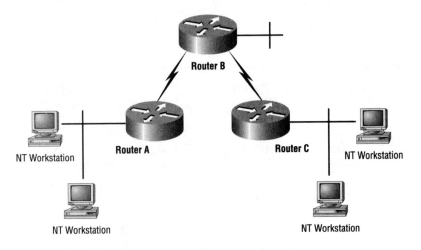

Here is the configuration:

```
RouterB#config t
Enter configuration commands, one per line.  End with
    CNTL/Z.
RouterB(config)#bridge irb
RouterB(config)#interface bvi1
RouterB(config-if)#ip address 171.16.20.2 255.255.255.0
RouterB(config-if)#exit
RouterB(config)#bridge 1 route ip
RouterB(config)#no bridge 1 bridge ip
RouterB(config)#^Z
RouterB#
```

Here is your final configuration:

```
RouterB#show running

<clip>

interface Ethernet0
 ip address 172.16.30.1 255.255.255.0
!
interface Serial0
 no ip address
 bandwidth 56
 clockrate 56000
 bridge-group 1
!
interface Serial1
 no ip address
 bandwidth 56
 clockrate 56000
 bridge-group 1
!
interface BVI1
 ip address 171.16.20.2 255.255.255.0
!
router rip
 network 172.16.0.0
!
no ip classless
bridge irb
bridge 1 protocol ieee
 bridge 1 route ip
 no bridge 1 bridge ip
bridge 1 priority 0
```

You can verify the function of the BVI by using the show interface command, and you can verify the status of bridged and routed protocols in individual interfaces by using the show interface int irb command. Output from these commands follows:

```
RouterB#show int bvi1
BVI1 is up, line protocol is up
  Hardware is BVI, address is 0000.0ced.e620 (bia
    0000.0000.0000)
  Internet address is 171.16.20.2/24
  MTU 1500 bytes, BW 10000 Kbit, DLY 5000 usec,
    rely 255/   255, load 1/255
  Encapsulation ARPA, loopback not set, keepalive set
    (10 sec)
  ARP type: ARPA, ARP Timeout 04:00:00
  Last input never, output never, output hang never
  Last clearing of "show interface" counters never
  Queueing strategy: fifo
  Output queue 0/0, 0 drops; input queue 0/75, 0 drops
  5 minute input rate 0 bits/sec, 0 packets/sec
  5 minute output rate 0 bits/sec, 0 packets/sec
    0 packets input, 0 bytes, 0 no buffer
    Received 0 broadcasts, 0 runts, 0 giants,
0 throttles
    0 input errors, 0 CRC, 0 frame, 0 overrun,
0 ignored, 0      abort
    0 packets output, 0 bytes, 0 underruns
    0 output errors, 0 collisions, 0 interface resets
    0 output buffer failures, 0 output buffers
swapped out
RouterB#show int s0 irb

Serial0

  Routed protocols on Serial0:
    ip

  Bridged protocols on Serial0:
    appletalk  decnet     ip          ipx
```

```
Software MAC address filter on Serial0
Hash Len    Address      Matches  Act      Type
0x00:  0  ffff.ffff.ffff        0 RCV  Physical
broadcast
0x2A:  0  0900.2b01.0001        0 RCV  DEC spanning
tree
0x2C:  0  0000.0ced.e620        0 RCV  Bridge-group
Virtual    Interface
0xC2:  0  0180.c200.0000        0 RCV  IEEE spanning
tree
0xC4:  0  0000.0c5d.6ec8        0 RCV  Interface MAC
address
RouterB#
```

Exam Essentials

Remember the commands to run integrated routing and bridging. The steps for integrated routing and bridging follow:

- Use the `bridge irb` command to enable IRB.

- Use the `interface bvi1` command to create the BVI with the appropriate bridge-group number.

- Configure the BVI. (you gave it an IP address)

- Back in Global Configuration mode, enter the `bridge 1 route ip` command. (This allows the BVI to accept IP packets from bridge group 1 and route them.)

- Enter the `no bridge 1 bridge ip` command to tell the BVI *not* to bridge IP packets. (You already told it to route them. By default, it will bridge them unless you route them.)

Remember how to verify your configuration. You can verify your configuration of integrated routing and bridging by using the `show interface bvi1` command as well as the `show interface s0 irb` command.

Key Terms and Concepts

IRB (integrated routing and bridging)   Used to basically make your router a brouter (or a bridge and router simultaneously).

BVI (bridge-group virtual interface)   Represents the bridge group in the routed environment.

Sample Questions

1. What is the correct ordering of the steps to configure IRB on your router?

1. Use the `bridge irb` command to enable IRB.

2. Configure the BVI.

3. Use the `interface bvi1` command to create the BVI with the appropriate bridge-group number.

4. Back in Global Configuration mode, enter the `bridge 1 route ip` command.

5. Enter the `no bridge 1 bridge ip` command to tell the BVI *not* to bridge IP packets.

   A. 5, 3, 4, 2, 1

   B. 1, 3, 2, 4, 5

   C. 2, 4, 3, 1, 5

   D. 3, 1, 2, 5, 4

   Answer: B—Turn on IRB, create a BVI interface, configure the BVI, turn on routing, and tell the router which ports are not bridged.

2. Enter the command to create a BVI.

   Answer: `interface bvi1`

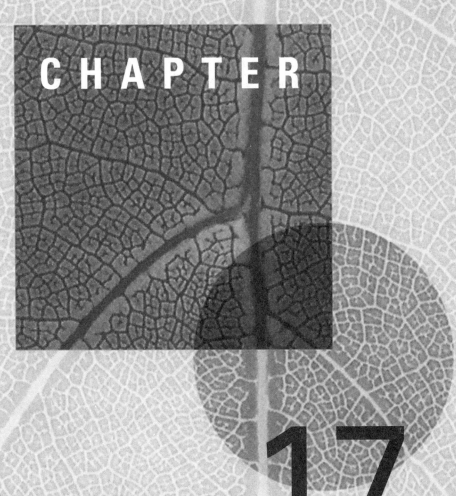

CHAPTER

17

Configuring
Source-Route Bridging

Cisco ACRC Exam Objectives Covered in This Chapter:

▶ **Describe the basic functions of source-route bridging (SRB).** *(pages 339 – 342)*

▶ **Configure SRB.** *(pages 342 – 346)*

▶ **Configure source-route transparent bridging (SRT).** *(pages 347 – 350)*

▶ **Configure source-route translational bridging (SR/TLB).** *(pages 350 – 358)*

▶ **Verify SRB operation.** *(pages 358 – 363)*

IBM created the source-route bridging (SRB) algorithm to bridge between local area networks (LANs). It was then adopted into the IEEE 802.5 Token Ring LAN specification. IBM has created new bridging standards since that time called source-route transparent (SRT) bridging. This chapter builds on information in preceding chapters by discussing the difference between SRB and SRT.

Source-route bridging got its name from the fact that the transmitting host knows the complete path to the destination host before transmitting. This information is put into the frame. Source-route transparent bridging was designed to replace source-route bridging. This has not yet happened, as is evidenced by the many plain source-route bridges running today. Transparent bridging is a bridging scheme used in Ethernet and IEEE 802.3 networks. It passes frames along one hop at a time, using routing information stored in tables that associate end nodes within bridge ports. This type of bridging is considered transparent because the source node doesn't need to know the entire route, as it does with source-route bridging. Translational bridging—called source-route translational bridging (SR/TLB)—allows source-route devices to communicate with transparent bridge devices.

This chapter shows you the basic functions of source-route bridging and also how to configure source-route bridging on your Cisco routers. It then discusses source-route transparent bridging, source-route translational bridging, and also how to configure both on your Cisco routers. The chapter finishes by showing you the commands to verify source-route operations. This chapter has only four objectives; however, remember that size doesn't matter when studying for the ACRC exam.

Describe the basic functions of source-route bridging (SRB).

To run both routable and nonroutable protocols together on your Cisco router, you can use source-route bridging. When source-route bridging is enabled, the router can then make routing decisions based on the MAC address in the frame. The advantage to this is that, if the routing functions are used at the Data Link layer, the Network-layer protocols can run their tasks more efficiently.

In this objective, the basic functions of source-route bridging are discussed. This is important to understand before moving into the next objective, which covers configuring SRB. Make sure you have a firm understanding of source-route bridging when studying for your ACRC exam.

Critical Information

As has already been indicated, IBM designed source-route bridging to extend Token Ring LANs. This is now handled completely by the IEEE 802.5 committee. The routing information field (RIF) in a Token Ring frame is used by the transmitting host to tell the frame which rings or Token Ring network segments the packet must transit to get to the destination device. The transmitting station, or source station, inserts the RIF into the MAC header immediately following the source address field in every frame, which is where the name *source-route* comes from.

When the destination station sends information back to the originating station, it just reverses the RIF field. The originating device finds the information to place in a RIF field by using explorer packets. Explorer packets are generated by the source node and traverse the entire network looking for possible paths to the destination device.

SRB was not designed for large internetworks. The specifications for IBM Token Ring define a maximum of eight rings and seven bridges. 802.5 defines up to 14 rings and 13 bridges.

Types of Explorer Packets

A source device determines the best path to a destination device by sending explorer packets. The following are the three types of explorer packets and what they are used for:

All-routes explorer packets   Find all routes to a destination host by checking all rings.

Local explorer packets   Find local destination devices.

Spanning explorer packets   Find the best route to the final destination.

NOTE   All-routes explorer packets are also known as *all-rings explorer packets,* and spanning explorer packets are also known as *single-route* and *limited-route explorer packets.*

Here is how the three types of explorer packets work together to find a route to a destination device:

1. A NetBIOS or SNA device generates a local explorer packet to determine if the destination device is connected to the local ring.

2. If the destination device is not located on the local ring, the transmitting device sends either a spanning or an all-routes explorer packet. (A NetBIOS device sends a spanning explorer packet, while the SNA device sends an all-routes explorer packet.)

3. The destination device responds to the explorer packets, which then return to the originating device. By examining the RIF, the source can determine the route to take to the destination.

From that point forward, the source will determine the path—hence the name *source-route bridging.*

Exam Essentials

Understand what source-route bridging is. The routing information field in a Token Ring frame is used by the transmitting host to tell the frame which rings or Token Ring network segments the packet must transit to get to the destination device. The source host understands the complete path to the remote network—hence the name *source-routing.*

Understand what local explorer packets are used for. Local explorer packets are used to find local destination devices.

Understand what spanning explorer packets are used for. Spanning explorer packets are used to find the best route to the final destination.

Understand what all-routes explorer packets are used for. All-routes explorer packets are used to find all routes to a destination host by checking all rings.

Key Terms and Concepts

Explorer packets   Used to find a destination device.

SNA (Systems Network Architecture)   A protocol stack created by IBM to connect devices—local and remote—to IBM mainframes.

Source-route bridging algorithm   Bridging protocol that finds the complete route to a destination device before transmitting.

Sample Questions

1. Which of the following statements accurately describes what a RIF is used for?

   A. Directs the frame to a source network

   B. Directs the frame to a destination network

   C. Identifies the upper-layer protocol

   D. Identifies the Transport-layer protocol

   Answer: B—The routing information field in a Token Ring frame is used by the transmitting host to tell the frame which rings or Token Ring network segments the packet must transit to get to the destination device.

2. Which of the following statements is true regarding the RIF?

   A. The RIF is placed in the LLC header after the source address.

   B. The RIF is placed in the LLC header after the destination address.

   C. The RIF is placed in the MAC header after the source address.

   D. The RIF is placed in the MAC header after the destination address.

   Answer: C—The transmitting station, or source station, inserts the RIF into the MAC header immediately following the source address field in every frame, which is where the name *source-route* comes from.

Configure SRB.

The purpose of a source-route bridge is to connect multiple physical Token Rings into one logical network segment. When only Token Ring networks are used to bridge between networks, it is called source-route bridging. It is referred to as remote source-route bridging when you bridge between a Token Ring network and another type of network (for example, Ethernet).

This objective focuses on how to configure source-route bridging on a Cisco router. This is important if you have a Token Ring network and run protocols that cannot be routed. When studying for the ACRC exam, configure SRB by writing out the answers on paper.

Critical Information

This section shows you the commands used in configuring source-route bridging. It is important to understand how to configure SRB with both the manual Spanning-Tree configuration and the automatic Spanning-Tree configuration.

To configure source-route bridging with the manual Spanning-Tree configuration, use the following commands:

- `config t` takes you to global configuration mode.

- `interface to0` chooses your interface to configure.

- `source-bridge 401 5 400` chooses the local ring number of 401, the target ring of 400, and the bridge number of 5.

- `source-bridge spanning` turns on manual Spanning Tree Protocol (STP).

- `interface to1` chooses the interface to bridge with.

- `source-bridge 400 5 401`, on the second interface (to1), chooses the local ring number of 400, the target ring of 401, and the bridge number of 5.

- `source-bridge spanning` turns on the Spanning Tree Protocol.

To enable the automatic Spanning Tree configuration, use the following commands:

- `config t` takes you to global configuration mode.

- **bridge 10 protocol ibm** creates a bridge number of 10, using the IBM protocol. (You can choose three protocols: DEC protocol, IBM protocol, and the IEEE 802.1 protocol.)

- **interface to0** chooses the first interface.

- **source-bridge 401 5 400** chooses the local ring number of 401, the target ring of 400, and the ring number of 5.

- **source-bridge spanning 10** uses an automatic SpanningTree Protocol.

- **interface to1** chooses the other interface on the router that is participating in the bridging.

- **source-bridge 400 5 401** chooses the local ring number of 400, the target ring of 401, and the bridge number of 5.

- **source-bridge spanning 10** turns on the automatic Spanning Tree Protocol (1–63), which is the SRB spanning-group number.

Necessary Procedures

This section demonstrates the commands used in configuring source-route bridging. Use figure 17.1 as an example of how to configure source-route bridging.

FIGURE 17.1: SRB example

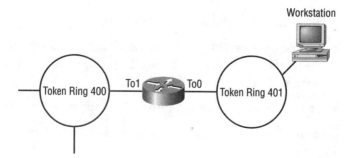

In this situation, you use a manual Spanning Tree configuration. Here is the configuration example:

```
RouterB#config t
Enter configuration commands, one per line. End with
   CNTL/Z.
RouterB(config)#interface to0
RouterB(config-if)#source-bridge 401 5 400
RouterB(config-if)#source-bridge spanning
RouterB(config-if)#interface to1
RouterB(config-if)#source-bridge 400 5 401
RouterB(config-if)#source-bridge spanning
RouterB(config-if)#^Z
RouterB#
```

Use the `source-bridge 401 5 400` command on interface to0 to indicate that the local ring is 401, the target ring is 400, and the bridge number is 5. You do the inverse on interface to1. The `source-bridge spanning` command indicates that you are using a manual Spanning Tree configuration. If you want to enable automatic Spanning Tree configuration, proceed as follows:

```
RouterB#config t
Enter configuration commands, one per line. End with
   CNTL/Z.
RouterB(config)#bridge 10 protocol ibm
RouterB(config)#interface to0
RouterB(config-if)#source-bridge 401 5 400
RouterB(config-if)#source-bridge spanning 10
RouterB(config-if)#interface to1
RouterB(config-if)#source-bridge 400 5 401
RouterB(config-if)#source-bridge spanning 10
```

The first configuration in this section uses the `source-bridge spanning` command, which enables the forwarding of spanning-tree explorers on all ring interfaces. The second configuration uses the automatic spanning-tree configuration. The `source-bridge spanning 10` command configures a bridge group to run the automatic spanning-tree function.

Exam Essentials

You must understand what the command string is to configure source-route bridging. `source-bridge 401 5 400` chooses the local ring number of 401, the target ring of 400, and the bridge number of 5.

Remember the three bridging protocols available. IEEE is used between disparate bridges; IBM is used with IBM bridges; and DEC is used with DEC bridges.

Key Terms and Concepts

Local ring   Where the source device is located.

Source-route bridging algorithm   Bridging protocol that finds the complete route to a destination device before transmitting.

Spanning Tree Protocol   Created by IBM to stop network loops for sites that have more than one link to a remote network. Works only at layer two.

Target Ring   Where the destination device is located.

Sample Questions

1. Type in the command to create a source bridge ring of 400, target ring of 401, with a bridge number of 6.

Answer: `source-bridge 400 6 401` chooses the local ring of 400, the target ring of 401, and the bridge number of 6.

2. Type in the command to set a bridge number of 5 with the protocol IBM.

Answer: `bridge 5 protocol ibm`–The global command bridge followed by the bridge number and then the protocol is the correct syntax.

Configure source-route transparent bridging (SRT).

As you already know, Cisco routers can run a combination of bridging and routing protocols, which allows you to run both the Spanning Tree Protocol and multiple layer-three protocols simultaneously. The advantage to this is that you can get the speed and protocol-transparency of a bridge without giving up the functionality and security of a router.

This chapter tells you about source-route transparent bridging and how to configure it on a Cisco router. This is important when working in a production environment that needs bridging. Also, remember that bridging is heavily tested upon when taking the ACRC exam, and SRT is a part of that.

Critical Information

The specification for source-route transparent bridging says that packets without a RIF field can be transparently bridged. If it has a RIF field, the frame is passed to the interface configured with source-route bridging. However, a Token Ring interface can have both a source-route configuration and a source-route–transparent configuration.

Frames sent from a source host without a RIF filed can never have a RIF field, and frames that start with a RIF can never lose that RIF field. If an interface is configured with both types of bridging (SR and SRT), it will use the SRT configuration if a SRT frame is received, and the same goes for SR. Also, you need to remember that source-route transparent bridging cannot handle Token-Ring-to-Ethernet media conversion.

Token Ring interfaces use the bridge-group command to configure source-route and source-route transparent bridging. These interfaces can use either the IEEE or DEC protocols. The IEEE specification is the Spanning Tree Protocol set by the IEEE 802.5 committee. If you have a bridge configured with the IEEE standard, it will communicate with any other IEEE bridge to build a loop-free network. If you use the DEC Spanning Tree Protocol, it can only communicate with other bridges running the DEC protocol. The DEC and IEEE protocols are not compatible.

Necessary Procedures

Configuration of source-route transparent bridging is simply a marriage of transparent bridging and SRB. Using the preceding example, to implement SRT instead of SRB you simply do as follows:

```
RouterB#config t
Enter configuration commands, one per line. End with
    CNTL/Z.
RouterB(config)#bridge 1 protocol ieee
RouterB(config)#interface to0
RouterB(config-if)#source-bridge 401 5 400
RouterB(config-if)#source-bridge spanning
RouterB(config-if)#bridge-group 1
RouterB(config-if)#interface to1
RouterB(config-if)#source-bridge 400 5 401
RouterB(config-if)#source-bridge spanning
RouterB(config-if)#bridge-group 1
RouterB(config-if)#^Z
RouterB#
```

Notice that, as mentioned, this is simply the combination of transparent bridging with SRB commands.

Exam Essentials

Understand that the commands for configuring SRT are used in combination. Use the `source-bridge` command and the `bridge-group` command to configure SRT.

Remember the three protocols that are used to configure SRT. IEEE is used between disparate bridges; IBM is used with IBM bridges; and DEC is used with DEC bridges.

Understand the SRT limitations. You need to remember that source-route transparent bridging cannot handle Token-Ring-to-Ethernet media conversion.

Key Terms and Concepts

IEEE (Institute of Electrical and Electronics Engineers) An organization that develops communications and network standards.

Transparent bridging The bridging scheme used in Ethernet and IEEE 802.3 networks, which passes frames along one hop at a time, using routing information stored in tables that associate end nodes within bridge ports. This type of bridging is considered transparent because the source node doesn't need to know the entire route, as it does with source-route bridging.

Sample Questions

1. What does the following command mean? (Choose all that apply.)

```
source-bridge 401 5 400
```

A. The local ring number is 400, the target ring is 401, and the bridge number is 5.

B. The local ring number is 401, the target ring is 400, and the bridge number is 5.

C. The local ring number is 401, the target ring is 5, and the bridge number is 400.

D. The local ring number is 5, the target ring is 400, and the bridge number is 401.

Answer: B—When you use the `source-bridge` command, the first parameter is the local ring, then the bridge number, and then the destination ring number.

2. Which of the followng would you use to configure your router to use DEC bridging?

A. `protocol dec bridging`

B. `bridge 2 protocol ieee`

C. `bridge 1 protocol digital`

D. `bridge 1 protocol dec`

Answer: D—`bridge 1 protocol dec` is the correct syntax for using DEC bridging.

Configure source-route translational bridging (SR/TLB).

Source-route translational bridging is used when you need to bridge packets between an interface running source-route bridging and source-route transparent bridging. To accomplish this, the Cisco router creates a type of software bridge between a virtual ring group and transparent bridge. By creating the software bridge, the source-route device actually thinks it is communicating to another source-route device on another network, and the same is true for the source-route transparent device. It does this by removing and caching the RIF field for when the frame is returned.

This objective shows you how to configure source-route translational bridging on a Cisco router. This is important if you have a production environment that bridges between Token Ring networks and Ethernet networks. When studying for the Cisco ACRC exam, you must know the differences between bridging types and how to configure each type. SR/TLB should be no exception.

Critical Information

Source-route translational bridging (SR/TLB) is used when bridging domains must be crossed. With SRT, it is possible to do both SRB and transparent bridging. With SR/TLB, SRB and transparent bridging domains can communicate. With SRT, communication from Ethernet to Token Ring is not supported, but SR/TLB addresses that issue. SRB generally runs on a Token Ring network, while transparent bridging is generally associated with Ethernet. It should be noted that SR/TLB is a Cisco IOS feature and is not an industry standard.

WARNING The spanning-tree packets used to prevent loops in transparent bridging environments will *not* cross SRB environments. It is crucial that no redundant paths are configured between the two domains, because spanning tree will not be able to detect and then disable them.

When bridging between Ethernet and Token Ring, a number of issues must be addressed:

- MTU size

- Lack of support for RIF in Ethernet frames

- Different systems for MAC addresses

WARNING There are significant technical challenges when bridging between dissimilar media. Cisco has documented problems with bridging Novell IPX, DECnet Phase IV, AppleTalk, VINES, XNS, and IP from Token Ring to other media and recommends that these protocols be routed rather than bridged whenever possible.

To configure SR/TLB, you must first configure multi-port SRB and transparent bridging as described earlier in this chapter. Then you use the source-bridge ring-group command to configure a virtual ring to which all SRB interfaces bridge. Finally, you use the source-bridge transparent command to enable bridging between the two environments. The syntax for this command is as follows:

```
Source-bridge transparent [ring-group] [psuedo-ring]
[bridge-number] [tb-group] [oui]
```

- ring-group is the virtual ring created by the source-bridge ring-group command.

- pseudo-ring is the ring number by which the transparent bridging domain will be known to the SRB domain.

- bridge-number is the SRB number of the router.

- tb-group is the number of the translational bridge group.

- oui is the organizational unit identifier. (This optional parameter can be set to 90-compatible, Cisco, or standard.)

Necessary Procedures

This section shows you how to configure SR/TLB. It sets the bridging protocol that will be used and then configures transparent bridging by using the source-bridge command.

```
RouterB#config t
Enter configuration commands, one per line. End with
  CNTL/Z.
Router(config)#bridge ?
  <1-63>  Bridge Group number for Bridging.
  cmf     Constrained multicast flooding
  crb     Concurrent routing and bridging
  irb     Integrated routing and bridging
```

Router(config)#**bridge 1 ?**
    acquire   Dynamically learn new,
        unconfigured stations
    address   Block or forward a particular
        Ethernet address
    aging-time   Set forwarding entry
        aging time
    bridge   Specify a protocol to be bridged in this
        bridge group
    circuit-group   Circuit-group
    domain   Establish multiple bridging
        domains
    forward-time   Set forwarding delay time
    hello-time   Set interval between HELLOs
    lat-service-filtering   Perform LAT service filtering
    max-age   Maximum allowed message age of received
        Hello BPDUs
    multicast-source   Forward datagrams with multicast
        source addresses
    priority   Set bridge priority
    protocol   Specify spanning tree protocol
    route   Specify a protocol to be routed in this
        bridge group

Router(config)#**bridge 1 protocol ?**
    dec   DEC protocol
    ibm   IBM protocol
    ieee   IEEE 802.1 protocol

Router(config)#**bridge 1 protocol ieee**
Router(config)#**source-bridge ?**
    connection-timeout   Connection timeout
    cos-enable   Prioritize traffic by Class
        of Service
    enable-80d5 Convert TR LLC2 frames to Ethernet type
        80d5 frames
    explorer-dup-ARE-filter Enable filtering of duplicate
        all-routes explorers

explorer-fastswitch	Enable local explorer fastswitching
explorer-maxrate	Maximum SRB local explorer data rate in bytes/sec
explorerQ-depth	Maximum SRB explorer queue depth per interface
fst-peername	Fast Sequence Transport local interface address
keepalive	Enable RSRB remote peer keepalive
lack-connection-timeout	Local ACK connection timeout
largest-frame	Largest frame size to use in a ring-group
passthrough	Do not local-ack frames to the specified ring
proxy-netbios-only	Proxy explorers only for NetBIOS
qllc-local-ack	Locally terminate QLLC sessions
remote-peer	Specify a remote peer for remote SRB
ring-group	Define a ring group
sap-80d5	Translate specified SAP frames to 80d5 frames
sdllc-local-ack	Locally terminate SDLC sessions
tcp-queue-max	Maximum TCP queue size for SRB
transparent	Bridging between a transparent and a source-route bridge

```
Router(config)#source-bridge ring
Router(config)#source-bridge ring-group ?
  <1-4095>  Virtual Ring Number
  H.H.H     Virtual MAC address for the ring
  <cr>

Router(config)#source-bridge ring-group 450 ?
  H.H.H  Virtual MAC address for the ring
  <cr>
```

```
Router(config)#source-bridge transparent ?
  <1-4095>  Source-route ring group attached to the
            transparent bridge

Router(config)#source-bridge transparent 450 ?
  <1-4095>    Pseudo-ring number of the transparent
              bridge
  fastswitch  Enable/disable fastswitching on sr/tlb
              bridge

Router(config)#source-bridge transparent 450 451 ?
  <1-15>  Bridge number to the transparent bridge

Router(config)#source-bridge transparent 450 451 5 ?
  <1-63>  Transparent bridge group attached to the
          virtual ring

Router(config)#source-bridge transparent 450 451 5 1 ?
  90-compatible      Cisco release 9.0 compatible OUI
  cisco              Cisco specific OUI
  enable-name-cache  Enable Netbios name cache
  standard           Standard OUI
  <cr>

Router(config)#source-bridge transparent 450 451 5 1

Router(config)#int to0
Router(config-if)#source
Router(config-if)#source-bridge ?
  <1-4095>            Ring number of local interface
  input-address-list  Filter input packets by MAC
                      address
  input-lsap-list    Filter input IEEE 802.5
                      encapsulated packets

  input-type-list    Filter input packets by type code
  max-hops           Set maximum number of hops a SRB
                     packet may take

  max-in-hops        Set maximum number of Span Input
                     hops a SRB packet may take
```

```
max-out-hops           Set maximum number of Span
  Output hops a SRB packet may take

max-rd                 Set maximum number of Routing
  descriptors
old-sna                Enable IBM PC/3270 compatibility
  mode
output-address-list  Filter output packets by MAC
  address
output-lsap-list       Filter output IEEE 802.5
  encapsulated packets

output-type-list       Filter output packets by
  type code
proxy-explorer         Enable proxy explorer packets
route-cache            Enable route-caching
spanning               Enables use of spanning
  explorers
```

Router(config-if)#**source-bridge 401** ?
<1-15> Bridge number

Router(config-if)#**source-bridge 401 5** ?
<1-4095> Target ring number

Router(config-if)#**source-bridge 401 5 405**
Router(config-if)#

Router(config-if)#**source-bridge span** ?
<1-63> SRB spanning group number
<cr>

When configuring translational bridging, you first configure the protocol that will be used. In the above example, the IEEE protocol is configured. Then the source-bridge command is used to configure the bridge. The example configuration allows the SRB environment out interface to0, seeing the entire bridge group 1 as ring 451.

Exam Essentials

Remember when to use SR/TLB. When you need to cross a bridging domain (for example, from Token Ring to Ethernet) you use SR/TLB.

Understand the command sequence for configuring SR/TLB. The command string for configuring translational bridging is:

```
Source-bridge transparent [ring-group] [psuedo-ring]
    [bridge-number] [tb-group] [oui]
```

Remember the command to set the spanning group number. The command to set the spanning group number is `source-bridge spanning`.

Key Terms and Concepts

Source-route bridging algorithm   Bridging protocol that finds the complete route to a destination device before transmitting.

Source-route translational bridging algorithm   Used when you need to bridge packets between an interface running source-route bridging and source-route transparent bridging.

Sample Questions

1. For which one of the following scenarios is source-route translational bridging used?

    A. Only when you have no other bridging support available

    B. When you need the bridge number of the transparent bridge

    C. When the source-route ring group attached to the transparent bridge is used

    D. When bridging domains must be crossed

Answer: D—SR/TLB is used when bridging domains must be crossed.

2. What does the following command mean? (Choose all that apply.)

```
source-bridge transparent 450 451 5 1
```

A. The 450 is the source-route ring group attached to the transparent bridge.

B. The 451 is the source-route ring group attached to the transparent bridge.

C. The 451 is the pseudo-ring number of the transparent bridge.

D. The 450 is the pseudo-ring number of the transparent bridge.

E. The 5 is the bridge number to the transparent bridge.

F. The 1 is the bridge number to the transparent bridge.

G. The 1 is the transparent bridge group attached to the virtual ring.

H. The 5 is the transparent bridge group attached to the virtual ring.

Answer: A, C, E, G—source-bridge transparent *(source ring group) (ring number of transparent bridge) (bridge number) (bridge group)* is the command sequence for configuring source-bridge.

Verify SRB operation.

As you can tell from all chapters in this book, it is important to be able to verify and monitor your configuration. Bridging is no exception to this rule. To be able to monitor the operation of bridging on Cisco routers, you need to study this objective section. There are not too many commands associated with source-route bridging, but some of the more complex bridging configurations can have more complete lists of commands that can be used for verifying your configuration.

This objective only covers the commands needed to verify source-route bridging, which are also the commands you need to know when studying for the ACRC exam.

Critical Information

You can use several commands to verify operation of SRB. As always, the show running-config command is useful to display configuration operations. There are also the show rif, show source-bridge, and show source-bridge interface commands.

- show running-config shows the configuration running in DRAM.
- show rif displays the routing information field cache.
- show source-bridge gathers information and statisitcs about source-route bridging running on your router.
- show source-bridge interface command gives you specific statistics about each configured interface.

Necessary Procedures

Let's run through the show running-config, show rif, and show source-bridge interface commands.

The *show running-config* Command

This is a helpful command because it shows the current configuration, which includes all the source-route configuration information.

```
Router#sh running-config
%SYS-5-CONFIG_I: Configured from console by console
Building configuration...

Current configuration:
!
version 11.2
```

```
!
hostname Router
!
!
source-bridge ring-group 450
source-bridge transparent 450 451 5 1
!
interface Serial0
 ip address 172.16.160.2 255.255.255.0
!
interface Serial1
 no ip address
 shutdown
!
interface TokenRing0
 no ip address
 ring-speed 16
 source-bridge 401 5 405
 source-bridge spanning
!
interface TokenRing1
 no ip address
 shutdown
!
no ip classless
!
bridge 1 protocol ieee
!
line con 0
line aux 0
line vty 0 4
 login
!
end

Router#
```

The *show rif* Command

This command displays information about the routing information field data in a Token Ring frame.

```
RouterB#show rif
Codes: * interface, - static, + remote
Hardware Addr  How   Idle (min)  Routing Information
     Field

RouterB#
```

As you can see, this command displays four pieces of information about each RIF entry:

- `Hardware Addr` is the hardware address.

- `How` indicates how the information was learned—via either a specific interface or ring group.

- `Idle` is the amount of time since this node was last heard from.

- `Routing Information Field` includes the contents of the RIF.

There is another command you can use to display the routing information field data of Token Ring frames passing through the router. That command is `Debug rif`.

The *show source-bridge* Command

This command gives you statistics about the source bridge.

```
Router#sh source-bridge

Local Interfaces:                    receive transmit
      srn bn  trn r p s n  max hops  cnt  cnt  drops
To0       401 5  405 * f   7   7  7  0    0    0

Global RSRB Parameters:
 TCP Queue Length maximum: 100

Ring Group 450:
  No TCP peername set, TCP transport disabled
    Maximum output TCP queue length, per peer: 100
  Rings:
    bn: 5 rn: 451 locvrt ma: 40e0.1e42.acae Bridge-group 1  fwd: 0
```

```
Explorers: ------- input -------        ------- output -------
    spanning all-rings    total    spanning all-rings    total
  To0   0        0          0          0        0          0

  Local: fastswitched 0           flushed 0           max Bps 38400

  rings   inputs   bursts   throttles   output   drops
  To0       0        0          0          0
```

The show source-bridge interface command gives you specific
statistics about each configured interface.

```
Router#sh source-bridge interface
                                  v p s n r                    Packets
Interface St   MAC-Address  srn bn  trn r x p b c IP-Address   In   Out
To0     dn 0007.7842.3575  401  5  405    f F                   0    0
To1     dn 0007.7842.35f5                                       0    0
```

Exam Essentials

Remember the commands to verify RIF. The commands you use
to verify RIF are show rif and debug rif.

Remember what the debug rif command does. debug rif displays the routing information field data of a Token Ring frame as it
passes through a router.

Remember the commands to verify source-route bridging. The
show run, show rif, and show source-bridge commands are all
used to verify source-route bridging on a Cisco router.

Key Terms and Concepts

Debug commands Can be run on a Cisco router to see what is
happening within a frame or packet when going through the
router.

RIF (routing information field) A field within a frame that is used
to direct a frame to a destination device.

Source-route bridging algorithm Bridging protocol that finds the
complete route to a destination device before transmitting.

Sample Questions

1. Type the command to display the routing information field data of Token Ring frames passing through a router?

   Answer: Debug rif

2. Which of the following commands are valid for verifying source-route bridging on a Cisco router?

   A. show running-config

   B. show rif

   C. show token-ring bridge

   D. show source-route

   Answer: A, B, D—show running-config, show rif, and show source-route are all commands you can use to verify your source-route running on your router.

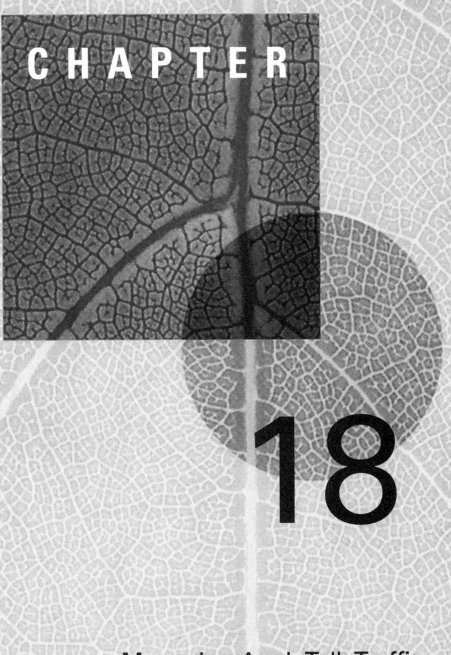

CHAPTER

18

Managing AppleTalk Traffic

Cisco ACRC Exam Objectives Covered in This Chapter:

▸ **Identify potential sources of congestion in an AppleTalk network.** *(pages 367 – 370)*

▸ **Configure zone filters.** *(pages 370 – 374)*

▸ **Configure RTMP filters.** *(pages 375 – 379)*

▸ **Configure NBP filters.** *(pages 379 – 382)*

AppleTalk is a protocol stack created by Apple Computer to run over Ethernet, Token Ring, FDDI, and LocalTalk, which is Apple's proprietary twisted-pair media access system. AppleTalk refers to the protocol stack itself, while the calls that the network media defines at both the Physical layer and the MAC sub-layer of the Data Link layer are known as LocalTalk, EtherTalk, TokenTalk, and FDDITalk. AppleTalk can also be run over X.25, HDLC, Frame Relay, and SMDS.

Just as IP and IPX have their own rules, AppleTalk has its own way of doing things. Addressing, location of services, and communication are a bit different than with other protocols. AppleTalk uses zones to let nodes find and advertise network services on a network. Technically, a *zone* is a logical network, independent of the physical network segment. A logical network is a network that you define based on your users instead of your wiring.

This chapter explains why AppleTalk has problems in larger internetworks and how to solve some of the problems created on your internetwork when running AppleTalk. The objectives covered in this chapter are dedicated to improving network response when running AppleTalk. This is a very important chapter if you have to run AppleTalk on your internetwork. When studying for the ACRC exam, make sure you are aware of the AppleTalk objectives and how to set the different AppleTalk filters.

Identify potential sources of congestion in an AppleTalk network.

AppleTalk is considered a "chatty" protocol. This, of course, makes it a dynamic and resilient protocol suite. Because AppleTalk uses an abundance of broadcasts, Macs are plug-and-play. Some of the features of AppleTalk are dynamic addressing and automatic name lookup.

When any network grows, so do the broadcasts needed to keep it running, which occur at the cost of the bandwidth available to users. Cisco provides filters that you can use on your Cisco routers to help cut down on bandwidth-consuming broadcasts. This chapter discusses those filters, but this objective focuses on the sources for congestion in an AppleTalk network. This is extremely important to understand before further reading within this chapter since it explains the basic problems in an AppleTalk network.

Critical Information

AppleTalk is a wonderfully dynamic protocol for users who are locating network services, but it depends on broadcasts to be able to do this. End nodes within a department need to be able to send and receive broadcast traffic to every other end node in the network, regardless of the physical topology of the network.

AppleTalk uses Routing Table Maintenance Protocol (RTMP) to build routing tables in routers. The entire routing table is broadcasted out all active interfaces every 10 seconds! (How about that as a reason for congestion on an AppleTalk network?) In addition, the Chooser on a MAC uses GetZoneList (GZL) to obtain a list of all zones on the internetwork, and Name Binding Protocol (NBP) uses broadcasts to resolve network names. All three of these protocols—RTMP, GZL, and NBP—are major reasons for congestion on an

AppleTalk network. The following objectives in this chapter are dedicated to showing how to restrict the broadcasts from these protocols.

Consider an example of how AppleTalk uses broadcasts to help users find resources on the network. Mac users launch the Chooser application to locate resources on the internetwork. Once users launch the Chooser, they select an AppleTalk zone and type of resource (file server, printer, etc.). Chooser then builds a dynamic list of workstations that offer the requested service in the selected zone. The user selects one of the names and then proceeds with their work. Let's get a more detailed idea of how this works:

1. The user launches the Chooser application.

2. The Chooser queries the router for available zones and presents the list of available zones to the user.

3. The user selects a zone and the type of resource requested.

4. The user's Mac issues an NBP request identifying the requested type of resource and zone.

5. The routers ensure that the NBP broadcast is forwarded to all specified network segments for that zone.

6. All nodes in the requested zone receive the NBP broadcast, and the nodes that provide the requested service reply to the requesting workstation.

7. Routers forward the responses to the requesting workstation's segment.

8. The Chooser builds a list of available services.

9. The user selects a service and proceeds with their work.

With this arrangement, it's obvious that the proper forwarding of broadcasts is crucial to locating resources on the internetwork. From the users' perspective, they can just use the dynamic Chooser to find out which resources are available on the internetwork. If you get a new laser printer, for instance, you simply plug it in and tell it which zone it's in, and the Chooser will automatically let users looking for that type of printer know that it's available.

Exam Essentials

Remember what causes network congestion on AppleTalk networks. The AppleTalk protocol stack is very chatty. For example, RTMP sends the complete routing table out all active interfaces every 10 seconds. To find network resources, GZL broadcasts are forwarded throughout the entire internetwork. And NBP is used to resolve network names and is broadcast intensive.

Understand what a zone is. A zone is a logical network, somewhat like a virtual LAN, which is independent of the physical location of devices. Zones allow you to create workgroups regardless of user location. These are not efficient like a VLAN is, but they do work.

Key Terms and Concepts

AppleTalk   Protocol stack created by Apple for the network connectivity of Apple devices.

GZL (GetZoneList)   Used by the Chooser on a MAC to obtain a list of all zones on the internetwork.

NBP (Name Binding Protocol)   Used on an AppleTalk network to resolve names.

Zone   A logical grouping of users and resources independent of physical location.

Sample Questions

1. Which of the following causes network congestion in an Apple-Talk network?

   A. TRMP

   B. RTMP

   C. Chooser

D. Network access

Answer: B, C—RTMP sends out the complete routing table every ten seconds to connected interfaces. The Chooser uses GZL and NBP broadcasts to find network resources throughout the internetwork.

2. What is the NBP protocol used for?

A. Resolving IP addresses to MAC addresses

B. Resolving network names

C. Converting bit to byte

D. Forwarding AppleTalk through a router

Answer: B—The Name Binding Protocol uses network broadcasts to resolve network names for transmission of data in the lower layers.

Configure zone filters.

Macintosh's Chooser uses GetZoneList requests to compile a list of zones from which the user can select services. As in IPX networking, a Cisco router on the same local network as the device can respond to these requests with a GZL reply. You can create zone filters by using a GZL filter on the router to control which zones the router advertises in its GZL replies. This allows you to control the list of zones that are displayed by the Chooser.

This objective section shows you how to configure a zone filter to filter both GZLs, which control zone information being sent between Macs and routers, and ZIP replies, which can control zone information from router to router. This is important to understand when configuring AppleTalk on your internetwork to solve bandwidth issues. When studying for the ACRC exam, you must remember the different types of zone filters available.

Critical Information

When a Macintosh user fires up Chooser to locate a remote device, the Mac sends a directed request to a router on its segment with a GZL request. The router is supposed to respond with a list of all available zones on the internetwork. If you can control the router's response (which zones the router tells the workstation about, i.e.), you can control the workstation's access to zones. Here are a few points to keep in mind:

- You cannot control which router a workstation will query on a given segment. Therefore, if you have multiple routers on any segment, you must configure them all to respond identically (i.e., they must have the same GZL filters).

- A very clever user can get around this if they know the actual AppleTalk address of a device, which is highly unlikely but not impossible. (This method controls only the GZL response.)

- Since this filter affects only the communication between clients and routers, there is no reason to use it on a serial interface, where there cannot be any AppleTalk clients.

The access list is composed to deny zone WAN and permit any other zone. The trick to making this access list a GZL filter comes when you apply it to an interface. You can use the `appletalk getzonelist-filter 610` command on the Ethernet interface. This tells the router that whenever it responds to a GZL request on the Ethernet interface it must use access list 610 when composing the reply. The end result is that workstations on the Ethernet segment with cable range 500-510 will no longer see zone WAN in their Chooser windows; the first line of access list 610 takes care of this. However, they will be able to see every other zone that the router knows about; the second line of access list 610 does this.

ZIP Reply Filters

GetZoneList filters work between clients and routers, and ZIP reply filters work between routers. After all, if you can prevent routers from learning about zones, you don't have to worry about clients serviced by those routers learning about them either.

Suppose that you have a small group called Payroll in Building C. You can create a zone for them—associated with cable range 500-510— along with zone BldgC. Suppose that you don't want any other sites to learn about the Payroll zone. You would first add the Payroll zone to the Ethernet interface. As you know, it's perfectly legal to assign two zone names to the same cable segment with phase two addressing. The access list is similar to the one previously mentioned concerning GZL filters. Once again, the trick is in *how* the access list is applied. This time, you would use the `appletalk zip-reply-filter 611` command on the serial interface. The end result is that Router C will advertise out cable range 500-510, but it won't tell anyone else about the Payroll zone—only the original zone.

Necessary Procedures

This section shows you how to configure both the GZL filter and the ZIP reply filter.

GZL Filters

Suppose that in your internetwork you want to prevent users from seeing your WAN zone, where you have been placing all of your serial interfaces. You would proceed as follows:

```
RouterC#config t
Enter configuration commands, one per line.  End with
  CNTL/Z.
RouterC(config)#access-list 610 deny zone WAN
RouterC(config)#access-list 610 permit additional-zones
RouterC(config)#int e0
RouterC(config-if)#appletalk getzonelist-filter 610
RouterC(config-if)#^Z
RouterC#
```

ZIP Reply Filters

Suppose again that you have a small group called Payroll in Building C. You create a zone for them—associated with cable range 500-510—along with zone BldgC. Suppose also that you don't want any other sites to learn about the Payroll zone. You would proceed as follows:

```
RouterC#config t
Enter configuration commands, one per line.  End with
    CNTL/Z.
RouterC(config)#interface ethernet0
RouterC(config-if)#appletalk zone Payroll
RouterC(config-if)#exit
RouterC(config)#access-list 611 deny zone Payroll
RouterC(config)#access-list 611 permit additional-zones
RouterC(config)#int s0
RouterC(config-if)#appletalk zip-reply-filter 611
RouterC(config-if)#^Z
RouterC#
```

Exam Essentials

Remember when to use a ZIP filter. Use a ZIP filter when you want to limit the updates sent between routers.

Remember when to use a GZL filter. Use a GZL filter when you want to limit the updates sent between routers and MACs.

Understand the command for configuring a ZIP filter. The command to configure a ZIP filter on a router is AppleTalk zip-reply-filter [access-list number].

Understand the command for configuring a GZL filter. The command to configure a GZL filter on a router is appletalk getzonelist-filter [access-list number].

Key Terms and Concepts

AppleTalk Protocol stack created by Apple for the network connectivity of Apple devices.

GZL (GetZoneList) Used by the Chooser on a MAC to obtain a list of all zones on the internetwork.

NBP (Name Binding Protocol) Used on an AppleTalk network to resolve names.

ZIP (Zone Information Protocol) Used to respond to a GZL with a list of all available zones on the internetwork.

Zone A logical grouping of users and resources independent of physical location.

Sample Questions

1. When is a ZIP reply filter used?

   A. Between MACs

   B. Between clients and routers

   C. Between routers

   D. Between cable ranges

   Answer: C—ZIP replies are used to update routers.

2. When is a GZL filter used?

   A. Between MACs

   B. Between clients and routers

   C. Between routers

   D. Between cable ranges

   Answer: B—GZLs are used by clients to get zone information from a router.

◢ Configure RTMP filters.

AppleTalk uses the RTMP routing protocol to update routers about networks (cable ranges). Routing Table Maintenance Protocol is a distance-vector routing algorithm that uses split horizon and a maximum hop count of 15 hops. However, unlike IP RIP, which sends updates every 30 seconds, and IPX RIP, which sends updates every 60 seconds, AppleTalk RTMP sends updates every 10 seconds. The RTMP update includes cable ranges and hop counts.

This objective shows you how to configure RTMP filters on a Cisco router. This is important because of the enormous number of updates that can be sent by default from a Cisco router running AppleTalk. It is important to understand how to control these broadcasts. When studying for your exam, remember that all AppleTalk filters are fair game on the ACRC exam.

Critical Information

As has already been stated, the Routing Table Maintenance Protocol is used by AppleTalk to update routing tables on routers. To control the RTMP broadcasts and even add security to your internetwork, RTMP filters can:

- Stop the routing of RTMP packets

- Stop routing updates

- Stop the advertisement of routes to networks with no associated zones

- Change routing update timers

RTMP filters can be used to reduce the number of AppleTalk routing table updates or stop routes from being advertised to users. The two commands used to filter RTMP are the distribute-list command and the access-list command. The distribute-list command is used to reduce or block updates of cable ranges between routers. The access-list command defines access to a single cable range or network resource.

To configure the routes advertised by a router, use the appletalk distribute-list [access-list] [in/out] command.

AppleTalk access lists all fall in the 600–699 range, and there are no extended or standard versions like there are with IP and IPX; there are just plain-old AppleTalk access lists. The same rules that you've been following all along still apply, and the patterns of use are pretty much the same too—create the access list and then apply it to an interface.

As you'll see, you can get pretty creative with the application of AppleTalk access lists to interfaces and, as always, online help can walk you through the many options. Here is an example of the range of options available via online help:

```
RouterC#config t
Enter configuration commands, one per line.  End with
   CNTL/Z.
RouterC(config)#access-list 600 permit ?
  <1-65279>        Appletalk network number
  additional-zones Default filter action for unspecified
   zones
  cable-range      Filter on cable range
  includes         Filter on cable range inclusively
  nbp              Specify nbp filter
  network          Filter an appletalk network
  other-access     Default filter action
  other-nbps       Default filter action for nbp
  within           Filter on cable range exclusively
  zone             Filter on appletalk zone
RouterC(config)#
```

When working with AppleTalk access lists, much of the magic occurs when the list is applied to an interface. There are many ways to apply a list, and functionality varies greatly depending on which method you use. The next section looks at some specific applications and examples.

Necessary Procedures

RTMP filtering gives you control over cable-range information. With RTMP filters, you can control the actual AppleTalk cable ranges that you advertise to the outside world.

In your network, suppose that you don't want Router B forwarding information about range 100–110 to Router C. You can use the following technique to achieve this goal:

```
RouterB#config t
Enter configuration commands, one per line.  End with
    CNTL/Z.
RouterB(config)#access-list 612 deny cable-range 100-110
RouterB(config)#access-list 612 permit other-access
RouterB(config)#access-list 612 permit additional-zones
RouterB(config)#int s1
RouterB(config-if)#appletalk distribute-list 612 out
RouterB(config-if)#^Z
RouterB#
```

This access list is similar to others that you have done. The application to an interface bears some explanation. First, note that when you use the distribute-list command access list 612 will not filter *packets* from cable range 100–110 but will filter *routing updates* about network 100–110. Also, notice that you use a direction when applying the access list to the interface. Out filters what a router advertises; in filters what a router listens to in the routing updates that it hears. The other-access and additional-zones tell the router that other networks are included in the update and that all zones not part of the specified zone are permitted.

Exam Essentials

Understand what RTMP does. Routing Table Maintenance Protocol is a distance-vector routing algorithm used to update routers about cable ranges.

Understand how RTMP updates other routers. RTMP uses hop counts and cable ranges to create routing tables, and it sends the complete routing table out every active interface every 10 seconds.

Remember the commands to filter RTMP updates. The distribute-list command is used to reduce or block updates of cable ranges between routers. The access-list command defines access to a single cable-range or network resource.

Key Terms and Concepts

GZL (GetZoneList)   Used by the Chooser on a MAC to obtain a list of all zones on the internetwork.

NBP (Name Binding Protocol)   Used on an AppleTalk network to resolve names.

RTMP (Routing Table Maintenance Protocol)   Used to update routers' update cable ranges (networks) between AppleTalk routers. Somewhat equivalent to RIP in an IP network.

ZIP (Zone Information Protocol)   Used to respond to a GZL with a list of all available zones on the internetwork.

Sample Questions

1. Which RTMP filter can be used to stop updates of networks between routers?

   A. GZL

   B. distribute-list

   C. access-list

   D. RTMP

   Answer: B—RTMP is used to propagate cable-ranges between routers. The distribute-list command is used to reduce or block updates of cable ranges between routers.

2. Which command can be applied to limit visibility of networks in an AppleTalk internetwork?

A. GZL

B. distribute-list

C. access-list

D. RTMP

Answer: C—The access-list command defines access to a single cable range or network resource.

Configure NBP filters.

The Name Binding Protocol is used to resolve network names that are used in the upper layers into addresses that can be used by lower layers for sending data across an internetwork. Since NBP lookups can be bandwidth intensive on an internetwork, NBP filters can be used to manage traffic in an AppleTalk network.

This objective section shows you how and why to use NBP filters to help manage your network. This is important to keep broadcasts from consuming your bandwidth, as well as for possibly adding security between zones. For the ACRC exam, you need to understand how to apply all AppleTalk filters, including NBP.

Critical Information

So far, you have seen how to control both zone and network address propagation. These tools will cover many situations. However, what if you need more granular control, such as limiting access to a particular file server or printer within a zone? NBP allows you to filter on network services. When configuring NBP filters, you must know the object name used in AppleTalk. This is referred to as a network-visible entity (NVE). The actual nodes are not considered to be NVEs, but the communications through sockets are NVEs.

To filter access to specific devices within zones, you can use NBP filtering. NBP uses broadcast requests for an object, type, and zone. AppleTalk nodes are classified by these three properties:

Object Refers to the name of the node. (The = sign is a wildcard for any object.)

Type Refers to the service the node offers (e.g., AFP Server, LaserWriter, etc.). (The = sign is a wildcard for any type.)

Zone Refers to the zone name. (The * signifies the user's current zone.)

You can use the help screen in the router to get some NVE names, but here is a small list of the most common ones used:

- AFPSerser
- LaserWriter
- Workstation
- 2.0MailServer
- ciscoRouter

To create an NBP filter, use the `access-list` command. Here is the command string:

```
Access-list [access-list number] {deny/permit} nbp seq
    {type | object | zone } string.
```

The next section presents an example to show you how to use this command to filter NBP.

Necessary Procedures

Suppose you have three buildings in your internetwork, and you don't want AppleTalk users in Buildings A or B to access any resources in Building C (other than file services). You can create the following NBP filter to accomplish this:

```
RouterB#config t
Enter configuration commands, one per line.  End with
   CNTL/Z.
RouterB(config)#access-list 615 permit nbp 1 type
   AFPServer
RouterB(config)#access-list 615 permit nbp 1 object =
RouterB(config)#access-list 615 permit nbp 1 zone BldgC
RouterB(config)#access-list 615 permit other-access
RouterB(config)#int s1
RouterB(config-if)#appletalk access-group 615
RouterB(config-if)#^Z
RouterB#
```

The 1 after the nbp command is called a *sequence number*. It ties the type, object, and zone statements together. The permit other-access line is critical; it allows the rest of the DDP traffic to pass. AppleTalk access lists applied to interfaces using the access-group command are applied incoming; therefore, you apply this filter on Router B's S1 interface.

NBP filters are powerful tools, but don't be afraid to play with them. They offer a level of control beyond the capabilities of zone and RTMP filters.

Exam Essentials

Remember what the Name Binding Protocol is used for. NBP is used to resolve names on AppleTalk networks.

Understand the command used to filter NBP. The command is
access-list [*access-list number*] [*permit/deny*] nbp
sequence number type.

Key Terms and Concepts

GZL (GetZoneList) Used by the Chooser on a MAC to obtain a list of all zones on the internetwork.

NBP (Name Binding Protocol) Used on an AppleTalk network to resolve names.

Zone A logical grouping of users and resources independent of physical location.

Sample Questions

1. Which command is used to set an NBP filter?

   A. GZE

   B. access-list

   C. distribute-list

   D. ZIP

   Answer: B—Just like in RTMP filters, you use the access-list command.

2. What does the 4 in the following command string do?

   access-list 649 permit nbp 4 type AFPServer

   A. It permits only cable-range 649 to access the server.

   B. It ties this access list together with RTMP filter 4.

   C. It ties the type, object, and zone statements together.

   D. It means only users on network 4 can use the server.

   Answer: C—The 4 after the nbp command is called a *sequence number*. It ties the type, object, and zone statements together.

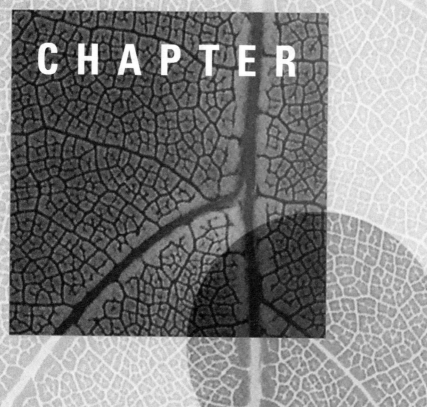

CHAPTER

19

Configuring T1/E1 and
ISDN PRI Options

Cisco ACRC Exam Objectives Covered in This Chapter:

▶ **Identify channelized T1 and E1 configuration.** *(pages 385 – 390)*

▶ **Identify ISDN PRI configuration commands.** *(pages 390 – 393)*

This chapter explains how to configure a Cisco router to run a T1 or E1 circuit. Part of this configuration will help you to understand how to break up a T1 or E1 into smaller channels. What this means is that you can use a partial-line or fractional T1 or E1, which can allow a company to save money by only buying the number of channels that will give them the bandwidth they need at the time. (If needed, other channels can be purchased later when the company grows.)

Each T1 circuit has 24 DS-0 channels of 64K each. Each E1 has 30 DS-0 ports. All of the channels in a T1 have a total bandwidth of 1.544Mbps. (In Europe, a full E1 totals 2.048Mbps.)

This chapter also talks about Integrated Services Digital Network (ISDN) Primary Rate Interface (PRI) configurations. Cisco IOS routers support PRI interfaces using MultiChannel Interface Processor (MIP) cards. MIP cards work to support channelized T1/E1 or PRI timeslots. MIP cards are available for Cisco 4x00, Cisco 36x0, Cisco 5x00, and Cisco 7x00 series routers.

It is important to understand the difference between a BRI and PRI and when you would use a T1. Also, since E1s are used in Europe, it is advantageous to understand their differences so you can order the right product for your company. This chapter shows you the configurations of a T1 and E1, helping you to understand how to perform these function at your job and for the exam.

Identify channelized T1 and E1 configuration.

The Cisco 7000 series of routers supports the Fast Serial Interface Processor (FSIP), which provides either four or eight serial ports, permitting the same number of point-to-point connections to remote offices. Cisco routers can be used to configure channelized ports using these interfaces or fractional T1s to remote offices.

As mentioned in the introduction, the Cisco series of routers also supports the MultiChannel Interface Processor, which furnishes support for two full T1/E1 ports in the 7000 series and one port in the 4000 series.

T1s run at 1.544Mbps, which use 24 channels in contrast to E1s, which use 30 channels and run at 2.048Mbps. E1 is mainly used in Europe, and both T1 and E1 are considered to be wide-area digital transmission schemes.

Each port in the MIP can support 24 DS-0 channels of 64Kbps each when using a T1, and 30 DS-0 channels when using an E1. The MIP refers to each line as a subchannel, which allows each channel to be configured individually. Subchannels have all the characteristics and options of regular serial interfaces.

Critical Information

This section presents the information needed to configure channelized T1s and E1s on a Cisco router.

Configuring a Channelized T1

The T1 serial links connect into either a private data network or a service provider's network. Both the line encoding and the framing must match the service provider's equipment. To configure a T1 on a serial link, you must supply the following information:

Channel type   Either T1 or E1.

Frame type   When using a T1, this can be either Super Frame (SF) or Extended Super Frame (ESF). Super Frame can also be referred to as D4 framing, which consists of 12 frames, each with 193 bits. The last bit is used for error checking. ESF is an enhanced version of SF that uses 24 frames, each with 192 bits. ESF is typically used in the U.S.

Linecode   This will be either alternate mark inversion (AMI) or binary 8-zero substitution (B8ZS). B8ZS is typically used in the U.S.; however, most legacy phone systems still use AMI.

Time slots used   For T1s, by using the `channel-group` command on your sub-channel, you can define the subchannels associated with each time slot.

Configuring a Channelized E1

The E1 configuration is similar to the T1 configuration but has different parameters.

Framing type   The E1 framing types available are *crc4*, *no-crc4*, and *australia*. The default is crc4, and it specifies CRC error checking, with no-crc4 specifying that CRC checking is disabled. The australia framing method is used when configuring an E1 in Australia.

Linecode   This is either AMI or HDB3 when configuring an E1, with AMI as the default.

Necessary Procedures

This section shows you how to configure your Cisco routers with both T1 and E1 configurations.

Configuring T1

The following example demonstrates how to configure slot 1, port 0 of the MIP card in a 7000 router, with ESF framing and B8ZS line coding. The channel-group 0 timeslots 1 line indicates that circuit 0 has only one time slot. Since no speed was specified, it's running the default of 56Kbps. If you have a different speed, you need to configure that.

Channel group one has six time slots running at 64Kbps. You can choose up to 24 DS-0s, but imagine that only six were purchased from your provider. Here's a look at the output:

```
Router#config t
Enter configuration commands, one per line. End with
    CNTL/Z.
Router(config)#controller T1 1/0
Router(config-if)#framing esf
Router(config-if)#linecode b8zs
Router(config-if)#channel-group 0 timeslots 1
Router(config-if)#channel-group 1 timeslots 6,3,4,8-11
    speed 64
Router(config-if)#^Z
```

An IP address and the serial encapsulation method (HDLC is the default) then need to be assigned to each interface, as shown in the following example:

```
Router#config t
Enter configuration commands, one per line. End with
    CNTL/Z.
Router(config)#int s 0/1:0
Router(config-if)#encap ppp
Router(config-if)#ip address 172.16.30.5 255.255.255.252

Router(config)#int s 0/1:1
Router(config-if)#encap hdlc
Router(config-if)#ip address 172.16.30.5 255.255.255.252
Router(config-if)#^Z
```

NOTE   When connecting two MIP cards together, you must specify the clock source. This is done with the `clock source` command.

Configuring E1

The following example uses slot 0, port 1 on your MIP card, and, by using the crc4 framing type, it's actually specifying the ESF frame type. The provider has defined HDB3 as the linecode (AMI is the default) to match the carrier's equipment. Primary group zero, with a time slot of 1, specifies that there is only one time slot with circuit 0. However, primary group one is using 12 time slots, with up to 30 available if purchased.

```
Router#config t
Enter configuration commands, one per line. End with
   CNTL/Z.
Router(config)#controller T1 1/0
Router(config-if)#framing esf
Router(config-if)#linecode b8zs
Router(config-if)#channel-group 0 timeslots 1
Router(config-if)#channel-group 1 timeslots 12 12-23
   speed 64
Router(config-if)#^Z
```

You then need to specify the IP address and encapsulation methods used—just as you did in the T1 example.

Exam Essentials

Remember the cards used to create channelized circuits.   Use MultiChannel Interface Processor (MIP), which furnishes support for two full T1/E1 ports in the 7000 series and one port in the 4000 series. The Cisco 7000 series of routers supports the Fast Serial Interface Processor.

Remember the commands to set up channels. The channel-group command is used to configure channels on an interface.

Remember the framing types for a T1. The framing types are Extended Super Frame, and Super Frame.

Remember the linecode types for a T1. The linecode will be either alternate mark inversion or binary 8-zero substitution (B8ZS).

Key Terms and Concepts

AMI (alternate mark inversion) A linecode for a T1 that is typically used in Europe but is sometimes used in the US.

B8ZS (binary 8-zero substitution) A linecode for a T1 that is typically used in US.

DS-0 (digital signal level 0) Timeslot for a T1, which is 64K.

ESF (Extended Super Frame) Made up of 24 frames with 192 bits each, with bit 193 providing other functions including timing a frame type for a T1.

Sample Questions

1. Which command is used to set up timeslots in T1?

   A. group-pri

   B. pri-group

   C. channel-group

   D. group-channel

   Answer: C—The channel-group command is used to set up timeslots in a T1.

2. What options are available for frame types when configuring a T1?

   A. FS

   B. SF

   C. SEF

   D. ESF

   Answer: B, D—Super Frame and Extended Super Frame are the framing types used in a T1 configuration.

Identify ISDN PRI configuration commands.

Y ou can purchase Cisco 7500 series, Cisco 7000 series, and Cisco 7200 series routers with a channelized T1/ISDN PRI port adapter, which can provide up to two channelized T1 or ISDN PRI interfaces. This can provide a rate of 1.544Mbps in a bidirectional data flow.

The Cisco E1 ISDN support works with the Cisco 7500 series, Cisco 7000 series, and Cisco 7200 series routers. You can have up to two channelized E1 ISDN PRI interfaces, which can transmit and receive data bidirectionally. (E1 are used in Europe and provide up to 2.049 Mbps.)

This objective focuses on how to configure ISDN PRI adapters. This is important if you happen to work for a company that has offices in Europe.

Critical Information

To configure an ISDN PRI interface, you need to provide the router with the line configuration, which most often is provided to you by the service provider. The first thing you need to get from your PRI provider is the switch type. Cisco routers can support the equipment of all major switch carriers.

You can set the type of switch with the isdn switch-type command. Once the switch type is configured, you need to specify the type of controller the router is using by using the controller [t1 | e1] [slot/port | unit-number] command. At this point, you can configure the PRI with the frame type by using the framing [sf | esf | crc4 | no-crc4] command. Also, the linecode command is used to set the line coding of the switch. The options are [ami | b8zs | hdb3]. Set PRI group timeslots for T1/E1 and indicate the speed used.

If you need to set the clock source, use the clock source {line [primary | secondary] | internal} command. To configure your router's time slots, use the pri-group [timeslots *range*] command.

Necessary Procedures

Let's go through the configuration on a Cisco router. The first thing you need to set is the switch type:

```
AS5200(config)#isdn switch-type ?
    primary-4ess      AT&T 4ESS switch type for the U.S.
    primary-5ess      AT&T 5ESS switch type for the U.S.
    primary-dms100    Northern Telecom switch type for the
    U.S.
    primary-net5      European switch type for NET5
    primary-ntt       Japan switch type
    primary-ts014     Australia switch type
```

Then you configure the frame and linecode in the controller interface:

```
controller T1 0
    framing esf
    clock source line primary
    linecode b8zs
    pri-group timeslots 1-24
```

```
controller T1 1
  framing esf
  clock source line secondary
  linecode b8zs
  pri-group timeslots 1-24
```

By using timeslots 1–24, you indicate that you are using the complete T1. To configure a T1-based PRI, apply the configuration commands to the PRI D channel (i.e., interface Serial0:23). All B channels in an ISDN PRI (or BRI) interface are automatically bundled into a dialer interface. When calls are made or received on the B channels, the configuration is cloned from the dialer interface (Serial0:23).

Exam Essentials

Remember the controller interfaces.   To configure a controller interface, the first T1 you have is T1 0, and the second is T1 1.

Remember the clock source.   You can set the clock by using the clock source line primary and clock source line secondary commands.

Understand how to configure the timeslots.   By using the pri-group timeslots command, you can set your router's controller interface with the timeslots you have purchased.

Key Terms and Concepts

PRI (Primary Rate Interface)   An ISDN specification that uses timeslots in a T1. It has 23 B channels of 64K each and 1 D channel for signaling at 64K.

BRI (Basic Rate Interface)   Uses two B (bearer) channels of 64K each for data transfer and one D (data) channel of 16K for signaling.

Sample Questions

1. ISDN PRI can use how many time slots?

A. 2

B. 8

C. 16

D. 24

E. 32

F. 38

Answer: D—An ISDN can use up to 24 ISDN time slots.

2. What command is used to configure timeslot in an ISDN PRI?

A. `groupp-pri timeslots`

B. `pri-group timeslots`

C. `timeslots-pri groups`

D. `groups-pri timeslots`

Answer: B—The `pri-group timeslots` command is used to specify the slots purchased in a T1.

Index

Note to the Reader: Page numbers in **bold** indicate the principal discussion of a topic or the definition of a term. Page numbers in *italic* indicate illustrations.

A

ABR (area border router)
  configuring
    default cost route on, 179–180
    inter-area route summarization on, 178, 180
    totally stubby areas on, 179
  defined, **168, 169**
  LSAs generated by, 173
access. *See* managing traffic and access
Access layer, 27, 28, **29**, *29*
access lists. *See also* extended access lists; standard access lists
  alternative to IP, 50–52
  AppleTalk, 376, 377
  defined, **72**
  IP
    extended, 40–42
    standard, 30–36
    verifying operation of, 44–49
  IPX
    categories of, 66–67
    extended, 69–70, 72
access-class command, 38, **39**
access-group command, 35, 40, **43**
accessibility and security, 12
  authentication protocols, 12
  dedicated and switched WAN support, 12
  exterior protocol support, 12
  scalable internetworks and, 4
access-list command, 33, 35, **43**, 375–376, 378
access-list 101 command, 266, 267
Ack packet, 189
adaptability
  balancing multiple network protocols, 11
  bridging and, 11
  creating network islands, 11
  redistribution and, 11
  with routable and nonroutable network protocols, 4
  scalable internetworks and, 4
  using EIGRP, 11
administrative distance
  assigning, 215–216
  changing assigned EIGRP, 208
  defined, **205, 214**

IGRP default, 215, 218
of static routing, 228
aggregation. *See* route summarization
algorithms
  DUAL, **192**, 193
  routing, 108–110
    distance-vector, 110, **113**, 119, 375
    link-state, 109, 110, *110*, **113**
  source-route bridging, **341**, 346, 357, 362
  source-route translational bridging, **357**
  SPF (shortest path first), 145, 148, 173
all-routes explorer packets, 340–341
alternate path routing, 8
AMI (alternate mark inversion), **389**
appletalk getzonelist-filter command, 372, 373
AppleTalk networks, **366–382**
  configuring NBP filters, **379–382**
    command used to filter NBP, 380, 382
    example, 381
    function of NBP, 379, 381
  configuring RTMP filters, **375–379**
    commands to filter RTMP updates, 375–376, 378
    function of, 375–376, 377
    updating routers with RTMP, 375, 378
  configuring zone filters, **370–374**
    GZL filters, 370, 371, 372, 373, **374**
    ZIP reply filters, 370, 371–372, 373, **374**
  defined, **369**
  GZL broadcasts, 367, **369**
  identifying potential congestion for, 367–370
  overview, 366
  zones, **369**
appletalk zip-reply-filter command, 373
application traffic on WAN networks, 248
area border router. *See* ABR
AS (autonomous system)
  autonomous system LSA, 173, *174*
  defined, **205, 221, 226**
  used by BGP routing, 229–230
AS (autonomous system) number
  defined, 195, **196**
  overview of, 202
  selecting for BGP routing, 232, 233

ASBR (autonomous system boundary router)
  configuring external route summarization
    on, 178, 180
  defined, **168, 169**
  LSAs generated by, 173, 174
  route redistribution and, 208
asynchronous dial-in products, 238, 240
ATM (asynchronous transfer mode), 5
authentication protocols, 12
automatic Spanning Tree configuration,
  343–344
autonomous system. *See* AS
autonomous system boundary router. *See*
  ASBR

B

B8ZS (binary 8-zero substitution), **389**
backbone area, 170, 171, 174, **180**, **184**
backbone router, **168, 169**
backup delay command, 279–280
backup load command, 279–280
bandwidth
  calculating best route to network with
    EIGRP, 188, 191, 192
  configuring router to handle over-satura-
    tion of, 280, 281
  custom queuing and, 98–99, *99*, 101
  defined, **88, 97, 214, 249**
  doubling with multilink PPP, 243
  interface, 194, **196**
  IPX and, 61
  legacy DDR and, 261
  in link-state routing algorithms, 109, 110
  managing over WANs, 74
  network congestion and, 18, 19
  primary-link bandwidth saturation,
    280–281
  of T1 and E1 channels, 384
  WAN connectivity and requirements for,
    248
Basic Rate Interface. *See* ISDN BRI
BDR (backup designated router), 150
Bellman-Ford routing algorithm, 147
BGP (Border Gateway Protocol), 224–234. *See
  also* BGP routing
  default administrative distance for, 216,
    217
  defined, **5, 226, 233**
  external, 216, **225, 226**
  internal, 217, **225, 226**
  methods of connecting to ISP, 228–234

  overview, 224
  situations requiring, 224–227
  types of, 225, 226
BGP routing
  connecting ISP with, 229–230
  methods of, 228–234
    BGP routing, 229–230, 232, **233**
    default routing, 229, 231, 232
    static routing, 228–229, 230, 232
    overview, 224
    situations requiring, 224–227
    scenarios requiring, 225
    types of BGP protocol, 225, 226
  creating, 232, 233
  defined, *233*
BootP (Boostrap Protocol), **57**
BRI (Basic Rate Interface). *See* ISDN BRI
BRI port, 281
bridge 1 protocol command, 323, 329, 331, 335
bridge irb command, 331, 335
bridge-group command, 347–348
bridging, **312–363**
  adaptability and, 11
  bridge performance on MAC sublayer,
    21–22, 215
  dissimilar media with Token Ring, 351
  Integrated Routing and Bridging (IRB),
    330–336
    commands for configuring, 331, 335
    configuring, 332–335, *332*
    defined, **336**
    overview, 322, 330–331
    verifying configuration, 331, 335
  OSI-model bridge routing, 312–313, *312*
  purpose of, 314, 315
  routable and nonroutable protocols,
    313–317
    broadcast domains and bridges, 313, 315
    overview, 313
    routers and protocol dependencies, 314
  segmenting networks with, 21–22, 25
  source-route, **338–363**
    about, 317, 318, **319**, 319
    basic functions of, 339–342
    configuring, 342–346
    verifying operation of, 358–363
  source-route translational
    about, 317, 319
    configuring, 350–358
    function of, 350–351
  source-route transparent
    about, 317, 318
    configuring, 347–350

transparent, 322–330
about, 317–318, **319**, 322
avoiding loops, 324–325, *325*
configuring, 323–324, *323*, 326–327, 329
defined, **319**, **330**
Spanning Tree Protocol, 325–326, 329
verifying configurations, 326, 328–329
types of, **317–320**
broadcast domains and bridges, 313, 315
broadcasts
defined, 57
frequency of SAP, 65
managing, **52–58**
enabling protocols with ip helper-address command, 52, 57
routing broadcasts to multiple servers, 54–56, *55*, 57
syntax for, 53–54
using ip forward-protocol command, 56, 57
of SAP, IP RIP, and IPX RIP protocols, 65
BVI (bridge-group virtual interface), 330, **336**

C

Carrier Sense Multiple Access/Collision Detection (CSMA/CD), **19**
cell switching (ATM), **23**
channel-group command, 387, 389
channelized T1 and E1 configuration, 385–390
commands for setting up, 389
configuring channelized E1, 386, 388
configuring channelized T1, 385–386, 387
framing types and linecodes for, 386, 389
FSIP, 385, 388
MIP cards, 384, 385, 388
overview, 384
CHAP (Challenge Handshake Authentication Protocol), **12**
CIDR (classless interdomain routing), **147**
Cisco IOS (internetwork operating system)
defined, **5**
features solving internetwork requirements, 7–14
Cisco routers, configuring OSPF on, overview, 155–156
Class A private networks, 134, 135
Class B private networks, 134, 135
Class C private networks, 134, 135
clear interface bri n command, 295, 297

clients
configuring for snapshot routing, 303–304, 305
setting up dialer map for, 303–304, 305
clock source command, 391, 392
commands. *See also specific commands*
configuring
Integrated Routing and Bridging (IRB), 331, 335
IPX spoofing, 309
ISDN PRI, 390–393
ISDN PRI controller interface, 392
debug, **362**
filtering
NBP, 380, 382
RTMP updates, 375–376, 378
setting
ISDN PRI clock source, 391, 392
ISDN PRI router's controller interface, 392
showing interfaces set by IP access lists, 49
spelling of queueing commands, 103, 106
testing, DDR operation, 274–275
verifying
access list operation, 44, 48
EIGRP operation, 198–199, **200**
IPX connectivity, 76–84
OSPF operations in multiple OSPF areas, 182–183
queuing operation, 102, 103, 105
for viewing routing tables, 220
configuring
alternatives to IP access lists, 50–52
BRI ports, 258
channelized E1, 386, 388
channelized T1, 385–386, 387
clients for snapshot routing, 303, 305
dialer interface, 270, 272
dialer profiles, 271–272
EIGRP, 194–197
helper addresses for multiple servers and subnets, 54–56, *55*, 57
hop counts in routing algorithms, 109, 110
Integrated Routing and Bridging (IRB), 332–335, *332*
IP extended access lists, 40–43
IP helper address to manage broadcasts, 52–58
IP standard access lists, 30–36
IPX spoofing, 309
ISDN BRI, 257–260
ISDN PRI, 390–393
ISDN switch types, 259

legacy DDR, 262
load and MTU in routing algorithms, 109, 110
multiarea OSPF network, 176–181
NAT, 137, 138
NBP filters, 379–382
OSPF in single area, **142–164**
   advantages over RIP in large internetworks, 143–149
   on Cisco routers, 155–159
   discovering, choosing, and maintaining routes, 149–155
   overview, 142
   verifying operations, 159–164
priority queuing, 95–96
queuing, **86–106**, 86–106
   custom, 98–102
   for large internetworks, 87–89
   overview, 86
   priority, 93–98
   verifying, 102–106
   weighted fair, 89–93, *90*
redistribution
   with redundant paths, 210–215
   without redundant paths, 206–209
servers for snapshot routing, 305
source-route bridging (SRB), 342–346
source-route translational bridging (SR/TLB), 350–358
source-route transparent bridging (SRT), 347–350
SPT
   automatic, 343–344
   manual, 343
stub area, 172, 174, 178–179, **180**
stub routers, 173
totally stubby areas, 179
transparent bridging, 323–324, *323*, 326–327, 329
variable cost links, 211, 213
vty ports, 37–38
congestive-discard-threshold option, 91, 92
connected interface, 216
contiguous networks
   defined, **127**
   using route summarization with, 132
controlling route update traffic, 203–206
   advertising specific networks, **204**, 204
   preventing broadcasts exiting interface, 203–204, **204**
   route filtering, 204
convergence
   defined, **13**, **119**, **147**

with distance-vector routing protocols, 114–115
   in link-state routing, 117
   of scalable routing protocols, 8
   speed of RIP, 144–145, 146
Core layer, 27, 28, **29**, 29
cost links, 211, 213
costs, WAN connectivity and, 248
CSMA/CD (Carrier Sense Multiple Access/Collision Detection), **19**
custom queuing, 88, 88, 98–102. *See also* queuing
   bandwidth and, 98–99, 99, 101
   configuring, 100–101
   maximum number of configurable queues, 98, 101
   responsiveness and, 9
   verifying queuing operations, 105
cut-through switching, **26**

D

data link connection identifier (DLCI), 92
Data Link layer
   bridging on, 312, *312*
   checking with debug isdn q921 command, 275
   as Layer two, **276**, **290**
   using addresses in nonroutable addresses, 313
databases
   synchronizing with LSAs, 152
   topological, 183, 187, 193
DDPs (database description packets), 152
DDR (dial-on-demand routing), **260–310**. *See also* ISDN
   defined, **240**
   dial backup, 279–291
      backup delay and backup load commands, 279–280
      debug dialer command, 284, 289–290
      debug isdn q921 command, 284, 287–288, 290
      debug isdn q931 command, 284, 288–289, 290
      debug ppp negotiation command, 284, 288, 290
      failure for DDR connections, 279
      overview, 279
      ping command, 283, 285, 290
      primary-link bandwidth saturation, 280–281

primary-link failure, 280
show dialer command, 284, 285–286, 290
show isdn status command, 284, 286–287, 290
dialer profiles, 268–273
  configuring dialer interface, 270, 272
  example of, 271–272
  running DDR with encapsulation method, 270–271
  steps for creating profiles, 269–270
IPX spoofing, 306–310
  commands for, 309
  entering no ipx route-cache command first, 308, 309
  syntax for, 308
legacy, 260–268
  advantages of DDR, 261–262
  configuration steps, 262
  creating a dialer list, 264–266
  specifying access lists, 266–267
  static routing, 262–264
  using IPX protocol, 267
  when to use redistribute command, 267
MultiLink PPP, 291–301
  clear interface bri n command, 295, 297
  commands for, 292, 293
  debug ppp multilink fragments command, 295, 296–297, 300
  overview, 295
  show controller bri command, 296, 300
  show dialer command, 295
  show interface bri n 1 2 command, 295, 299, 300
  show interface bri n command, 295, 297–299, 300
  syntax for, 293
  overview of, 260–261
PPP encapsulation method with, 270, 272
snapshot routing, 302–306
  configuring clients, 303, 305
  configuring servers, 305
  overview, 302
  setting up client and server with, 303–304
  setting up dialer map for client and server, 303–304, 305
  verifying, 274–276
  commands for, 274–275
  dial backup operation, 283–291
  MultiLink PPP operation, 295–301
WAN connectivity and, 239
debug commands, **362**

debug dialer command, 274, 275, 284
debug isdn q921 command, 275, 284
debug isdn q931 command, 275, 284
debug ppp multilink fragments command, 295, 296–297, 300
debug ppp negotiation command, 284
debug rif command, 362
DEC bridging protocol, 346, 347–348, 349
decimal to binary conversion of IP addresses, 31–33, 35, 131, 132
dedicated and switched WAN support, 12
dedicated-leased lines, 237–238, 238, 240
default, **101**
default routing
  connecting to ISP with, 229, 232
  cost of, 179–180
  creating with ip route command, 231, 233
  defined, **226, 233**
default-metric command, 207–208
delay
  in EIGRP metrics, 191
  in link-state routing algorithm, 109, 110
delay of line, 147
designated router. *See* DR
DHCP (Dynamic Host Configuration Protocol), **57**
dial backup, 279–283
  backup delay and backup load commands, 279–280
  failure for DDR connections, 279
  overview, 279
  primary-link bandwidth saturation, 280–281
  primary-link failure, 280
  verifying, 283–291
    with debug dialer command, 284, 289–290
    with debug isdn q921 command, 284, 287–288, 290
    with debug isdn q931 command, 284, 288–289, 290
    with debug ppp negotiation command, 284, 288, 290
    with ping command, 283, 285, 290
    with show dialer command, 284, 285–286, 290
    with show isdn status command, 284, 286–287, 290
dial-backup links, 9
dialer interface, 270, 272
dialer lists, 264–266
dialer load-threshold command, 292, 293
dialer map command, 303–304, 305

dialer profiles, 268–273
  example of configuration, 271–272
  running DDR with encapsulation method,
    270–271
  steps for creating, 269–270
dial-on-demand routing. *See* DDR
digital signal level 0 (DS-0), **389**
Dijkstra, E. W., 145
discontiguous IP addresses, 125, 127
discontiguous networks
  avoiding route summarization with, 132
  defined, **127**
dispatching algorithm in priority queuing, 95
distance-vector routing algorithms
  defined, **110, 113, 119**
  RTMP as, 375
distance-vector routing protocol, 112–120
  convergence, 114–115
  defined, **147**
  differences between link-state and, 118,
    119, 147
  handling routing loops, 115–116
  overview, 112
  snapshot routing and, 302
distribute-list command, 195, 196, 197, 204,
    375–376, 378
Distribution layer, 27, 28, **29,** 29
DLCI (data link connection identifier), 92
DR (designated router)
  defined, **154**
  discovering OSPF neighbors, 150
  present with Broadcast or NBMA network
    types, 150
DS-0 (digital signal level 0), **389**
DUAL (diffused update algorothim) algorithm,
    192, 193
dynamic routing, **226**

E

E1 lines. *See* channelized T1 and E1
    configuration
E protocol, 254, **256**
eBGP (external Border Gateway Protocol)
  default administrative distance for, 216
  defined, **225,** 226
efficiency, 9–10
  access lists and, 10
  compression over WANs, 10
  dial-on-demand routing, 10
  reduction in routing table entries, 10

scalable internetworks and, 4
  snapshot routing and, 10
EFS (Extended Super Frame), **389**
EGP (Exterior Gateway Protocol)
  default administrative distance for, 217
  defined, **5**
EIGRP (Enhanced Interior Gateway Routing
    Protocol), 186–200
  alternate path routing, 8
  configuring, 194–197
    autonomous system number, 195, **196**
    connection speeds, 194
    syntax for, **196**
  default administrative distance for, 216
  defined, **5**
  DUAL algorithm, **192,** 193
  features and operations of, 187–193
    establishing neighbor relationships,
      188–189, 191, 192
    updating routes, 189, *190*
  as hybrid distance-vector routing protocol,
    113
  load balancing and, 8, 191
  overview, 186
  reliability and availability of, 8
  route distribution and, 208
  topology database in, 187, 193
  verifying operation of, 197–200
    commands, 198–199, **200**
EIGRP distribution list, **196**
EIGRP events command, **200**
EIGRP network, **196**
EIGRP passive interface
  defined, **196**
  flagging updates as, 194
Ethernet, 351
explorer packets
  defined, **341**
  types of, 340–341
extended access lists. *See also* standard access
    lists
  IP
    applying with access-group command,
      40
    IP standard access lists vs., 40
    memorizing industry standard port
      numbers, 42
    number range for, 41, 42
    protocols and filtering, 42
    syntax for, 41

IPX, 69–70, 72
  defined, 67
  number ranges for, 72
  parameters for filtering, 72
Extended Super Frame (ESF), 386, 389, 389
extending IP addresses with VLSMs, 123–128
  adjusting host and network portions of IP
    addresses, 124–125, 124
  avoiding discontiguous IP addresses, 125, 127
  defining number of hosts on network,
    125–126, 126, 127
  using VLSMs on router, 127
Exterior Gateway Protocol (EGP), 5, 217
exterior routing protocols, 13

F

failure
  for DDR connections, 279
  primary-link, 280
fair-queue command, 91, 92
Fast Ethernet, 25
Fast Serial Interface Processor (FSIP), 385, 388
FDDI (Fiber Distributed Data Interface)
  defined, 19
  function of, 25
  lack of contention with, 25
feedback
  causing, 217
  defined, 218
  resolving, 218
FIFO (first in, first out), 87, 88
flat networks, 314
Frame Relay
  defined, 6
  using IETF encapsulation with, 245
frame switching, 23
frame types
  for channelized T1 and E1 configurations,
    386, 389
  for LAPB, 244
FSIP (Fast Serial Interface Processor), 385, 388
full-duplex communications, 26
full-duplex Ethernet devices, 24, 25
  defined, 24
  lack of contention with, 25

G

GNS (get nearest server), 63, 65

GZL (GetZoneList)
  defined, 369, 378
  as reason for AppleTalk congestion, 367, 369
GZL filters, 370, 371, 372, 373, 374

H

HDLC (High-Level Data Link Control)
  defined, 245
  as encapsulation method with DDR, 270
  LAPB's advantages over, 244, 245
  when to use with WANs, 241, 243–244,
    245
Hello packets
  establishing neighbor relationships with
    EIGRP, 188–189, 191, 192
  LSPs as, 116
Hello protocol
  defined, 154
  establishing peering sessions between
    routers, 150, 151
  maintaining route information with, 152, 154
  making peer relationships with neighbors, 147
help screens for OSPF verification, 163
hierarchical routing, 167, 169
holddown state, 115
hop counts
  configuring in routing algorithms, 109, 110
  defined, 110
  as difference between OSPF and RIP
    protocols, 147
  maximum number of, 115, 118
  used in RIP protocol, 110
hops, 65

I

I protocol, 254, 256
IANA (Internet Assigned Numbers Authority),
  133–134
iBGP (internal Border Gateway Protocol), 217,
  225, 226
IBM bridging protocol, 346, 347–348, 349
IEEE bridging protocol, 346, 347–348, 349
IEEE (Institute of Electrical and Electronics
  Engineering), 349
IETF (Internet Engineering Task Force)
  defined, 246
  when to use with WANs, 241, 245

IGRP (Interior Gateway Routing Protocol)
  default administrative distance for, 215, 216, 218
  as distance-vector routing protocol, 113
  maximum hop count for, 118
  route distribution into EIGRP, 208
IGRP global-router-configuration command, 217
implied *deny any* statements, 31, 35
Integrated Routing and Bridging. *See* IRB
inter-area routing
  defined, **167**, **169**
  intra-area routing vs., 167, 168
interconnecting multiple OSPF areas
  about areas, routers, and LSAs, 170–175
    backbone area, 170, 171, 174, **180**, **184**
    LSA types, 173–174
    not-so-stubby area (NSSA), 171, 172
    standard area, 170, 171, 174
    stub area, 171–172, 174, **180**
    totally stub area, 171, 172, **180**
  configuring multiarea OSPF network, 176–181
    configuring default route cost, 179–180
    configuring totally stubby areas, 179
    with network command and wildcard masking, 177, 180
    overview, 176
    route summarization, 177–178, 180
    stub area configuration, 178–179, 180
  issues and problems, 166–170
    inter-area routing vs. intra-area routing, 167, 168
    process ID values, 168
    types of routers, 168
  verifying OSPF operation in, 181–184
    commands for, 182–183
    overview, 181–182
interface bvi1 command, 331, 335
interfaces
  applying standard IP access lists to physical, 34, 35
  configuring dialer, 270, 272
  default administrative distance for connected, 216
  defined, **101**
  finding IPX address of, 83
  showing interfaces set by IP access lists, 49
internal router, **168**, **169**
Internet
  connecting BGP to ISPs, **224–234**

  network addresses and wildcard masks, 31–33, 35
  private network addresses and, 134
Internet Service Providers. *See* ISPs
internetworks
  choosing routing algorithm for, 110
  configuring queuing for large, 87–89
  defined, **6**, **19**
  IPX's support for, 63
  OSPF
    OSPF vs. RIP characteristics, 146
    scalability features of OSPF, 145–146
    scalability limitations of RIP, 144–145
  scalable, 2–14
    IOS features for internetwork requirements, 7–14
    key requirements of, **2–7**
    overview, 2–3
    solving network congestion for, 17–19
  solving network congestion for, 17–19
intra-area routing
  defined, **167**, **169**
  inter-area routing vs., 167, 168
IP access lists
  alternative to, 50–52
    configuring alternatives to Null 0 interface, 50, 51
    configuring helper addresses for multiple servers and subnets, 54–56, 55, 57
    protocols enabled with ip helper-address command, 52, 57
    using ip forward-protocol command, 56, 57
  commands showing interfaces set by, 49
  efficiency and, 10
  extended
    applying with access-group command, 40
    IP standard access lists vs., 40
    memorizing industry standard port numbers, 42
    number range for, 41, 42
    protocols and filtering, 42
    syntax for, 41
  serving accessibility and security with, 12
  standard, 30–36
    applying to physical interfaces, 34, 35
    creating, 33–34
    extended access lists vs., 40
    filtering from top to bottom, 35
    implied *deny any* at end of, 31, 35

locating near destination router, 30, 35
network addresses and wildcard masks,
    31–33, 35
syntax for access-list command, 33, 35
verifying operation of, 44–49
IP addresses, **122–139**
extending use of with VLSMs, **123–128**
about VLSMs, 122–123
adjusting host and network portions of
    addresses, 124–125, *124*
avoiding discontiguous IP addresses,
    125, 127
classless and classfull IP addresses,
    123–124
defining number of hosts on network,
    125–126, *126*, 127
using VLSMs on router, 127
IP helper addresses, **52–58**
enabling protocols with, 52, 57
routing broadcasts to multiple servers,
    54–56, *55*, 57
syntax for, 53–54
using ip forward-protocol command,
    56, 57
network address translation, **136–139**
Cisco proprietary version of, 136, 138
configuring, 137, 138
when to use, 138
private addressing, **133–136**
function of, 135
IANA assigned private networks, 134
ranges for Class A, B, and C private net-
    works, 135
route summarization, **128–133**
with contiguous networks, 132
decimal to binary conversion of IP
    addresses, 131, 132
when to use, 129, 132
significant bits, 130, **132**
ip forward-protocol command, 54, 56, 57
IP helper addresses, **52–58**
enabling protocols with, 52, 57
routing broadcasts to multiple servers,
    54–56, *55*, 57
syntax for, 53–54
using ip forward-protocol command, 56,
    57
ip helper-address command, 52, 54, 57
ip ospf priority command, 212, 214
IP RIP protocols, 65
ip route command, **52**, 230
IPX (Internetwork Packet Exchange)
commands for verifying connectivity, 76–82

defined, **65**, **75**
development as protocol suite, 61
mapping to OSI model, 62
uses of, 60, 267
IPX access lists
categories of, 66–67
extended, 69–70, **7**2
filtering IPX traffic with, 66–73
number ranges for, 72
standard, 68–69, 72
verifying IPX/SPX filtering operation,
    76–84
IPX networking
maintaining dialup connections across
    DDR, *307*
maintaining dialup connections with LAN,
    307
spoofing and, 306
IPX RIP protocol, 65
IPX SAP filters
defined, **67**
parameters for, 72
simplifying configuration with, 70–71
ipx sap-interval command, 74–75
IPX spoofing, **306–310**
commands for configuring, 309
entering no ipx route-cache command first,
    308, 309
syntax for, 308
ipx spx-idle-time command, 309
ipx spx-spoof command, 309
ipx watchdog-spoof command, 309
IRB (Integrated Routing and Bridging),
    330–336
commands for configuring, 331, 335
configuring, 332–335, *332*
defined, **336**
overview, 322
verifying configuration, 331, 335
ISDN (Integrated Services Digital Network),
    253–257. *See also* DDR; ISDN BRI; ISDN
    PRI
defined, **240, 256, 259, 272, 290**
overview, 252
protocols, 254, **256**
reference points, 254
switch types, 254–255, 259
terminals, 253
ISDN BRI (Basic Rate Interface)
commands for viewing B and D channels,
    274, 275
configuring, 257–260

defined, 255, 256, 259, 267, 273, 282, 294, 305
obtaining SPID for, 255
TE1 terminal adapter with, 257
ISDN PRI (Primary Rate Interface), 256
  configuration commands for, 390–393
    configuring controller interface, 392
    setting clock source, 391, 392
    setting router's controller interface, 392
  defined, 256
ISDN reference points, 254
ISDN switch types
  configuring, 259
  key word for configuring, 254–255
isdn switch-type command, 391
ISDN terminals, 253
ISPs (Internet Service Providers), 224–234
  connecting BGP to, 228–234
  overview, 224
  scenarios requiring BGP protocol, 225
  situations requiring BGP, 224–227

K

keepalive, defined, 309
keepalive packets, 306, 309

L

LAN switches
  cell switching, 23
  features supported with, 24
  frame switching, 23
  port-configuration switching, 23
  segmenting networks with, 23, 25
LAPB (Link Access Procedure, Balanced)
  advantages over HDLC, 244, 245
  defined, 246
  frame types for, 244
  when to use with WANs, 241, 244
LAT (Local Area Transport), 314, 315
latency, 6, 26
Layer one, as Physical layer, 276
Layer two
  bridging on, 312, 312
  as Data Link layer, 276, 290
Layer three, as Network layer, 276, 290
LCP (Link Control Protocol), 242
legacy DDR, 260–268
  advantages of, 261–262
  commands for testing, 283–284
  configuration steps for, 262

creating a dialer list, 264–266
overview of, 260–261
specifying access lists to define traffic on, 266–267
static routing, 262–264
using IPX protocol, 267
when to use redistribute command, 267
linecodes for channelized T1 and E1 configurations, 386, 389
Link Access Procedure, Balanced. *See* LAPB
Link Control Protocol (LCP), 242
link-state advertisements. *See* LSAs
link-state packets (LSPs), 116
link-state routing algorithm
  bandwidth in, 109, 110
  defined, 110, 113
  metrics used in, 110
link-state routing protocol, 112–120
  convergence in, 117
  defined, 148, 164
  distance-vector routing vs., 118, 119, 147
  with large internetworks, 147
  network discovery in, 116
  overview, 112
load, configuring in routing algorithms, 109, 110
load balancing
  for Cisco IOS, 8
  defined, 214
  in EIGRP, 8, 191
  in OSPF, 8
Local Area Transport (LAT), 314, 315
local explorer packets, 340–341
local ring, 346
loopback interface, 212–213
lowest-custom option, 101
LSAs (link-state advertisements)
  defined, 154, 184
  purpose of, 153, 154
  synchronizing databases with, 152
  types of, 173–174
LSPs (link-state packets), 116

M

MAC addresses, 318, 319
MAC sublayer, bridge performance on, 21–22, 315
Maintenance Operation Protocol (MOP), 314, 315
managing traffic and access, 16–58
  for AppleTalk networks, 366–382
    configuring NBP filters, 379–382

configuring RTMP filters, 375–379
configuring zone filters, 370–374
identifying potential congestion for, 367–370
causes of network congestion, 17–20
key terms and concepts, 19
overview, 17–19
configuring alternative to IP access lists, 50–52
Null 0 interface, 50, 51
configuring IP extended access lists, 40–43
memorizing industry standard port numbers, 42
number range for, 41, 42
protocols and filtering, 42
syntax for, 41
configuring IP helper address to manage broadcasts, 52–58
enabling protocols with ip helper-address command, 52, 57
routing broadcasts to multiple servers, 54–56, 55, 57
syntax for, 53–54
using ip forward-protocol command, 56, 57
configuring IP standard access lists, 30–36
applying lists to physical interfaces, 34, 35
creating access lists, 33–34
filtering from top to bottom, 35
implied *deny any* at end of, 31, 35
locating lists near destination router, 30, 35
network addresses and wildcard masks, 31–33, 35
syntax for access-list command, 33, 35
configuring queuing, 86–106
for large network, 87–89
overview, 86
priorities, 93–98
setting up custom queuing, 98–102
verifying queuing operation, 102–106
in weighted fair queuing operation, 89–93, 90
controlling network congestion, 20–26
with Fast Ethernet, 25
with FDDI, 25
with full-duplex Ethernet devices, 24, 25
with network switching technology, 23, 24
overview, 20–21
with physical segmentation, 21–23

exam objectives for, 16
limiting virtual terminal access, 37–39
Novell IPX/SPX traffic, 60–84
filtering IPX traffic with IPX access lists, 66–73
management issues for, 61–66
managing over WANs, 73–76
verifying IPX/SPX filtering operation, 76–84
three-layer hierarchical model and, 27–30
Access layer, 27, 28, **29**, 29
Core layer, 27, 28, **29**, 29
Distribution layer, 27, 28, **29**, 29
illustrated, 27
verifying access list operation, 44–49
commands for, 44, 48
manual Spanning-Tree configuration, 343
maximum transmission unit. *See* MTU
metrics. *See* routing metrics
MIP (MultiChannel Interface Processor) cards, 384, 385, 388
MOP (Maintenance Operation Protocol), 314, 315
MTU (maximum transmission unit)
configuring in routing algorithms, 109, 110
defined, **110**
in EIGRP metrics, 191
multicasts, 57
multilink, **294**, **305**
MultiLink PPP, 291–294
commands for configuring, 292, 293
doubling bandwidth with, 243
syntax for configuring, 293
verifying, 295–301
clear interface bri n command, 295, 297
debug ppp multilink fragments command, 295, 296–297, 300
overview, 295
show controller bri command, 296, 300
show dialer command, 295
show interface bri n 1 2 command, 295, 299, 300
show interface bri n command, 295, 297–299, 300

N

NAP (network access point), 225
NAT (Network Address Translation), 136–139
Cisco proprietary version of, 136, 138
configuring, 137, 138
defined, **135**

private network assignments and, 134
when to use, 138
NAT inside command, 138
NAT outside command, 138
NAT pool, 137, 138
NBP (Name Binding Protocol)
defined, **369**, **378**
as reason for AppleTalk congestion,
367–368, 369
NBP filters, **379–382**
command for filtering NBP, 380, 382
example of configuring, 381
function of NBP protocol, 379, 381
NCP (NetWare Core Protocol), 63
neighbor relationships
discovering OSPF, 150, *151*
establishing in EIGRP with Hello packets,
188–189, 191, 192, **193**
making peer relationships with Hello
protocol, 147
synchronizing routes with neighbors, 150,
151
viewing with show ip ospf neighbor command, 183, 184
neighbor tables
in calculating EIGRP best route and load
sharing, 192
SRTT in EIGRP, 188
neighboring routers, **154**
NetBEUI, as nonroutable protocol, 314, 315
network access point (NAP), 225
network address translation. *See* NAT
network addresses. *See also* NAT
creating supernet, 130
private, 134
wildcard masks and, 31–33, 35
network command, 177, 180
network congestion
bandwidth and, 18, 19
causes of, 17–20
controlling, 20–26
with Fast Ethernet, 25
with FDDI, 25
with full-duplex Ethernet devices, 24,
25
with network switching technology, 23,
24
overview, 20–21
with physical segmentation, 21–23, 25
identifying potentials for AppleTalk,
367–370
key terms and concepts, 19
network hosts, 125–126, *126*, 127

network islands, 11
Network layer
checking with debug isdn q931 command,
275
as Layer three, **276**, **290**
nonroutable protocols and, 313
routers function on, 22
network LSAs, 173, 174
network switching technology, 23, 24
NLSP (NetWare Link Services Protocol), 63
NLSP (Novel Link State Protocol), reachability
and, 8
no bridge 1 bridge command, 331, 335
no ipx route-cache command, 308, 309
nonroutable protocols
allowing routable and, 4
defined, **6**, **315**
list of, 314–315
overview, 313
not-so-stubby area (NSSA), 171, 172
Novell IPX protocol stack, **61–63**, *62*
development of, 61
IPX, 62, *62*
IPX, SAP, and RIP updates, 63–64
IPX's internetworking capability, 63
NCP, 63
NLSP, 63
RIP, 62, *62*, 65
SAP, 63
SPX, 62, *62*
Novell IPX/SPX traffic
filtering IPX traffic with IPX access lists,
66–73
extended IPX access lists, 69–70
IPX SAP filters, 70–71
standard IPX access lists, 68–69
management issues for, 61–66
Novell IPX protocol stack, 61–63, *62*
managing over WANs, 73–76
overview, 73
solving bandwidth issues, 74
verifying IPX/SPX filtering operation,
76–84
with show access-list command, 78, 82
with show ipx interface command, 78,
79–80
with show ipx servers command, 78–79
with show ipx traffic command, 78,
80–81
with show proto command, 78, 82
NSSA (not-so-stubby area), 171, 172
Null 0 interface
defined, **52**

key concepts about, 50, 51
static route to, *51*
number range for extended access lists, 41, 42

O

optimizing routing updates. *See* routing
    updates
OSI Reference model
    AppleTalk and, 366
    bridging and, 312–313, *312*, 315
    Data Link layer
        bridging on, 312, *312*
        checking with debug isdn q921
            command, 275
        as Layer two, **276, 290**
        using addresses in nonroutable
            addresses, 313
    IPX protocol stack and, 62
    Network layer
        checking with debug isdn q931
            command, 275
        as Layer three, **276, 290**
        nonroutable protocols and, 313
        routers function on, 22
    Physical layer
        checking with show controllers
            command, 275
        as Layer one, **276**
OSPF (Open Shortest Path First)
    alternate path routing, 8
    configuring in single area, **142–164**
        advantages over RIP in large
            internetworks, 143–149
        on Cisco routers, 155–159
        discovering, choosing, and maintaining
            routes, 149–155
        overview, 142
        verifying operations, 159–164
    default administrative distance for, 216
    defined, **6, 148**
    interconnecting multiple OSPF areas,
        165–184
        about areas, routers, and LSAs,
            170–175
        configuring multiarea OSPF network,
            176–181
        issues and problems, 166–170
        verifying OSPF operation in, 181–184
    as link-state routing protocol, 113
    load balancing and, 8
    reliability and availability of, 8

route distribution into EIGRP, 208
route redistribution
    changing cost of link with redundant
        paths, 213, 214
    configuring router priority with redun-
        dant paths, 212, 214
OSPF peer initialization, **151**

P

packet tunneling, 9
packets
    database description, 152
    defined, **249**
    ineffectiveness of spanning-tree in SR/TLB,
        351
    keepalive, 306, **309**
    link-state, 116
    priority queuing and, 93, 97
    types of explorer, 340–341
packet-switched services, 239, 240
PAP (Password Authentication Protocol), 12
passive interface command, 194, 196, 197, 203
performance. *See* network congestion; routing
    updates
physical interfaces, 34, 35
Physical layer
    checking with show controllers command,
        275
    as Layer one, **276**
physical segmentation
    with bridge, 21–22
    with LAN switches, 23
    with router, 22–23
ping command, 283
poison reverse, 115
port-configuration switching, **23**
ports
    configuring BRI, 258
    memorizing industry standard port num-
        bers, 42
    MIP support for T1 and E1 subchannels,
        385
    vty, 37–38, **39**, *39*
ppp multilink command, 292, 293
PPP (Point-to-Point Protocol)
    defined, **246, 291, 294, 305**
    as encapsulation method with DDR, 270,
        272
    using MultiLink PPP, 243
    using over HDLC, 245
    when to use with WANs, 241, 242, 245

PRI. *See* ISDN PRI
primary link
    bandwidth saturation of, 280–281
    defined, **282**
    failure of, 280
Primary Rate Interface. *See* ISDN PRI
priority queuing, 93–98. *See also* queuing
    categories for, 94, 97
    configuring, 95–96
    defined, **88**, 88
    overview, 93–94, *95*
    on packet basis, 93, 97
    responsiveness and, 9
    verifying operations of, 104
private addressing, 133–136
    function of, 135
    IANA assigned private networks, 134
    ranges for Class A, B, and C private
        networks, 135
process ID, 155–156, 158, 168
protocol option, **102**
protocols. *See also* routing protocols; *and
    specific protocols listed by name*
    authentication, 12
    balancing multiple network, 11
    bridges and, 314
    dynamic routing, 109
    filtering and extended access lists, 42
    forwarding using ip helper-address
        command, 52, 57
    ISDN, 254, **256**
    MOP as nonroutable protocol, 314, 315
    routing vs. routed, 5
    scalable routing, 143
    using route summarization with routing,
        129
proxy, **135**
PSN (packet switched networks), **240**
PSTN (Public Switched Telephone Network)
    as asynchronous dial-in product, 238
    private packet-switched services and, 239
    PSNs vs., 239

Q

Q921, **290**
Q931, **290**
Q protocol, 254, **256**
queueing, defined, **88**, **97**, **106**
queuing, 86–106
    custom, 98–102
        bandwidth and, 98–99, *99*, 101

        configuring, 100–101
        maximum number of configurable
            queues, 98, 101
    defined, **88**, **92**, **106**
    for large internetworks, 87–89
    priority, 93–98
        categories for, 94, 97
        configuring, 95–96
        defined, **88**, 88
        overview, 93–94, *95*
        on packet basis, 93, 97
    responsiveness and, 9
    verifying, 102–106
        commands for, 102, 103, 105
        for custom queuing, 105
        for priority queuing, 104
        showing queuing, 105
        spelling of queueing commands, 103, 106
        for weighted fair queuing, 104
    vs. queueing, **88**, **97**
    weighted fair, 89–93
        assigning priorities in, 90
        defined, **87**, 88
        overview, 89–91, *90*
        setting up, 91–92

R

R reference point, 254
redistribute command, 267
redistribution
    adaptability and, 11
    defined, **13**
    with redundant paths, 210–215
        adding loopback interface, 212–213
        changing cost of link in OSPF, 213, 214
        changing default metrics, 211–212
        configuring different cost links, 211, 213
        configuring OSPF priority, 212, 214
    without redundant paths, 206–209
        route distribution and EIGRP, 208
    resolving path selection problems, 215–219
        assigning administrative distances,
            215–216
        default administrative distances,
            216–217
        feedback, 218
        IGRP default administrative distance,
            215, 218
    verifying, 220–222
        commands for viewing routing tables,
            220

purpose of routing tables, 221
 reason for, 220, 221
reduction in routing table entries, 10
redundant bridges, *324*
reference points, 254
reliability and availability
 of alternate paths routing, 8
 configuring in routing algorithms, 109, 110
 convergence and, 8
 of dial-backup links, 9
 of load balancing, 8
 of packet tunneling, 9
 reachability and routing protocols, 8
 scalable internetworks and, 3–4
 WAN connectivity and network, 247
remote source-route bridging, 343
responsiveness, 9
 custom queuing and, 9
 priority queuing and, 9
 scalable internetworks and, 4
 weighted fair queuing and, 9
RFC 1918, **135**
RID (router ID), 182, 183
RIF (routing information field)
 defined, **362**
 source-route bridging and, 339, 341
 source-route transparent bridging of, 347
RIP (Routing Information Protocol)
 about, 62, *62*, 64, 65
 default administrative distance for, 216
 defined, **65, 76, 111, 148**
 as distance-vector routing protocol, 113
 hop counts and, 110
 IP RIP and IPX RIP protocols, 65
 OSPF advantage on large internetworks,
  143–149
  OSPF vs. RIP characteristics, 146
  overview, 143
  scalability features of OSPF, 145–146
  scalability limitations of RIP, 144–145
 route distribution into EIGRP, 208
 server updates, 63–64
RIP update intervals
 reducing over WANs, 74
 syntax for changing update timer, 75
routable protocols
 allowing nonroutable and, 4
 defined, **6, 315**
 overview, 313
route filtering, 204
route redistribution. *See* redistribution
route summarization, 128–133, 177–178, 180
 with contiguous networks, 132

decimal to binary conversion of IP
 addresses, 131, 132
 inter-area and external, 178
 on multiarea OSPF network, 177–178, 180
 configuring external summarization on
  ASBR, 178, 180
 configuring inter-area summarization
  on ABR, 178, 180
 when to use, 129, 132
route tagging
 defined, **192, 205**
 as EIGRP feature, 191
 overview, 202
routed protocols, routing protocol vs., 5, 199
router ID (RID), 182, 183
router LSAs, 173, 174
routers, 108–120. *See also* ABR; ASBR; routing
 updates
configuring
 helper addresses for, 54–56, *55, 57*
 ISDN PRI interface for, 391–392
 multiarea OSPF, 176–181
 OSPF on, 155–159
 stub area on, 179, 180
defining autonomous systems on, 202
distance-vector and link-state protocol
 operation, 112–120
 about distance-vector routing protocols, 113–116
 about link-state routing protocols,
  116–117, 119
 differences between, 118, 119
 hop-count limits of distance-vector
  routing algorithms, 118
 interior routing, 113
 overview, 112
DR
 defined, **154**
 discovering OSPF neighbors, 150
 present with Broadcast or NBMA network types, 150
information needed by, 108–111
 function of routers and routing tables,
  108–109
 metrics used in routing algorithms,
  109–110
internal, **168, 169**
limitations on configuring stub, 173
locating access lists near destination, 30, 35
neighboring, **154**
OSI-model bridge routing and, 312, *312*
OSPF peer initialization on, *151*
protocol dependencies and, 314

segmenting networks with, 22–23, 25
types of OSPF, 168
updating with RTMP filters, 375, 378
using SAP, 63, 64
using VLSMs on, 127
verifying EIGRP operations on, 198–199,
200
viewing neighbor relationships of, 183, 184
routes. *See also* routing updates
OSPF, **149–155**
discovering OSPF neighbors, 150, *151*
overview, 149
synchronizing routes with neighbors,
152–153
using Hello protocol to maintain route
information, 152, 154
using link-state advertisements (LSAs),
153, 154
redistributing routes, 215–219
updating EIGRP, 189, *190*
Routine Table Maintenance Protocol. *See*
RTMP
routing. *See also* DDR; routing updates
alternate path, 8
BGP
connecting ISP with, 229–230
creating, 232, 233
defined, *233*
CIDR, **147**
classless EIGRP, 191
default
connecting to ISP with, 229, 232
cost of, 179–180
creating with ip route command, 231,
233
defined, **226, 233**
dissimilar media with Token Ring, 351
distance-vector
convergence, 114–115
handling routing loops, 115–116
overview, 112
dynamic, **226**
hierarchical, **167, 169**
inter-area vs. intra-area, 167, 168
link-state, 112–120
convergence in, 117
distance-vector routing vs., 118, 119,
147
network discovery in, 116
overview, 112
managing routing broadcasts to multiple
servers, 54–56, 55, 57
optimizing routing updates, 202–222

configuring redistribution with redundant paths, 210–215
configuring redistribution without
redundant paths, 206–209
controlling route update traffic,
203–206
redistributing routes, 215–219
verifying redistribution, 220–222
snapshot, 10, **13**, 302–306
static
connecting ISP using, 228–229, 232
creating with ip route command, 230
default administrative distance for, 216
defined, **52, 226, 233**
routing algorithms, 108–110. *See also* EIGRP;
OSPF
Bellman-Ford, 147
running VLSMs with, 122
routing loops
avoiding with transparent bridging,
324–325, *325*
handling with distance-vector routing,
115–116
routing metrics
for calculating best route with EIGRP, 188,
191, 192
defined, **148, 158**
for redistributing protocols without redundant paths, 207–208
for route redistribution without redundant
paths, 206
for route redistribution with redundant
paths, 211–212
used in algorithms, 109–110
routing protocols
administrative distances associated with,
215, 216–217
balancing multiple network protocols, 11
convergence of scalable, 8
convergence of scalable routing, 8
defined, **249**
displaying IP, 182
distance-vector, 113–116
link-state, 116–117, 119
reachability and, 8
route distribution into EIGRP, 208
route redistribution between dissimilar,
206–215, **208, 214–215**
route tagging for, 202
routed protocols vs., 5, 199
WAN connectivity and, 248, **249, 249**
routing tables
defined, **205, 221**

displaying IP, 182
function of, 108–109
purpose of, 221
reading when running EIGRP, 208
using route summarization with, 129
routing updates, **202–222**
configuring redistribution with redundant
paths, 210–215
adding loopback interface, 212–213
changing cost of link in OSPF, 213, 214
changing default metrics, 211–212
configuring different cost links, 211,
213
configuring OSPF priority, 212, 214
configuring redistribution without redundant paths, 206–209
controlling route update traffic, 203–206
advertising specific networks, **204**, 204
preventing broadcasts exiting interface,
203–204, **204**
route filtering, 204
EIGRP, 191, **193**
filtering in AppleTalk, 377
resolving problems in redistributed networks, **215–219**
assigning administrative distances,
215–216
default administrative distances,
216–217
feedback, 218
IGRP default administrative distance,
215, 218
verifying route redistribution, 220–222
commands for viewing routing tables,
220
purpose of routing tables, 221
reason for, 220, 221
RTMP (Routine Table Maintenance Protocol)
defined, **378**
as reason for AppleTalk congestion, 367,
369
RTMP filters, **375–379**
commands to filter RTMP updates,
375–376, 378
function of, 375–376, 377
updating routers with, 375, 378

S

S reference point, 254
SAP (Service Advertising Protocol)
defined, **65**, 83

frequency of SAP broadcasts, 65
IPX SAP filters, 67, 70–71, 72
knowing why and how to change timer for
SAP updates, 75
reducing SAP intervals over WANs, 74
server updates, 63–64
uses for, 63, 64
SAP timer, 75
saturation, **282**
scalability
features of OSPF, 145–146
limitations of RIP, 144–145
scalable internetworks, 2–14
features solving internetwork requirements,
7–14
correlating IOS features with key
requirements, 8–12
overview, 7–8
key requirements of, **2–7**
overview, 2–3
solving network congestion for, 17–19
security, 4
servers
configuring helper addresses for multiple
subnets and, 54–56, 55, 57
setting up dialer map for, 303–304, 305
setting up for snapshot routing, 303–304
showing IPX servers from Cisco router, 83
shortest path first (SPF) algorithm, 145, **148**
show access-list command, 78, 82
show access-lists 187 command, 44–47
show access-lists command, 44–47
show command, **164**
show controller bri command, 274, 296, 300
show dialer command, 274, 284, 295
show interface bri 0 command, 274, 275
show interface bri command, 274, 275
show interface bri n 1 2 command, 295, 299,
300
show interface bri n command, 295, 297–299,
300
show interface bvi1 command, 335–336
show interface s0 irb command, 334, 335
show ip access-lists command, 44–47
show ip eigrp events command, 199, **200**
show ip eigrp neighbors command, 198, **200**
show ip eigrp topology command, 199, **200**
show ip eigrp traffic command, 199, **200**
show ip interface command, **49**
show ip ospf border-routers command, 160,
163, 183
show ip ospf command, 160, **161–162**, 163,
182

show ip ospf database command, 183
show ip ospf interface command, 160, **162**, 163, 182
show ip ospf neighbor command, 183, 184
show ip ospf virtual-links command, 183
show ip protocol command, 182, 199
show ip route command, 182
show ip route eigrp command, 198
show ipx interface command, 78, 79–80
show ipx servers command, 78–79
show ipx traffic command, 78, 80–81
show isdn status command, 274, 284
show ppp multilink, 275
show proto command, 78, 82
show rif command, 359, 361, 362
show running-config command, 49, 359–360, 362
show source-bridge command, 359, 361–362
show source-bridge interface command, 359
show startup-config, **49**
showing queuing, 105
significant bits, 130, **132**
SLIP (Serial Line Interface Protocol), 270
SMDS (Switched Multimegabit Data Service), 6
SNA (Systems Network Architecture), **341**
snapshot client command, 303–304
snapshot routing, 302–306
  configuring clients, 303, 305
  defined, **13**
  efficiency and, 10
  setting up client and server with, 303–304
  setting up dialer map for client and server, 303–304, 305
snapshot server command, 303–304
sockets, 72, **83**
source-bridge 401 5 400 command, 345, 346
source-bridge spanning command, 357
source-bridge transparent command, 352, 355–356, 357
source-route bridging algorithm, **341**, **346**, **357**, 362
source-route bridging (SRB), **338–363**
  about, 317, 318, **319**, 319
  basic functions of, 339–342
    explorer packets, 340–341
    routing information field, 339, 341
  bridging protocols available, 346
  configuring, 342–346
    automatic Spanning Tree configuration, 343–344
    example of, 344–345, *344*
    manual Spanning-Tree configuration, 343

defined, **319**
development of, 338
verifying operation of, **358–363**
  debug rif command, 362
  show rif command, 359, 361, 362
  show running-config command, 359–360, 362
  show source-bridge command, 359, 361–362
  show source-bridge interface command, 359
source-route translational bridging algorithm, **357**
source-route translational bridging (SR/TLB), 317, 319
  about, 317, 319
  configuring, 350–358
    example of, 352–356
    ineffectiveness of spanning-tree packets in, 351
    syntax for, 352
  development of, 338
  function of, 350–351
source-route transparent bridging (SRT), 317, 318
  about, 317, 318
  configuring, 347–350
    example of, 348
    information about, 347–348
  development of, 338
  Token-Ring-to-Ethernet media conversion, 347, 349
spanning explorer packets, 340–341
speed of line, 147
SPF (shortest path first) algorithm, 145, **148**, 173
spid command, 258
SPID (service profile identifier)
  about, 258–259
  defined, **259**, **267**
  obtaining when configuring ISDN BRI, 255
split horizon, 115
SPT (Spanning Tree Protocol), 325–326, 329
  commands for automatic Spanning Tree configuration, 343–344
  commands for manual Spanning-Tree configuration, 343
  defined, **330**, **346**
  supported for transparent bridging, 326, 329
SPX protocol, 62, 62, 64
SR/TLB. *See* source-route translational bridging

SRB. *See* source-route bridging
SRT. *See* source-route transparent bridging
SRTT (smooth round trip timer), 188
standard access lists. *See also* extended
   access lists
   IP, **30–36**
      applying to physical interfaces, 34, 35
      creating, 33–34
      extended access lists vs., 40
      filtering from top to bottom, 35
      implied *deny any* at end of, 31, 35
      locating near destination router, 30, 35
      network addresses and wildcard masks,
         31–33, 35
      syntax for access-list command, 33, 35
   IPX, 68–69, 72
      defined, **67**
      number ranges for, 72
      parameters for filtering, 72
standard area, 170, 171, 174
static routing, 262–264
   connecting ISP using, 228–229, 232
   creating with ip route command, 230
   default administrative distance for, 216
   defined, **52, 226, 233**
store-and-forward switching, 26
stub area, 171–172, 174
   configuring, 178–179, **180**
   configuring area as, 172, 174
   creating stub network, 179, 180
   defined, **180**
   unable to define as, 173
stub routers, 173
stun, **102**
subnet masks. *See also* VLSMs
   creating supernet network address, 130
   defined, **127**
subnet prefixes, **128**
subnets
   configuring helper addresses for multiple
      servers and, 54–56, *55*, 57
   supernets, 132
summarization, **132**
summary LSAs, 173, 174
Super Frame framing type, 386, 389
supernet network address, 130
supernets, 132
switching
   cell (ATM), **23**
   cut-through, **26**
   dedicated and switched WAN support, 12
   frame, **23**
   ISDN switch types

configuring, 259
   key word for configuring, 254–255
   network switching technology, 23, 24
   physical segmentation with LAN switches,
      23
   port-configuration, 23
   PSN, **240**
   PSTN, 238, 239
   segmenting networks with LAN switches,
      23, 25
   store-and-forward, **26**
switch-type command, 257, 258
synchronizing
   databases with LSAs, 152
   OSPF routes with neighbors, 150, *151*,
      152–153
syntax
   for access-list command, 33, 35
   for configuring IP extended access lists,
      41–42
   for configuring IPX spoofing, 308
   for configuring OSPF on router, 156, 158
   defined, **43, 158**
   for EIGRP configuration, 194–195, 196
   for IP helper address, 53–54
   of Null 0 command, 50, 51
   for SR/TLB configuration, 352

T

T1 lines. *See* channelized T1 and E1 configura-
   tion
T reference point, 254
Target Ring, **346**
TCP protocol, 42
TCP/IP protocol, 60
TE1 router, 257
TE1 terminals, **253**
TE2 terminals, **253**
terminals
   limiting access to virtual, 37–39
   TE1 and TE2, **253**
three-layer hierarchical model, 27–30, *27*
   Access layer, 27, 28, **29**
   Core layer, 27, 28, **29**
   Distribution layer, 27, 28, **29**
tick, defined, **65**
Token Ring
   bridging between Ethernet and, 351
   configuring source-route and source-route
      transparent bridging on, 346–347
   source-route bridging and, 342–343

Token-Ring-to-Ethernet media conversion, 347, 349
topological database
   in EIGRP, 187, 193
   viewing, 183
totally stub area
   about, 171, 172
   configuring area as, 172, 174
   defined, 175, 180
totally stubby areas, 179
traffic. *See also* managing traffic and access; Novell IPX/SPX traffic
   application traffic on WAN networks, 248
   controlling route update, 203–206
      advertising specific networks, 204, 204
      preventing broadcasts exiting interface, 203–204, 204
      route filtering, 204
   defining with access lists on legacy DDR, 266–267
   filtering IPX traffic with access lists, 66–73
   issues for managing Novell IPX/SPX traffic, 61–66
   managing Novell IPX/SPX traffic over WANs, 73–76
transparent bridging, 317–318, 322–330
   about, 317–318, 319, 322
   avoiding loops, 324–325, 325
   configuring, 323–324, 323, 326–327, 329
   defined, 319, 330, 349
   functions of, 318, 319
   Spanning Tree Protocol, 325–326, 329
   verifying configurations, 326, 328–329
triggered updates, 115

U

U reference point, 254
unicasts, 57
updates. *See also* routing updates
   IPX, SAP, and RIP server, 63–64
   triggered, 115

V

variable-length subnet masks. *See* VLSMs
variance command, 211, 213
verifying
   DDR operation, 274–276
   dial backup operation, 283–291
      with debug dialer command, 284, 289–290
      with debug isdn q921 command, 284, 287–288, 290
      with debug isdn q931 command, 284, 288–289, 290
      with debug ppp negotiation command, 284, 288, 290
      with ping command, 283, 285, 290
      with show dialer command, 284, 285–286, 290
      with show isdn status command, 284, 286–287, 290
   EIGRP operations, 197–200
   IPX/SPX filtering, 76–84
   IRB configuration, 331, 335
   MultiLink PPP operation, 295–301
      with clear interface bri n command, 295, 297
      with debug ppp multilink fragments command, 295, 296–297, 300
      overview, 295
      with show controller bri command, 296, 300
      with show dialer command, 295
      with show interface bri n 1 2 command, 295, 299, 300
      with show interface bri n command, 295, 297–299, 300
   operation of IP access lists, 44–49
   OSPF operations, 159–164
      in interconnecting multiple OSPF areas, 181–184
      overview, 159–160
      with show ip ospf border-routers command, 160, 163, 183
      with show ip ospf command, 160, 161–162, 163, 182
      with show ip ospf interface command, 160, 162, 163, 182
      using help screens, 163
   queuing operation, 102–106
      for custom queuing, 105
      showing queuing, 105
      spelling of queueing commands, 103, 106
      verifying priority queuing, 104
      for weighted fair, 104
   route redistribution, 220–222
      commands for viewing routing tables, 220
      purpose of routing tables, 221
      reason for, 220, 221
   SRB operation, 358–363
      with debug rif command, 362

with show rif command, 359, 361, 362
with show running-config command,
359–360, 362
with show source-bridge command,
359, 361–362
with show source-bridge interface command, 359
transparent bridging configuration, 326,
328–329
virtual links
defined, **184**
showing, 183
verifying, 183
virtual terminal lines, **37**
VLSMs (variable-length subnet masks)
about, 122–123
assigning network and host portions of IP
address, 124–125, *124*
defined, **128**, **148**
extending use of IP addresses, 123–128
adjusting host and network portions of
IP addresses, 124–125, *124*
avoiding discontiguous IP addresses,
125, 127
defining number of hosts on network,
125–126, *126*, 127
using VLSMs on router, 127
using with OSPF, 177
vty (Virtual TeleType) ports
configuring, 37–38
defined, **39**
number of, 38, 39

W

WANs (wide-area networks)
advantages of legacy DDR, 261–262
compression over, 10
defined, **14**
managing Novell IPX/SPX traffic over,
73–76
reducing SAP and RIP intervals over, 74
support for dedicated and switched, 12
WAN connectivity, **236–250**
differences in, **237–241**
asynchronous dial-in products, 238,
240
dedicated-leased lines, 237–238, *238*,
240
dial-on-demand routing, 239
packet-switched services, 239, 240

issues for evaluating WAN services,
247–250
bandwidth requirements, 248
costs, 248
management ease, 248
network availability, 247
routing protocols, 248, **249**, 249
type of application traffic, 248
overview, 236
when to use PPP, HDLC, LAPB, and IETF
encapsulation types, 241–246
watchdog packets, 308
weighted fair queuing, **89–93**. *See also* queuing
assigning priorities in, 90
defined, **87**, 88
overview, 89–91, *90*
responsiveness and, 9
setting up, 91–92
verifying queuing operations for, 104
wildcard masks
creating, 177, 180
decimal to binary conversion of, 31–33, 35
defined, 36

X

X.25
defined, **6**
as encapsulation method with DDR, 270
XNS (Xerox Network Systems), IPX and, 61

Z

ZIP (Zone Information Protocol), defined, 378
ZIP reply filters, 370, 371–372, 373, **374**
zone, **369**
zone filters, 370–374
GZL, 370, 371, 372, 373, **374**
ZIP reply filters, 370, 371–372, 373, **374**

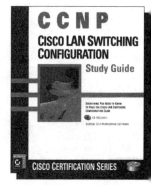